NEW DIRECTIONS IN RELIGIOUS EDUCATION

Edited and Introduced by
John Hull
(University of Birmingham)

The Falmer Press

(A member of the Taylor & Francis Group)

First published 1982

ISBN 0 905273 30 3 (paper)
0 905273 31 1 (cased)

Jacket design by Leonard Williams

Printed by Taylor and Francis (Printers) Ltd
Basingstoke, England
for
The Falmer Press
Falmer House
Barcombe
Lewes, Sussex
BN8 5DL

NEW DIRECTIONS IN RELIGIOUS EDUCATION

Contents

General Editor's Preface vii
Philip Taylor
Introduction: New Directions in Religious Education xi
John M. Hull

1 **RELIGION IN CHILDHOOD AND YOUTH: EMPIRICAL FOUNDATIONS FOR RELIGIOUS EDUCATION** 1
On Beyond Goldman: Religious Thinking and the 1970s 5
John H. Peatling
Measurement Reapplied: Research into the Child's Attitude Towards Religion 23
Leslie Francis
Towards a Standardized Test of Religious Language Comprehension 35
E.B. Turner

2 **THE NATURE OF RELIGIOUS EDUCATION: THE SEARCH FOR A RATIONALE** 49
Educational Religious Education 53
Edwin Cox
Taking Religious Education Seriously 59
John Wilson
Phenomenology and the Future of Religious Education 69
John Marvell
Conceptual Research in Religious Education 77
David Attfield
Religious Education: A Shocking Business 85
Edward A. Robinson

3 **THE SOCIAL CONTEXT: RELIGIOUS PLURALISM IN SCHOOL AND SOCIETY** 93
Teaching Religion in a Secular Plural Society 97
Lesslie Newbigin
Truth in Religious Education: Further Reflections on the Implications of Pluralism 109
Daniel W. Hardy

4 **DESIGNING THE CURRICULUM IN RELIGIOUS EDUCATION** 119
Problems of RE Syllabus Construction in a Democracy 123
John Elliott

Checklists for Study of the Religious Education Syllabus 133
H.E. Lupton
Discussing Religious Education: A Conceptual Framework for the Consideration of Curricular Issues 143
David Gooderham

5 **METHODS IN TEACHING RELIGION TODAY** 155
The Demands Made by RE on Pupils' Thinking 161
Trevor Kerry
Religion in the Multi-Faith School 171
W. Owen Cole
The Multi-Faith Situation in the Secondary School 179
Robin Minney
Teaching the Bible in School 187
Paul D. Fueter
Notes on Contributors 205

General Editor's Preface

The way we think about Religious Education, about the educational purposes it is to serve, how it is taught, the practical problems of designing a programme of Religious Education, a syllabus and the objectives to be achieved have been a matter of critical examination for more than thirty years. This collection of papers sets out to show something of the nature of that critical examination, where it originated and where it is leading.

The collection is edited by John Hull, one of this country's foremost authorities in Religious Education. He is the author of *Sense and Nonsense about God, Hellenistic Magic and the Synoptic Tradition* and *School Worship, An Obituary,* and edits the *British Journal of Religious Education.* With telling effect, John Hull organizes his selection of articles to illuminate those salient issues with which the teacher and the student of Religious Education must come to terms in the search for a viable classroom practice. More than this, to read this edited collection is, for the teacher of Religious Education, to rehearse the process of deciding what to teach, how and why.

Philip Taylor
General Editor

Acknowledgements

I would like to express my gratitude to the Christian Education Movement, 2 Chester House, Pages Lane, London N.10, publishers of the *British Journal of Religious Education*, and its predecessor *Learning for Living*, and particularly to the General Secretary, the Revd John Sutcliffe, for permission to publish the articles in this collection.

John M. Hull
Birmingham
July 1981

Introduction: New Directions in Religious Education

John M. Hull

In 1859 John Stuart Mill argued that it would not infringe the liberty of society or of the individual if the State were to *require* general education, provided that the State did not seek to *direct* that education:

> A general State education is a mere contrivance for moulding people to be exactly like one another: and as the mould in which it casts them is that which pleases the predominant power in the government, whether this be a monarch, a priesthood, an aristocracy, or the majority of the existing generation, in proportion as it is efficient and successful, it establishes a despotism over the mind, leading by natural tendency to one over the body.[1]

There would be a sufficient number of individuals and voluntary bodies ready to offer education with the necessary State support and financial help, but if this were not so, 'the government may, as the less of two great evils, take upon itself the business of schools and universities'.[2] Mill suggested that the State should set up a compulsory, public examination in order to ensure an acceptable standard of general education, but 'To prevent the State from exercising, through these arrangements, an improper influence over opinion, the knowledge required for passing an examination . . . should . . . be confined to facts and positive science exclusively'.[3] These arrangements would be quite compatible with a satisfactory education and examination in controversial subjects. 'The examinations on religion, politics or other disputed topics, should not turn on the truth or falsehood of opinions, but on the matter of fact that such and such an opinion is held, on such grounds, by such authors, or schools, or churches'.[4] Such a religious education would not conflict with the nurturing of a variety of religious faiths by various churches. Children 'would be brought up either churchmen or dissenters as they now are, the State merely taking care that they should be instructed churchmen, or instructed dissenters'. Although the State should not attempt 'to bias the conclusions of its citizens on disputed subjects', it would be quite in order for the State 'to ascertain and certify that a person possesses the knowledge, requisite to make his conclusions, on any given subject, worth attending to'. Thus 'there is no reasonable objection to examining an atheist in the evidences of Christianity, provided he is not required to profess a belief in them'.[5]

The enterprise of the State in the religious education of the people began eleven years later, with the passing of the 1870 Education Act and the creation of schools owned and maintained by local government. For nearly three-quarters of a century the State tolerated the teaching of religion, permitting it but not requiring it or inspecting it. The impartiality of this religious education in publicly-provided schools was secured (as it still is) by insisting that if and when the schools provided for the teaching of religion (and almost all were in fact to do so) such religious education should include 'no religious catechism or religious formulary which is distinctive of any particular denomination'.[6]

But there were limits to the impartiality of this religious education. Although the teacher was forbidden to use textbooks or aids which indicated a denominational imprint or origin, he was not to be prevented from expressing his own personal religious opinions, and an amendment which proposed that 'in any [board] school in which the Bible shall be read and taught, the teaching shall not be used or directed in favour of or against the distinctive tenets of any religious denomination' was overwhelmingly rejected.[7] Many local School Boards sought to interpret and enforce the religious neutrality which the Act expected. The Denbigh School Board, for instance, declared that religious instruction might include 'the history of the Jews and the Jewish nation and the geography and natural history of Ancient as well as Modern Palestine; but that in any use which may be made of the Bible in teaching or illustrating these subjects, it is to be distinctly understood that no reference whatever is to be made to the doctrines taught therein; except in cases of discipline and to enforce moral teaching'.[8]

With the 1944 Education Act, the policy of the State became more positive. Religious education was now required, not merely tolerated. But, in line with the vision of John Stuart Mill, the State still quite properly refused to be involved in any attempt to influence the minds of children on disputed questions of religion. This was made clear, not only in the repetition of the clause forbidding denominational instruction, but also in the requirement that religious education 'shall be given in accordance with an agreed syllabus'.[9]

It is most significant that, although detailed regulations are laid down in Schedule 5 of the Act for the procedure by which an agreed syllabus was to be drawn up, nothing whatever is said about the content and objectives of these syllabuses, apart from the mere fact that they are to be syllabuses of 'religious instruction'. Local agreement was a required condition of the required religious education. But in the meantime the rather arid and formal impartiality of the late nineteenth and early twentieth century religious education had passed away. The agreed syllabuses which preceded the 1944 Act, the earliest of them appearing in the early 1920s, had already adopted a tone of buoyant Christian optimism and had inaugurated the 'Christian nurture' period of British religious education.[10]

It might be argued that in a sense this was still consistent with Mill's ideals, since the nature of the agreement reached by the participating parties in the syllabus indicated that the questions were not disputed, while Anglicans would still bring their children up as Anglicans, and Non-conformists would bring theirs up as Non-conformists, regardless of, but in harmony with the religious teaching offered in the county schools. But with the increased plurality and secularity of British society in more recent years, and with the rise of a view of education which seeks to foster a more critical and more autonomous individual, the Christianising period of religious education has largely come to an end.

Mill's prophetic words indicated both the best and the worst in the religious education which was to come. The best was the ideal of a truly educational enterprise, appropriate to the common schools of a pluralist and freedom-loving democracy in which a wide variety of beliefs and values exist, a religious education which would not seek to mould the mind along sectarian lines or even in conformity with the wishes of a powerful majority, but would be informative and rational, enabling pupils to express and defend their positions, making them 'worth attending to' and thus raising the level of general intelligent participation in matters which are controversial precisely because they are so important. The worst was a religious education which was afraid of controversy, one which sought in fact to avoid the direct teaching of religion, one which was insufficiently vibrant, consisting of inert facts unrelated to pupils' lives, one which became falsely academic instead of truly liberating, and which failed to confront pupils with the rich religious experience of humanity.

The recent history of religious education in this country may be understood as an attempt to create a subject which would be faithful to its own natural content, and which would be impartial but not arid, personal but not proselytizing. The papers in this collection represent the attempt to articulate such a religious education. The Cambridgeshire Syllabus of 1924[11] helped to steer religious education away from the merely factual, often non-religious teaching of the Bible towards a fuller and richer teaching of Christianity as a faith involved in life, but the major impetus towards this more experiential teaching came from the work of Harold Loukes in the early and middle 1960s, especially his *Teenage Religion* (1961).[12] This led to a renewed interest in the capacity of children to understand and respond to religion. The studies by Ronald Goldman and Kenneth Hyde continue to be influential and their work has been verified and extended in several directions. This creative period also led to a resurgence of the agreed syllabuses, some of which (for example, West Riding 1966, Lancashire 1968, ILEA 1968) are significant documents of the child-centred approach in religious education and are probably more typical of what goes on in many schools than the more recent and more controversial World Religions syllabuses.

But this period was a brief Indian summer. Although an important start had been made in correcting what I have described as the worst aspect of the religious education envisaged by Mill, its arid factuality, the problem of creating a religious education which expressed the best of his vision had hardly been tackled at all. Three books from the later 1960s introduced this discussion. They were Edwin Cox: *Changing Aims in Religious Education* (1966), Ninian Smart: *Secular Education and the Logic of Religion* (1968) and J.W.D. Smith: *Religious Education in a Secular Setting* (1969). Ninian Smart saw the answer in an objective study of the religions of the world, while Smith sought a ground common to both believer and non-believer in fundamental existential questions of life, but both agreed that religious education could not continue as the attempt to foster Christian faith, and both pointed to the need to create a wholly new rationale for what was emerging as virtually a new subject.[13]

This new subject was to a large extent created during the 1970s. Its curriculum ideals were set out in writings such as those by Jean Holm, *Teaching Religion in School, A Practical Approach*, Oxford University Press, 1975, and Michael Grimmitt, *What Can I do in R.E.?*, Mayhew–McCrimmon, 2nd edition, 1978. Much of its nature and consequences, especially for school assembly, was discussed in my *School Worship, An Obituary*, SCM Press, 1975, and it has found formal expression in the agreed syllabuses of Birmingham (1975), Avon (1976), Hampshire (1978) and the City of Manchester: *Guidelines for Religious Education* (1980). Religious education is no longer to foster or nurture faith in any particular religion; it is to promote a sympathetic but critical understanding of religions. Its focus will no longer lie in far-off lands long ago but in the teeming religious life of the towns and cities in which we live. The teacher will no longer teach his own enthusiasms or project his own religious commitments but will be an educator, aiding his children's learning, and seeking to discover his curriculum and his method from educational theory, and not from the religious teaching of the churches or from the polemics of the religions themselves.

But what *is* it to learn from religion? It is not difficult to see why religious education has been facing questions of curriculum development at least as severe as those encountered by any other subject today. The received tradition of religious teaching presented a sort of 'common core' of ecumenical Christianity, whether reduced to its barest, most factual content and assertions in the biblical history and teaching, or whether more richly contemporary and more involved in life today. But the curriculum was created by ecumenical agreement, and although there were questions of local emphasis, problems about the selection and grading of material, and attempts to relate the material to the aptitude and experience of the pupil, the curriculum question was not an open one in any fundamental sense until the late 1960s and the early 1970s. So an ecumenical agreement is replaced by an educational agreement. One no longer seeks to agree about what is true but only about what is worth teaching. The 1977 report of a working party set up by the Religious Education Committee of the Schools Council *A Groundplan for the Study of Religion* is probably the clearest statement of the new conception of the religious curriculum and no doubt we will see its influence upon the agreed syllabuses of the 1980s.

How can the objective, descriptive study of world religions, resting upon the phenomenological approach to religious studies, engage the pupils' own lives and concerns? Religious education has only just emerged out of its faith-fostering period and it is only natural that teachers should scrupulously avoid anything which might smack of a desire to convert children, or to be more favourably disposed towards those young people moving in the direction of faith in God than towards those moving in the opposite direction. But, at the same time, there is a suspicion that once again the problem of teaching *religion* may be avoided by an exaggerated emphasis upon the observable facts about religion, and there is a renewed desire that pupils should learn from religion in ways which will enrich them and deepen their humanity, rather than merely informing them. It looks as if religious education in the last ten years or so has recapitulated the problem posed by Mill. The objective study of world religions has sought for his impartiality and his refusal to bias pupils' minds; the concentration upon facts and reasons is leading to a reaction in which, through poetry, drama and the arts, religious education seeks to avoid the worst – the inert imparting of facts.

Sometimes this ferment of new ideas and approaches is described as 'confusion' and religious education is criticised for 'not knowing where it is going'. Those who come to this subject with the naive expectation that they will find simple Christianity preached by Christians to Christians need to be confused first if they are going to be able to take modern religious education seriously. There is, of course, an important sense in which the subject does not know where it is going. This is why the emphasis upon research has increased in recent years and is still increasing. But religious education is no different in this respect from any other branch of education or indeed any of the social sciences in a time of rapid social change. What to simple and dogmatic minds appears confusing is seen as a mark of vitality and responsibility by those engaged in religious education in our county schools. It may once have been possible for critics of religious education to describe it as indoctrination, the apex of compulsion in a compulsory system, and as being uneducational through its lack of enquiry and criticism. It would be more accurate today to see in this subject a crucial focus for the examination of those beliefs and values without which education could not be true to itself and as a classroom example of that meeting between religions, and between the religious and the secular outlooks, which is changing the consciousness of humanity today.

Since it was founded in 1934 the *British Journal of Religious Education* (under the titles *Religion in Education* [1934–1961] and *Learning For Living* [1961–1978]) has been the main forum for the serious discussion of British religious education. The task of selecting some of the most significant articles which have appeared in the journal during the ten years I have been editing it (1971–1981) has not been easy, and no doubt many readers of the journal, to say nothing of the authors of the many good articles which have not been included, will disagree with my choice. I hope that what has been selected will be sufficient to illustrate at least some of the many new directions which religious education is taking today.

Notes and references

1 Mill, J.S., 'On Liberty' in Robson, J.M. (ed.). *Collected Works of John Stuart Mill*, Vol. XVIII, University of Toronto Press, Toronto and Routledge and Kegan Paul, London, 1977, p. 302.
2 *Op. cit.*, p. 303.
3 *Ibid.*
4 *Ibid.*
5 *Op. cit.*, p. 304.
6 Murphy, J., *Church, State and Schools in Britain, 1800–1970*, Routledge and Kegan Paul, London, 1971, p. 58.
7 *Op. cit.*, p. 60.
8 Quoted by Adamson, J.W., *English Education 1789–1902*, CUP, 1930, p. 163*f.*
9 1944 Education Act, Section 26.
10 See the Appendix of my *School Worship, An Obituary*, SCM Press, 1975, pp. 137–144 for detailed examples of the ethos of pre 1944 syllabuses.
11 *The Cambridgeshire Syllabus of Religious Teaching for Schools*, Cambridge University Press, 1924.
12 For a description and an appraisal of the work of Harold Loukes see the editorial Obituary to him in the *British Journal of Religious Education*, Spring, 1981.
13 Grimmitt, M., 'When is "commitment" a problem in religious education?', *British Journal of Educational Studies*, 29, 1981, pp. 42–53.

1
Religion in Childhood and Youth: Empirical Foundations for Religious Education

Introduction

Studies of the religious psychology of children for the guidance of clergy and classroom teachers have been appearing for over a century. Amongst earlier works, one thinks of Thomas Stephens' *The Child and Religion,* published in 1905,[1] Edith E. Read Mumford's *The Religious Difficulties of Children,* also published at the turn of the century,[2] Basil A. Yeaxlee's *Religion and the Growing Mind,*[3] and J.W.D. Smith's *Psychology and Religion in Early Childhood,*[4] both published in the 1930s.

From the early years of the century, syllabus makers were advising teachers to consider carefully whether various passages from the Bible were suitable for the age and development of the child. But it was not until the 1960s, with the increased emphasis upon experiential religious education, that the psychology of religion in childhood and youth, as it is affected by religious education in county schools, was placed on a secure research basis. The work of Ronald Goldman in developing a stage theory of religious development has been influential on both sides of the Atlantic, and has received its most probing criticism and confirmation in the work of Dr John Peatling. While Goldman and Peatling have concentrated mainly on the development of religious thinking, the work of Kenneth Hyde on the formation of religious attitudes is continued today in the work of Dr Leslie Francis and others. Peatling, Francis and E.B. Turner have developed a range of test instruments which enable the religious education teacher to diagnose the intellectual and attitudinal situation of the pupil *vis-à-vis* his education in religion, leaving it open for the teacher in a church context to develop this for the formation of religious faith, or for the religious education teacher in the county school to develop an increased insight into religion appropriate to a secular educational context. With the formation in 1978 of the International Seminar for Religious Education and Values (ISREV) many British researchers are in regular contact with colleagues in several countries, and although the difficulties in this area of investigation must never be under-estimated, it does seem possible, as John Peatling remarks, that 'the future may hold a "science" of religious education'.

References

1 Stephens, T., *The Child and Religion*, London, Wm. Norgate, 1905.
2 Read Mumford, E.R., *The Religious Difficulties of Children*, London, The Sunday School Union, undated.
3 Yeaxlee, B.A., *Religion and the Growing Mind*, London, Nisbet & Co., 1939.
4 Smith, J.W.D., *Psychology and Religion in Early Childhood*, London, Student Christian Movement, 1936.

*On Beyond Goldman: Religious Thinking and the 1970s**

John H. Peatling

Parents (and other alert adults) in the United States are familiar with the work of a delightful spinner of tales who writes under the pseudonym of Dr Seuss. One of his numerous works bore the title, *On Beyond Zebra.*[1] The hero of that tale was a precocious boy whose reaction to the claim of a classmate that Z is 'all there is; there is no more!' was to announce (and demonstrate!) that 'where his alphabet left off, mine began!' With broad humour the author and his hero demonstrate that an ending can be a beginning, that only a kind of intellectual arthritis assumes finality, or (inferently) that it requires an SQ in excess of 145 to presume that the creative burst of the 1960s provided religious education with all there was, let alone all there is to know.[2] Seuss provided a delightful 'alphabet' on beyond Z. The author and his colleagues have provided a series of focused studies on beyond the seminal work of Ronald J. Goldman in the early 1960s.

The beginning of the author's work on the construct Religious Thinking, like many a good thing, goes back to a post-meeting supper. Over good food and wine, good conversation sometimes flourishes. The place was New York City. The year was 1965. The question was whether or not Goldman's findings could be 'replicated' with a large sample of children and adolescents in the United States via a paper-and-pencil instrument. Goldman, the author and several educational researchers were involved. Goldman fielded the question by suggesting that the attempt be made: both a psychologically safe and (given the time) a scientifically correct response. That meeting has, with appropriate scholarly care, been recognized as a beginning and referenced in the author's 1973 dissertation.[3] But it was only a start. There was an 'on beyond' initial encouragement

*This article first appeared in *Learning for Living*, Vol. 16, No. 3, Spring, 1977.

that involved years of work, a goodly sum of money, and the co-operation of many schools and their pupils. To the question of how one does that sort of thing there is really only one answer: *Very Carefully!*

The author and his colleagues in the then Department of Christian Education of The Episcopal Church spent the remainder of 1965, all of 1966, 1967, 1968 and most of 1969 preparing for the study envisioned and encouraged over a supper in mid-town Manhattan. In addition, The Episcopal Church itself supported that work with a series of generous grants, plus the administrative decisions that enabled the author to devote an increasing proportion of his time to the preparation for and conduct of the final study. It was not 'cheap' research by any measure one would care to use.

The instruments: 'Thinking about the Bible'

The research very early focused upon the development of Religious Thinking itself: the projective pictures Goldman used were bypassed in favour of three biblical miracle stories, plus criterion-referenced responses.[4] In view of Goldman's pre-dissertation study of story stimuli,[5] and because of a desire to create a body of 'comparable' data from North America, the three stories of (a) Moses and the Burning Bush (Exodus 3:1–6), (b) the Crossing of the Red Sea (selections from Exodus 14), and (c) the Temptations of Jesus (Luke 4:1–13 and Matthew 4:1–9) were used. Initially these three stories were taken to a sample of 330 subjects, each of whom supplied a response to a set of questions based upon Goldman's interview schedule.[6] Then these responses were subjected to a lengthy content analysis, which judged them against a combination of Goldman's stated criteria and Piaget's criteria for the several stages of cognitive development. As one might guess, this process created reams of paper, took an almost inordinate amount of time, and occasionally left the author feeling that the major difference between middle Elementary school children and Secondary school students had something to do with spelling and sentence construction. But the process did not stop.

As a result of the content analysis of student-supplied responses to a set of standard questions, a series of 'typical' responses for the Stages of Concrete and Abstract Religious Thinking were identified. These responses were put into a multiple-choice format and tested with another, second sample of 403 students. The results were submitted to a careful and thorough item analysis; a normal psychometric procedure that helps one discover which items 'work' and which simply have no discriminating 'power'. As a result, the multiple-choice format was revised and taken to a third sample of 401 students, and the item analyses repeated. By this time the instrument was performing as one would wish: it was discriminating between the youngest Elementary school students and the oldest Secondary school students, two criterion groups whose average response one could presume should be both noticeably different and, as well, different in a theoretically expected direction. Finally, a core of highly discriminating item responses was identified and, from the open-ended responses of the first sample, parallel sets of 'extreme' responses at the Concrete and the Abstract ends of the cognitive development continuum were added. This revision was, during mid-1969, carefully programmed, formatted, and printed: the resulting instrument was entitled *Thinking about the Bible*.

The initial study: On beyond Z

During 1969 the author had the co-operation of the National Association of Episcopal Schools and, as a result, was able to conduct a random sample of classes (within each grade-level from 4 through 12) that was a genuinely nation-wide, representative sample of schools in the NAES.[7] During late 1969 and early 1970 some 91 schools co-operated in this sample, and 1994 students across the nine grade-levels completed and returned usable instruments. Although the instrument was an *un*timed test, actual experience indicated that the average administration took 49 minutes (a confidence band of two standard errors ran from 46 to 52 minutes). Thus, in actual practice in North American private schools it was possible to use *Thinking about the Bible* in its long, research edition well within the limits of a 'normal' one-hour class period. In terms of the sheer pragmatics of many school settings this was an excellent and an important result: assessment of levels of Religious Thinking was possible within the constraints imposed by normal school scheduling.

In addition to completing the research instrument, most of the co-operating schools provided information on the measured intelligence of each student in the sample. Thus it was possible to calculate a mental age for something more than 80 per cent of the students.[8] In addition, each student identified his or her chronological age. As a result, in addition to a school grade-level and a calculated mental age, each student respondent could be identified by age-level. In the resulting analyses three basic metrics were used: Grade, Age, and Mental Age. Developmental curves for each of these metrics were drawn, and adjacent-group means were tested for statistically significant differences. As a result, over all 'growth' in Religious Thinking could be (and was) described in terms of periods of slower and more rapid 'growth', or change.

For example, periods of noticeably 'slower' growth in Religious Thinking appeared to approximate plateaus, as specified in Piaget's theory of cognitive development, where periods of relative equilibrium are posited as a part of the sequence of developmental advance. Periods of noticeably 'rapid' growth in Religious Thinking, then, appeared to indicate times of transition from one such plateau to a next higher one. This pattern of plateaus was markedly evident under the metric of school grade-level, evident under the metric of chronological age, and still statistically significant under the metric of mental age-level. For this sample of North American students, then, Religious Thinking grew or progressed in a step-wise manner toward increasingly 'higher' levels of Abstract Stage Religious Thinking across the nine school grades 4–12.

Goldman was right, but . . .

Basically, Goldman was right: children and adolescents do become increasingly abstract in their Religious Thinking. However, Goldman and Piaget are wrong, if one reads either of them in such a way that the transition from a Concrete Stage to an Abstract Stage of thinking is presumed to be rapid (or, even, quasi-instantaneous). The transition itself appears to be a much slower, step-wise progression through an identifiable 'intermediate' stage for the North American students in this sample. For example, two plateaus were clearly identified under the grade-level metric well within such an 'intermediate' stage, while two plateaus were equally clearly within an Abstract Stage of Religious Thinking.[9] While students in the United States are not exact equivalents of students in England, the author's sample does represent a carefully considered attempt to create (as nearly as possible) an equivalent sample of students. Thus, the finding that it was not until a school grade-level of 8 that a plateau exceeded the operationally defined limits of an 'intermediate' stage, and not until a grade-level of 10 that one could confidently speak of a dominance of Abstract Stage Religious Thinking, posed a peculiarly pointed challenge to a simple interpretation of Goldman's thesis that the transition occurred between 13 and 14 years M.A.[10] In the author's study of North American students it simply happened much later. Moreover, it appears that the students in that sample 'entered' such an 'intermediate' stage much earlier than Goldman's English students.[11] (Those hardy readers who wish to check this result are referred to either the author's 695-page 1973 dissertation text, which is available in microfilm or hard copy from Xerox University Microfilms, or to a much shorter yet thorough report published in the journal *Character Potential: A Record of Research*, Vol. 7, No. 1, October, 1974, pp 52–61.)

Goldman was right, and (perhaps) also 'wrong'. There is more that can be learned about Religious Thinking via large-sample research than reading the 1964 report of Goldman's Birmingham dissertation will tell one.[12] However, that is as it should be. Seminal research should lead toward more refined research, which should confirm some things and correct other things. Only a stale and static discipline without either curiosity or competence settles for the beginning of a process of research: religious education has no need to fall under such strictures, although at times it may seem to almost desire the state. Fortunately, what began with the author's study of 1994 North American students has across the years of the 1970s, grown into a body of research that currently is both interdenominational and international in scope. By the end of 1976 more than 11,000 students and adults will have used the author's research instrument, *Thinking about the Bible*. Most of this expansion of the data has been accomplished by independent investigators who, while corresponding with the author, have conducted their own studies for their own purposes, using samples available to them. Although most of these studies have been undertaken in North America, a large and careful study of students in the Finnish school system during 1975 has been successfully completed by Dr Kalevi Tamminen of the University of Helsinki's Institute of Practical Theology. Thus, one can learn considerably more about the construct Religious Thinking now in the late 1970s than one could during the 1960s. Minimally, one would hope that current data would inform the thinking of religious educators on both sides of the Atlantic.

Additional studies of religious thinking

Even as the author was in the midst of extensive computer-based analyses of the data from his basic study of students in schools affiliated with The Episcopal Church, two researchers became aware of his work and asked permission to use *Thinking about the Bible* in their own studies.

1 A study of United Methodist Adults

One of these researchers, Thomas B. Newton, was then Co-ordinator of the Office of Central Research for The Methodist Publishing House, which was faced with important decisions regarding a 'new' programme of adult Bible study. With permission, Newton and his associates used a special, shortened form of *Thinking about the Bible* that included only the three biblical stories while omitting a moral puzzle, a measure of socioeconomic class, and some questions on religious behaviour. Along with some other instruments, they conducted a pre-publication market survey during which 2896 adult students and 393 adult teachers, in a carefully constructed stratified random sample of Methodist churches across the United States, completed and returned usable instruments. Thus, for a large sample of 3289 adult Methodists scores on the six Scales of Religious Thinking could be (and were) calculated.[13] Not too surprisingly, albeit quite importantly, these adults consistently exhibited mean scale scores on all six scales that indicated that they were 'adult': that is, they scored 'higher' on the scales of Abstract Stage Religious Thinking and 'lower' on the scales of Concrete Stage Religious Thinking than Peatling's sample of students.[14]

2 A study of Lutheran students

The second researcher to request permission to use *Thinking about the Bible* during 1971 was Dr Charles W. Laabs, a professor of education at Concordia Teachers College in River Forest, Illinois. The author and Laabs co-operated closely in this study, although the sample was created solely by Laabs and his students from schools serviced by Concordia and affiliated with the Lutheran Church–Missouri Synod. The sample was geographically limited to schools in the northern part of the State of Illinois, which includes the metropolitan area around Chicago. In this study, Laabs collected 988 instruments from children and adolescents in the school grade-levels 4–9, 12. All of this data was collected by Laabs and his students, reduced to punched card format at Concordia, and, in the form of punched cards, shared with the author. Parallel and independent analyses were undertaken of this data. The author, who had moved from New York City to Schenectady in late 1971, used the same computer programs he had used in his basic study to analyse the data from Lutheran schools.[15] Copies of the resulting print-outs were shared, and a joint interpretative effort was begun.

Two research problems were uppermost in our minds: (a) would we see a similar step-wise progression in grade-level means? and (b) would we be able to distinguish the two student populations from one another, since we hypothesized a difference in the two denominationally-supported school systems? The analyses enabled us to answer both questions. The same pattern of a step-wise progression in grade-level means was clearly evident: the data suggested a similar developmental sequence of periods of relative equilibrium followed by periods of transition. Moreover, we could quite readily distinguish the two student populations in terms of mean scores on the Scales of Religious Thinking. The plateaus came at different places and, upon reflection, it was evident that although they were at similar levels they were evidence of a different rate of 'growth'. For example, the Lutheran schools' students evidenced the first three of the plateaus found for the Episcopalian schools' students, but not the final and 'highest' one. Given our hypothesis that the two denominationally-supported school systems were different (that is, one was theologically and biblically more 'conservative' than the other), the statistical lagging of plateaus pictured what one might expect. Thus, in a fair and reasonable manner we were able to describe a similar developmental process in two noticeably different student populations.

However, the author and Laabs realized that the data provided them with a peculiarly knotty interpretative problem. Given describable difference, was it possible to speak of evidence that one system's religious education was 'better' or more 'effective' than that in the other system? Without wanting to avoid the issue, in one paper and in a detailed article educational goals and values in one's 'interpretation' of relatively 'objective' data.[16] Obviously, either school system could be judged 'better', given a select set of goals and values. As researchers, we were not prepared to do more than point to our findings. As educators, we both hoped that the data would encourage and (even) permit systems to determine whether or not the results pictured their goals and values. If that happened, it was our belief that something akin to educational responsibility would be exercised.

While the Newton and Laabs studies were in their data collection phase, and after most of the data analyses had been run for the author's own study, he arranged to spend three weeks in directed library research at the School of Education of the University of Birmingham. Thus, in the late spring of 1971 he talked with Professor E.A. Peel, who had directed Goldman's original dissertation research, and other faculty at the then School of Education. He read as widely as he could into then extant (and available) post-Goldman/Piaget-related research. With considerable good fortune, he was able to spend a number of meetings with Peel considering the interpretative problem inherent in his North American data. All of that experience helped in the process of creating a thorough research report in the form of a doctoral dissertation for New York University. However, the author must assume responsibility for both that document and for any of the subsequent research into the development of Religious Thinking with which he has been associated, although he can be and is grateful for help generously and freely given in 1971, and for friendships begun and acquaintances made. Those weeks are a special memory, a thing to be cherished.

3 *A study of Finnish students*

Shortly before the author's dissertation was accepted by New York University in the summer of 1973, an almost chance meeting took place in Boston, Massachusetts. The author met Dr Kalevi Tamminen at an annual meeting of several professional groups concerned with research into various aspects of religion. As a result of that meeting (and a goodly correspondence), Tamminen decided to use the Scales of Religious Thinking as one of many measures in an extensive study of children in the Finnish school system.[17] Naturally, that decision meant that an English-language instrument had to be translated into Finnish. However, Tamminen and his students and colleagues at the Institute of Practical Theology at the University of Helsinki accomplished that task and successfully completed an extensive study of children, adolescents and university students during 1975. The Finnish edition of *Thinking about the Bible*, as distinct from the shorter North American editions, included a Piagetian moral puzzle. Thus, while scores on the Scales of Religious Thinking could be (and were) calculated, it is also possible to compare North American Episcopalian students and Finnish students on their responses to that particular puzzle, which probes one aspect of what Piaget long ago termed a sense of justice.

The Finnish study sampled 1374 children and adolescents in every other school grade-level from the Finnish grade III through the Finnish grade XI, plus some 96 second-year students at the University of Helsinki's School of Theology. A comparison of average ages for students in the Finnish grades indicated that they were comparable to students in the United States in a grade-level one higher than the Finnish numbering: for example, Finnish grade III is equivalent to United States grade 4. Thus, grade-level averages for the Finnish data may quite readily (and with reasonable accuracy) be compared to and contrasted with 'equivalent' data from North American studies. Doing that should address the question of whether or not the developmental progression discerned in prior studies was (or was not) simply a North American cultural phenomenon or, more generally, something like a cross-cultural, trans-national reflection of some basic human process of cognitive development.

In a recent issue of the journal *Character Potential: A Record of Research* Tamminen reported the Finnish results extensively,[18] and the author compared and contrasted the results of his, Laabs' and Tamminen's studies of students.[19] While Tamminen's results clearly indicate that the several Scales of Religious Thinking survived translation, his process of sampling every other grade-level made the identification of plateaus hard. However, the author's comparative study indicated that the Finnish data did witness to each and every such plateau that had been identified in previous research by Laabs and Peatling. Moreover, the Finnish grade-level means tended generally to occupy a 'middle position' between Peatling's sample means and Laabs' sample means, for equivalent grade-levels. Thus, it would appear that the two North American studies identified something very like an upper and lower bound, grade-level by grade-level, for what seems to be a remarkably general process of cognitive development (as that is expressed in or through Religious Thinking). If this interpretation be true, then Religious Thinking appears to be a reflection of some very basic human developmental process that religious educators can only 'encounter', not ignore.[20]

4 On beyond students – a select sample of adults

Between late 1969, when the author's student sampling began, and the summer of 1975, when Tamminen's Finnish study was completed, the research instrument *Thinking about the Bible* was administered in four studies to 4452 students and to 3289 adults. Data on 7741 administrations provided scores on six Scales of Religious Thinking and, of course, group means on each of those scales. During this same period, the author received a number of requests from groups of religious educators in the north-eastern part of the United States to share his findings about the development of Religious Education. Partly as an instructional strategy and partly as a research strategy he administered the original research edition of *Thinking about the Bible* to each group of adults to whom he went to make an address. In this way, he collected a highly select sample of 107 adult responses. This sample included professional and lay religious educators from Jewish synagogues, Roman Catholic, Eastern Orthodox, Anglican and Protestant churches. Moreover, the chronological ages of these adults ran from the late teens to the early fifties, with one each in the sixties and the seventies. For each of these adults it was possible to calculate a score on each of the six Scales of Religious Thinking, plus scores on a scale of prior exposure, a scale of literalism, and a moral judgment scale (in a word, everything one could calculate for the author's original student sample). Thus, it has been possible to gain some clue to the progress of Religious Thinking across much of the human life-cycle.

Much of the author's time across the period 1974–1976 has been devoted to the analysis and interpretation of the data from this select sample of adult religious educators. As of the writing of this article, it seems quite clear that Religious Thinking undergoes a slight 'regression' during the early and middle twenties, 'recovers' its direction and tends generally to increase through a seeming plateau during the thirties and early forties to a yet further plateau in the fifties. Interestingly, the data from this select sample suggests that the exact theoretical ordering of Abstract Stage Religious Thinking does not characterize any age-level sample before the late forties or early fifties.[21] If this finding should be confirmed by other more extensive studies of adults, the importance for adult religious education programmes should be considerable. Equally interesting, the adult responses to a Piagetian moral puzzle are distinctly *unlike* those of the Secondary school students in the author's original study, and distinctly *like* those of the Elementary and Junior High School students in that same study. This finding has led to a number of papers across the past several years, and to a thorough pattern analysis of adult responses, all of which suggest that the development of Religious Thinking and the development of Moral Judgment are noticeably different processes across that portion of the human life span from 9–10 years C.A. to approximately 55 years C.A.[22] Implicitly, this idea raises a fundamental theoretical question: just what does one mean by 'development' across the human life span?

5 *Further studies now in progress*

As of late 1976, four further studies are under way in the United States. Dr Laabs has completed the data gathering phase of a nation-wide study of students in school grades 4–12 in schools affilated with the Lutheran

Church–Missouri Synod. Private communication indicates that he has approximately 2890 responses to *Thinking about the Bible*, and he and the author plan to replicate their analytical and interpretative procedures on this new body of data. In addition, two studies of students in Roman Catholic schools are under way or planned. One involves a student of Dr Laabs, who intends to administer *Thinking about the Bible* to 300 students in grade-levels 4 through 8 in a school in Illinois. The second study is a dissertation project undertaken by Sr Catherine Killeen as part of her doctoral work at Rutgers University. This study will focus upon approximately 250 students in grade-levels 7–12, gather information on Religious Thinking, and study with particular care the relation between levels of cognitive operation and levels of moral judgment. Finally, Dr Dean R. Hoge and Fr Gregory Petrillo of the Sociology Department at The Catholic University of America's Boys Town Center for the Study of Youth Development are using the author's scales of Religious Thinking in a study of approximately 360 students at grade-level 10. They hope to discover some of the determinants of Religious Thinking (and of religious attitudes toward the church) among adolescents living in the metropolitan Washington, D.C., area.[23]

The four studies presently under way will, if all their plans work out, elicit responses from another 3770 students during 1976. Added to the 107 adults in the author's select sample of adults, and the 7741 students and adults involved in previous studies, 1977 should see data in hand for 8222 students and 3396 adults, or a total of 11,618. That is a lot of data. Interpretation of individual studies and, especially, of the relationships of the several studies will take some months (or years). But we should be coming close to a time when, rather generally, the simple incidence of the measurable types of Religious Thinking may be discernible. Then, and perhaps only then, will religious education be able to move with considerable *precision* and *confidence* to *adapt* both content and method to the *student*: insight, experience, philosophy and theology may always be necessary, but religious education may be close to having some verifiable knowledge, as well as an abundance of wisdom.[24] If so, the future may hold a 'science' of religious education. But whether or not that be so, the future may well construct a rigorous experimental pedagogy as a base for religious education.[25] If nothing else, that would be rather noticeably different than what now is.

Commentary, conclusions and speculations

Data on the development of Religious Thinking is far in excess of what a reader of either *Religious Thinking From Childhood to Adolescence* or *Readiness for Religion*[26] might presume; diagnosis is now far easier, but prescription is still a matter of attending to ignored or all too easily overlooked problems. Religious education is not yet a 'science', at least it is not in North America! Nor is there much of anything like a rigorous experimental pedagogy presently available. But a basic requirement for both, a way of assessing the levels of various types of Religious Thinking in student and adult populations, is in hand. Moreover, it is an objective, standardized, practical way of assessment that could be useful at a classroom level, as well as a tool for large-sample research studies. With that help, one can readily imagine a new level of realism for local curriculum decisions, the construction of assessment-based curricular units, and (perhaps) the freeing of religious education from an all too pervasive and debilitating 'adultomorphism'.[27]

In sum, studies undertaken during the eleven years 1965–1976 indicate that Religious Thinking is developmental in an almost classic Piagetian sense;[28] that Religious Thinking continues throughout middle and late adolescence;[29] that the school system's *milieu* has some determinable effect;[30] that there are grade-levels where thinking is more similar than dissimilar;[31] that the idea of readiness can have a clearly specifiable meaning;[32] that the earliest and most 'concrete' type of Religious Thinking declines but does not simply disappear;[33] that the theoretically most 'advanced' type of Religious Thinking is a preference largely of middle adulthood and beyond;[34] that the transition from 'concrete' to 'abstract' Religious Thinking is likely to be a far lengthier process than one might think;[35] that Religious Thinking is a phenomenon that is not limited to English-speaking nations;[36] that there is a discernible and different effect of aural-oral communication and visual communication upon the development of Religious Thinking toward an 'abstract' level;[37] that the levels of literalism and level of Religious Thinking tend to pull apart for many adults;[38] and that across the life-span the development of Religious Thinking and Moral Judgment have distinctly different courses;[39] and that mental age is an efficient predictor of level of Religious Thinking.[40] Moreover, all of these indications come from studies that can be (and should be!) replicated; comparisons and contrasts across differing populations need to be made, if the wisdom of the mid-1960s is to become the verifiable knowledge of the late 1970s. That possibility seems realistic, as well as a thing to be desired. But it will take more than simple interest in a theoretical problem. It will take guts – dedication and courage – for time, money, effort, and a certain level of competence must all be put to work.

The author is a research-orientated religious educator, and he has spent much of the past eleven years working with the data from the studies listed above. However, he also recognizes that data rarely speak directly; interpretation is both necessary and inevitable. Therefore, in what follows we want to interpret or speculate about some 'meanings' that seem evident after more than a decade of work.

(a) To the degree that 'understanding' is a goal of religious education, the use of legendary/mythical material must be reassessed far more realistically than it has yet been.[41] A match between probable student interpretations of such material and the goals of the religious educator must be carefully considered: in fact, a fair amount of trial is probably necessary before one will know for certain what happens when Bible and student are put together within a course of religious education.

(b) The comfortable thesis that 'something honest' about any subject can be taught at any age must be questioned.[42] Minimally, religious educators need to be very clear just what it is that will, in all probability, be learned from their 'subject' by students at given age-levels. And they must assume the educational responsibility for deciding whether or not that is 'honest'.

(c) Given a reasonable ability to assess a student's level of Religious Thinking, pedagogy can (and perhaps had best) shift from the search for 'motivations' to a consideration of 'relevance'.[43] While it may be true, as Piaget has suggested, that humans are cognitively resilient – that is, what can not be assimilated to existing cognitive structures will be overlooked – such resilience is more like insurance against 'damage' than it is a positive encouragement for educational practice. Religious education should think rigorously and extensively about how it can adjust to the pervasive effect of levels of cognition upon human understanding. In this effort, however, religious education may not be alone, for other school disciplines may also need similar periods of rigorous re-examination and adjustment.

(d) If mental age is a remarkably effective predictor of the level of 'abstract' Religious Thinking, and if increasingly 'abstract' levels are desired (either for theoretical/theological reasons or, pragmatically, because 'adults' seem increasingly to be characterized by such 'advanced' levels of thought), religious education should consider its own stake in efforts to support, advance, or accelerate the growth of general intelligence in any population.[44] Perhaps measured intelligence is a fundamentally 'religious' quality of humans, and religious education should be as concerned with the results as is any other kind of education.

(e) Since there is evidence from both Finland and the United States that traditional piety (for example, saying an evening prayer) and practice (for example, frequency of attendance at church services) *declines* as the level of 'abstract' Religious Thinking *increases*,[45] the need for (a) alternative rationales for such behaviour, and/or (b) alternative albeit acceptable behaviours, and/or (c) alternative understandings of what is meant to be a 'religious' person, becomes increasingly pressing. This need is both broad and fundamental, it will call for a new synthesis of available wisdom and verifiable knowledge, and is a quite contemporary challenge.

(f) Since levels of Religious Thinking can be assessed at a known and/or know-able level of reliability,[46] religious education (and religious educators) should get about the business of determining the differential effects of varying curricular sequences, pedagogical methods, educational settings, and teacher-related personological variables upon students' development of Religious Thinking. Some curriculum sequences may be worse than useless, while others may vary from neutrality to a positive contribution. Some methods may be self-defeating, while others may be remarkably supportive of growth, *and* that result may depend very much on the age or mental age of the students. Some settings may support growth in Religious Thinking, while other settings may suppress such growth. Some teacher personalities may be absolutely unsuited for religious education, while others may be almost ideally suited to that task. None of these is exactly a 'new' idea, but the answers may now be more approachable than ever before.

Concluding comments

It would seem like a perversity bordering upon culpable 'ignorance' to believe that there was no On Beyond the work of the 1960s in religious education, generally, or Religious Thinking, specifically. There is. Increasingly, the excuses are falling away. While the challenge increases with each excuse that drops by the wayside, there does not appear to be any *a priori* reason to believe the challenge cannot be met with an adequate response. Certainly, only a deeply pessimistic view would assign religious education *per se* to Toynbee's category of 'cultures' that could not respond to their challenge. Even if much suggests that analogue, it need not be. Yet, that is not to argue that success is certain, or the way ahead 'easy': only that a way ahead is possible, discernible, realistic, and rigorously challenging.

Notes and references

1 Seuss, D., *On Beyond Zebra*, New York, Random House, o.p.
2 An SQ is the conceptual reciprocal of an IQ, with a mean of 100 and a standard deviation of 15. The abbreviation SQ stands for the phrase 'stupidity quotient' and refers to a sometimes useful concept, albeit a presently imprecise psychometric measure.
3 Peatling, John H., *The Incidence of Concrete and Abstract Religious Thinking in the Interpretation of Three Bible Stories by Pupils Enrolled in Grades Four Through Twelve in Selected Schools in The Episcopal Church in the United States of America*, Unpublished Doctoral Dissertation, New York University, 1973, 695 pp. (Xerox University Microfilms, Ann Arbor, Michigan, No. 74–12, 859).

[A copy of this thesis is in the Birmingham University Faculty of Education Library – Ed.]

4 The criteria used for four basic types of Religious Thinking, which the author terms Very Concrete, Concrete, Abstract and Very Abstract, are listed in his dissertation text (Item 3) on pp. 153, 155, 170 and 173.

5 Goldman's preliminary studies of Religious Thinking used eight Bible stories, but his final study focused upon only three. This information may be found in: Goldman, R.J., *Religious Thinking From Childhood to Adolescence,* London, Routledge & Kegan Paul Ltd, 1964, pp. 37–38.

6 The standard set of questions used by the author in the instrument *Thinking about the Bible* is based upon the following questions listed by Goldman in Appendix A, The Picture and Story Religious Thinking Test, found in *Religious Thinking From Childhood to Adolescence* (1964) on pp. 254–257: S.1, Q.2.A; S.1, Q.4.A; S.1, Q.5; S.1, Q.6; S.2, Q.2.A; S.2, Q.2.B; S.2, Q.4; S.2, Q.5; S.3, Q.2.A; S.3, Q.2.D; S.3, Q.4; S.3, Q.5. Scale scores of Religious Thinking are based upon the student response pattern to criterion-referenced choices for all 12 questions.

7 The assistance of The Rev. John Paul Carter, Executive Secretary, National Association of Episcopal Schools, 815 Second Avenue, New York, NY. 10017, USA, was invaluable at this stage of the research. A complete listing of schools (by grade-levels) is found in Appendix B of the author's dissertation (Note 3, above), pp. 639–641.

8 Actual school-reported IQs were received for 1631 of the 1994 students, or 82 per cent of the total sample. Tests indicate that the performance of these students does not differ significantly from the performance of the total sample.

9 While the first two grade-level plateaus – grades 4 and 5, and grades 6 and 7 – are statistically significantly different from one another, both fall within 0.67 sigma of the chance mean, a band where by chance 50 per cent of all scores would be presumed to fall. Thus, both plateaus fall well within the operational definition of an 'intermediate' stage as a range of scale scores plus and minus one standard deviation about the chance mean. On the other hand, the third plateau – grades 8 and 9 – is slightly more than one standard deviation above the chance mean, while the fourth plateau – grades 10, 11 and 12 – is in excess of two standard deviations above the chance mean.

10 Goldman, Ronald J., *Religious Thinking From Childhood to Adolescence,* London, Routledge & Kegan Paul Ltd, 1964, p. 64.

11 Peatling, John H., *Op. cit.,* pp. 537–540.

12 The reference is, obviously, to *Religious Thinking From Childhood to Adolescence,* which is based solidly upon Goldman's 1962 doctoral dissertation at the University of Birmingham.

13 Newton, Thomas B., *Report on Development Testing,* Sub-System 03/00 of the NABS Project. Report No. 093, August 31, 1971. Nashville, Tennessee: Central Research, The Methodist Publishing House, 1971.

14 Peatling, John H., Charles W. Laabs and Thomas B. Newton. 'Cognitive Development: A Three-Sample Comparison of Means on the Peatling Scale of Religious Thinking', in *Character Potential: A Record of Research,* Vol. 7, No. 3, August, 1975, pp. 159–162.

15 The author used programs described in Dixon, W.J. (Ed.). *BMD Biomedical Computer Programs,* Berkeley, California, University of California Press, 2nd

ed., 1968; and in Dixon, W.J. (Ed.). *BMD Biomedical Computer Programs: X-Series Supplement*, Berkeley, California, University of California Press, 1969. Program BMD-X70, T Program and Program BMD-02D, Correlation with Transgeneration, were particularly useful.

16 Peatling, John H. and Charles W. Laabs. 'A Comparison of Data From a Sample of Students Enrolled in Schools Affiliated with The Lutheran Church–Missouri Synod with Data Reported by Peatling for a National Sample of Students Enrolled in Schools Affiliated with The Episcopal Church, Plus Some Reference to a Three-Denominational Comparison of Lutheran, Episcopalian, and a United Methodist Adult Sample, as well as Reference to Other Selected Analyses of the Lutheran Data.' A paper read at the Convention of the Religious Education Association of the United States and Canada, in Toronto, Ontario, on November 20, 1973.

Peatling, John H. and Charles W. Laabs. 'Cognitive Development of Pupils in Grades Four Through Twelve: A Comparative Study of Lutheran and Episcopalian Children and Youth', in *Character Potential: A Record of Research*, Vol. 7, No. 2, March, 1975, pp. 107–115.

17 The plans for this Finnish study were described in Kalevi Tamminen, 'Religious-Educational Research in the Faculty of Theology of the University of Helsinki', in *Character Potential: A Record of Research*, Vol. 6, No. 4, February, 1974, pp. 188–199.

18 Tamminen, Kalevi. 'Research Concerning the Development of Religious Thinking in Finnish Students: A Report of Results', in *Character Potential: A Record of Research*, Vol. 7, No. 4, April, 1976, pp. 206–219.

19 Peatling, John H., 'Finn and American: Reflections on a Comparison', in *Character Potential: A Record of Research*, Vol. 7, No. 4, April, 1976, pp. 220–225.

20 Peatling and Laabs had reached much the same conclusion after an examination of the data from their two studies (see Note 16), for they concluded that, '. . . it looks to us as if the development of Religious Thinking toward ever more "abstract" levels is close to a fact of life. . . . We think educators must recognize that this development will influence the nature of what their students can or do regard as "relevant".' Note 16, p. 114.

21 Data supporting these statements will be published in *Character Potential: A Record of Research*, Vol. 8, No. 2, *c.* May, 1977, in an article now titled, 'Cognitive Development: Religious Thinking in Children, Youth and Adults'.

22 During 1974, 1975 and 1976 the author's analyses of the data generated by students and adult responses to a Piagetian moral puzzle led to the following four papers:

Peatling, John H., *Truth Telling and Peer Protection: A Report*, Schenectady, New York, The Author, 1974, 64 pp.

Peatling, J.H., *A Piagetian Perspective on the Development of an Aspect of the Sense of Justice*, Schenectady, New York, The Author, 1975, 67 pp.

Peatling, J.H., *Signs of Structure and Signs of Dissonance: Adult Responses to a Piagetian Moral Puzzle*, Schenectady, New York, The Author, 1976, 54 pp.

Peatling, J.H., 'Continuing Development of a Sense of Justice in Life'. A paper read as part of a symposium on Career Development & Crises in Mid-Life at the Convention of the American Personnel and Guidance Association in Chicago, Illinois, on April 13, 1976, 12 pp.

23 The Maryland Youth Study of Hoge and Petrillo intends to also check on the Goldman thesis that a gap between how a student thinks about science and how a student thinks about religion accounts for a 'loss' of adolescents to religion and/or the church. Information may be secured by writing: Dr Dean R. Hoge, Department of Sociology, The Catholic University of America, Washington, D.C. 20064, USA.

24 The potentially helpful distinction between wisdom and verifiable knowledge is suggested by Jean Piaget in *Insights and Illusions of Philosophy*, New York, The World Publishing Company, 1971. It is clearly and pointedly put on pp. 230–232, which might well form the core of a lengthy meditation for many (religious) educators.

25 The author has in mind a reference specifically to: Jean Piaget, *Science of Education and the Psychology of the Child*, New York, The Viking Press, 1969/1970, pp. 8–9, 20–24, where Piaget identifies psychologically-related but pedagogically-specific problems for such a discipline. It is possible that the ability to measure Religious Thinking types and levels could make an important contribution to such an experimental pedagogy.

26 Goldman, Ronald J., *Readiness for Religion. A Basis for Developmental Religious Education*, London, Routledge and Kegan Paul, 1965.

27 The word 'adultomorphism' is used by Piaget and Inhelder in their book *The Psychology of the Child*, New York, Basic Books, Inc, 1966/1969, p. 21, with specific reference to studies of very early affectivity, which are criticized for being '. . . limited to the reconstruction of the early stage in the emotional life of the child in terms of adult psychopathology.' The use of the term here suggests that, analogically, religious education may be all too limited by a reconstruction of student 'religion' in terms of adult-level theologies, pieties, or 'philosophies'.

28 Peatling, John H., 'Cognitive Development in Pupils in Grades Four through Twelve: the Incidence of Concrete and Abstract Religious Thinking in American Children', in *Character Potential: A Record of Research*, Vol. 7, No. 1, October, 1974, pp. 52–61.

29 *Ibid.*, Also see Tamminen (1976), Note 18, above.

30 See especially Peatling and Laabs (1975), Note 16, above.

31 *Op. cit.*, Also see Peatling (1976), Note 19, above.

32 See Peatling (1973), Note 3, above.

33 *Ibid.*, Also see Notes 14, 16, 17, above.

34 This indication is based upon the author's most recent data analyses of Religious Thinking scale score means for a select sample of adults. Also see Note 21, above.

35 See Notes 14, 16 and 28, above.

36 This is a clear implication of Tamminen (1976), Note 18, above.

37 This differential effect was noted by Peatling and Laabs in their 1973 paper at the Religious Education Association convention in Toronto, Ontario; see Note 16, above. They particularly noted a positive effect of what they termed 'memorable hearing' upon Abstract Stage Religious Thinking, a phenomenon not matched by students who reported seeing biblical stories on film or television. Further research needs to be done.

38 See especially Note 13, above.

39 See Peatling (1976), in Note 22, above. Also see Peatling, John H., 'A Sense of Justice: Moral Judgement in Children, Adolescents and Adults', in *Character*

Potential: A Record of Research, Vol. 8, No. 1, December, 1976, pp. 25–34.

40 See Note 3, above; especially Table CXXXVI, Results of Running Mental Age-Level RTTA Means Against Program ***POLFIT, p. 453. The coefficient of determination for a third order polynomial is there reported to be 0.965437, which suggests a remarkably high degree of predictive efficiency from the metric of mental age to an estimate of total Abstract Stage Religious Thinking scale score mean. See also Peatling, John H., 'The slow Learner and Religious Education: A Research Note' in *Learning for Living*, 14, No. 3, January, 1975, pp. 102–106.

41 The three biblical miracle stories used by Goldman and the author as story-stimuli in the assessment of levels of Religious Thinking are examples of a much broader category of biblical material, which here is identified as 'legendary/mythical material'.

42 While this thesis of Jerome Bruner has, undoubtedly, contributed a good deal to many school subjects, far too often religious educators have taken Bruner's thesis to be license to continue their grossly optimistic attempts to teach 'adult' concepts to children. The realistic caution that was implicit in Bruner's original thesis has, at least in North American religious education, tended to be ignored. Thus, the thesis has proved far too comfortable to have produced any genuine progress.

43 See Note 3, especially pp. 559–573.

44 See Note 3, especially pp. 451–453, which report on the possibility of predicting observed mental age-level means by fitting that data to a third order polynomial (that is, an equation that takes account of a step-wise progression in the observed means). The association between mental age-level and level of Abstract Stage Religious Thinking is so close that, inferentially, one might speculate about the 'religious' quality or aspect of measured intelligence.

45 See Note 18, above, for Tamminen's examination of this association. Previously unpublished analyses of the author's student data suggest much the same phenomenon for his sample of Episcopalian students: for example, when contingency table analysis of responses to questions of religious behaviour *vs.* ranges of 'abstract' Religious Thinking scale scores was done the more 'abstract' scorers were less likely to affirm traditional acts.

46 See Note 3, Appendix D, Estimates of Reliability, pp. 665–668. The author there reported that the Abstract Stage Religious Thinking scale (RTTA) had a split-half estimate of reliability of 0.7297.

*Measurement Reapplied: Research into the Child's Attitude Towards Religion**

Leslie Francis

In an earlier article, in *Learning for Living*, Spring 1977, I argued the case that research in the area of religious development in childhood and adolescence can best be advanced by means of the development of rigorous measurement techniques.[1] In that paper I described the construction of one particular research instrument developed according to stringent psychometric scaling criteria and I presented the findings of a preliminary survey which employed that instrument. The present paper proposes to strengthen the case in three ways. First, I shall present the summary findings of further recently completed research, and discuss the implications of these findings for the religious educationalist. Second, I shall indicate the ways in which the research employing this instrument and currently in hand stands to advance the state of knowledge regarding the young person's religion. Third, I shall propose ways in which further research can profitably build upon the work so far completed.

Introduction

There is a tendency among some religious educationalists to disparage the role of measurement in education and in educational research.[2] I believe that this is unfortunate for three reasons. It ignores the contribution which measurement has made to a number of areas of study. It detracts from the contribution which measurement can already make to the area of religious education. It deters potential researchers from investing their skills in the area of religious education and, in the long term, this is to

*This article first appeared in *British Journal of Religious Education*, Vol. 1, No. 2, Winter, 1978/9.

the detriment of the religious field. The emphasis on the inadequacy of existing research underestimates the extent of the task involved in the development of measurement processes in a new field of study.

The case for measurement

Many of the principles and methods of the social sciences have been taken over from the physical sciences. It is difficult to imagine how the physical sciences could have developed to their present degree of sophistication without the prior development of precise measurement instruments. Something as simple as the foot ruler, for example, plays a very important part in building up our knowledge of the physical world and in determining our ability to respond to it.

In the area of the study of the child's physical development, the foot-ruler has eight important and distinct functions. First, the ruler functions as a descriptive tool. It enables us to chart exactly the child's development and height according to age. Second, it functions as a prescriptive tool. It enables us to prescribe the dimensions of the environment appropriate for different ages of children. Third, it functions as a predictive tool. It enables us to predict the average height for children at any given age. Fourth, it functions as a monitoring tool. It enables us to observe exactly how a given child grows over time. Fifth, it functions as a comparative tool. It enables us to compare the height of children whom we are never able to see side-by-side because they live in different countries or different times in history. Sixth, it functions as an experimental tool. It enables us to gain an understanding of the relationship between development of height and other factors, like vitamin intake. Seventh, it functions as a diagnostic tool. It draws our attention to any irregularity or abnormalities in an individual's pattern of growth, and, on the basis of such diagnosis, corrective and therapeutic strategies can be initiated. Eighth, it functions as a heuristic tool. It enables us to discover new information about the nature of growth and the situation in which healthy growth occurs. It is at this level in particular that measurement leads on to new insights which are not strictly accessible to intuition alone.

In the sphere of the social sciences the situation is less straightforward than in the sphere of the physical sciences. The problem here is two-fold. The constructs employed by the social scientist are less easy to define than those employed by the physical scientist. Attitude is less easy to define than length. The social scientists' span of working experience is considerably less. The measurement of length, weight and temperature are now well established techniques: the period of trial and error are over. The measurement of attitude, anxiety and belief are not yet well established: the period of trial and error is still under way.

However, the research techniques of the social scientist have become sufficiently well established to make the construction of measuring instruments rigorous enough to be of some service to the educationalist. As with the physical sciences, these measuring instruments, when constructed, can function in eight different ways, as descriptive, prescriptive, predictive, monitoring, comparative, experimental, diagnostic and heuristic tools.

The measurement of attitudes towards religion

The way in which attitudes are generally measured is through the careful construction of a questionnaire. The questionnaire contains a series of statements. Each statement expresses one specific opinion. The respondent is required to rate his response to each opinion item in turn. A person's attitude is something less specific than an opinion. Attitude underlies and informs opinions. We can, therefore, infer a person's attitude from his response to a number of opinion-statements. We can discover which opinion items can best indicate a specific attitude by a number of statistical criteria.[3] It is on the basis of these statistical criteria that Attitude Questionnaires can be constructed. Well constructed Attitude Questionnaires permit a considerable degree of confidence to be placed in the level of attitude measurement achieved.

One major problem exists in the area of the questionnaire measurement of attitudes which does not exist in the area of the measurement of such physical dimensions as length. It is meaningful to compare measurements of length recorded according to different metrical systems. It is possible by means of a simple transformation formula to compare information recorded in inches with information recorded in centimetres. It is considerably less easy to compare information collected by means of different attitude questionnaires, or even by means of the same questionnaire administered under different conditions.[4]

In the past there has been a tendency for each researcher working in the area of the measurement of attitudes towards religion to develop his own measuring instrument.[5] For this reason it has not been possible to co-ordinate closely the information already available in the field and a somewhat piecemeal picture has emerged.

When considering my own first attitude study I considered it worthwhile to invest, what appeared at the time, a disproportionate amount of energy into the process of the construction of the measuring instrument. My hope was that once this instrument had been constructed it would be possible to employ it in a number of different research projects, and so begin to build up a bank of comparable data. The basic attitude scale is a twenty-four item instrument conforming to the scaling criteria originally proposed by Likert[6] and subsequently modified in a number of ways.[7] The scale is known to work with high levels of reliability and validity over a wide age-range from the first year of the junior school to the fifth year in the secondary school. It did not prove possible to extend the usefulness of the scale at the lower end of the age range into the infant school. As yet, data is not available on the usefulness of the scale among older age groups than the fifth year in the secondary school.

In addition to the basic attitude scale, a short lie-detection scale has been constructed. The purpose of the lie-detection scale is to detect conscious or unconscious tendencies towards response falsification.[8] Information is also available on the influence of aspects of the testing situation on the pupils' responses. For example, we know now the influence which the test administrator is likely to have on the pupils' response to these questions. We also know the degree to which anonymity is important in the completion of the questionnaires. We know the reading ages, presupposed by the questionnaire items and by the instruction which precedes them.[9]

Completed research

To date two research projects have been completed using my attitude scale and the data collected in the course of these projects has been analysed. Both projects were conducted in 1974.

1 Attitude change according to age

The first project was designed to monitor the change which occurs in the child's attitude towards religion during the period of schooling. The precise age limits embraced by the study were defined by two factors. The younger end of the age continuum was defined by the fact that the Attitude Scale was known not to function reliably earlier than the first year of the junior school. The older end of the age continuum was defined by the fact that after the fifth year of the secondary school, schools no longer contain a representative sample of the age group.

Attitude scales were therefore administered to children in the nine year groups from the first year of the junior school to the fifth year of the secondary school. This represents the widest age range so far investigated by any single attitude scale in English educational research.[10] More than one hundred children were tested from each age group. The schools and subjects within these schools were randomly selected to be representative of pupils in local education authority schools in Essex, Suffolk and Cambridgeshire. The variables included in the research design were sex, age, religious behaviour and religious involvement.

Four of the conclusions from this research project are of considerable importance. First, it was shown that a constant and persistent deterioration occurs in the child's attitude towards religion according to increase in age. This deterioration is not, however, characterized by any specific changes at certain ages. It has been suggested from time-to-time that a deterioration in attitude towards religion and religious education is associated with specific age levels, specific crisis of youth, and even with the transition from primary to secondary schooling. None of these suggestions is supported by the present empirical data. There is a simple and straight gradient of decline in attitude from the age of eight to the age of fifteen. This observation seems to define very clearly the situation in which the religious educationalist is working, and the situation which he needs to work to change.

Second, this study demonstrates that the deterioration of attitude towards religion, long suspected to be the case in the secondary school, in fact has its roots in the primary school. It follows from this new information that any corrective in the form of modified teaching programmes needs also to be given its roots in the primary school. There is need at the present time for a serious curriculum development initiative to review the needs of the primary school child in relationship to religious education.

Third, this study demonstrates that there is a specific movement towards more aggressively hostile attitudes among the pupils in the fifth year of the secondary school. This seems to be associated with the general hardening of attitudes towards compulsory schooling which occurs in relationship to the raising of the school leaving age.

Fourth, any tendency towards the maintenance of favourable attitudes in the secondary school is at present strongly associated with the extra curriculum influence of the churches among young people. This information should be of considerable importance to the churches in two ways. First, it emphasizes the influence which the church is still able to exercise on the young. Second, it emphasizes the minority nature of the young people with whom the churches currently appear to have contact. The problem remains very much one of the churches' failure to make contact with the young. At the present time the churches need to be prepared to invest much more by way of specialized skills and resources into coming to terms with the vital issue of the churches' work among young people.

2 Primary school influence on pupil attitude

The second project was designed to examine the influence of the school upon the primary school child's attitude towards religion. Two specific aspects of the school were isolated for research attention. The first issue concerns the form of religious education provided. Within local education authority primary schools, there seem to be three main approaches for religious education. Some primary schools still employ the form of teaching advocated by the type of agreed syllabus which emerged after the 1944 Education Act.[11] Some schools employ the form of agreed syllabus which emerged as a result of the West Riding initiative in 1966.[12] Other schools seem to provide no religious education at all. The second issue concerns the foundation of the school. Three different foundations seem worth comparing, the local education authority primary school, the Church of England aided primary school, and the Roman Catholic aided primary school.

Schools were selected to be representative of these different approaches to education within the three counties of Essex, Suffolk and Cambridgeshire. Within these schools the Attitude Questionnaire was administered to all third year and fourth year junior pupils. This involved nearly three thousand children. The variables included in this research project were age, sex, intelligence, reading age, social class, religious behaviour, religious involvement and parental religious behaviour.

Three of the conclusions from this research project are of considerable importance. First, this study questioned some of the claims made for the form of agreed syllabus which belongs to the West Riding mould. This new form of syllabus was promoted on the grounds that it would inhibit the deterioration of attitudes towards religion which was at that stage largely attributed to the content and organization of the old form of agreed syllabus. Strangely, no previous study among English school children had ever evaluated this claim until my 1974 project. The results of my project throw considerable doubt upon the claims made for the new style of syllabus. It was found that unfavourable attitudes were more associated with pupils taught according to the new style of syllabus than according to the old style of syllabus. This observation provides a strong case that curriculum innovation should be carefully monitored by research before it becomes too widely accepted.

Second, this study provides some disquieting information on Church of England aided primary schools. One of the main grounds on which the Church argues for the maintenance of church schools is that they contribute towards developing favourable attitudes towards religion in their pupils. The results of my study throw considerable doubt upon the realistic nature of this claim. It was found that unfavourable attitudes towards religion were more associated with pupils taught in some Church of England aided schools than in local education authority schools. This observation provides a strong case that the Church of England should give serious attention to what goes on in its aided primary schools.

Third, this study provides a great deal of encouragement for the Roman Catholic aided primary schools. Even if the influence of church attendance and parental religious behaviour in Roman Catholic families is taken into account, it was found that Roman Catholic schools contribute greatly to the pupils' favourable attitude towards religion. This finding gives considerable support to the value of research and curriculum development work currently being undertaken by the Roman Catholic Church for use in its aided schools. The allocation of skill and finance in this area is proving to be a very worthwhile investment for the Roman Catholic Church.

Research in progress

Since 1974 the two initial research projects have become the basis on which further research studies have been designed to employ the same attitude scale. It is in this way that a body of interrelated research data will be gradually assembled. During 1978, four years after the original projects, four separate research studies have been commenced. I propose now to provide a brief introduction to these studies which are currently in progress.

1 Mike Stubbs

Mike Stubbs is working in the area of Special Education within the context of a year's secondment at Culham College. He is employing the attitude scale in order to monitor the attitudes towards religion of the young people who are in the eight residential schools of the National Children's Home. Stubbs is concerned that as yet little research has been done in the area of the religious development of the slow-learning child. His own sample includes the physically handicapped, the ESN (M) child, and children in community homes. Stubbs' research data will make an important contribution to our knowledge of these groups of children. His intention is that this information should be employed in assessing and developing the religious education programme adopted within the schools of the National Children's Home.

Stubbs' research design has also taken into consideration a potentially important set of variables not included by my own studies. Stubbs' project incorporated the Junior Eysenck Personality Inventory.[13] It will be of interest and value to explore the relationship between attitudes towards religion and introversion, extraversion and neuroticism amongst slow-learning children.

Mike Stubbs regards his present project as a pilot study. He hopes, if time and funding become available, to design and execute a larger project in the important area of religion and special education. It is to be hoped that he finds appropriate sponsorship for this.

2 William Kay

William Kay is working in the area of comparative education within the context of Reading University. He is employing the attitude scale in order to obtain information about young peoples' attitudes towards religion in different countries. At present he is considering a comparison between children in England, Ireland and possibly Israel. It will, for example, be of considerable interest to learn how the attitude towards religion of those brought up in the atmosphere of religious conflict which prevails in Northern Ireland differs from the attitude of young people in England.

It is conceivable that this information might be of relevance both to understanding the conflict situation in Ireland, and to advancing an appropriate educational response to that situation.

Like Mike Stubbs' project, William Kay also intends to employ the Junior Eysenck Personality Inventory. In addition, he is using the Peatling Scale of Religious Thinking.[14] This project will therefore provide some important information about the relationship between attitudes towards religion and the development of religious thinking. This is an issue which has not been previously explored by means of carefully constructed psychometric instruments.

3 James Jones and Pete Meadows

Although the main intention of an attitude scale is to speak in terms of an overall attitude score, it is always worth keeping in mind the fact that the scale itself is composed of a number of opinion statements. As well as the overall attitude score, it is also possible to report the percentage responses to the individual opinion items. It is this property of my attitude scale which appeals to Jones and Meadows.

Jones and Meadows are in the process of conducting an Opinion Survey on behalf of certain Evangelical organizations which work among young people, namely Scripture Union, the Bible Society, the Evangelical Alliance and the *Buzz* Magazine. The objective of their project is to explore the best ways of communicating the Christian faith to young people. They believe that this process of communication is best advanced in relationship to a study of young people's beliefs and opinions. As part of their research questionnaire they propose to employ some of the opinion items from my own Attitude Questionnaire. In this way, it will be possible to relate their research data to the existing body of knowledge assembled by means of my own Attitude Scale.

4 Leslie Francis, John Rust and Boyd Wesley

John Rust and Leslie Francis have recently attracted Social Science Research Council funding in order to establish a research project based on the London University Institute of Education. The intention of the project is to replicate the two original studies which I conducted in 1974. The 1974 studies will be replicated in the sense that the same schools, the same sampling procedure, and the same questionnaire will be employed in establishing the two 1978 studies as were employed in establishing the original studies. The new studies are being conducted by Boyd Wesley, the Project Officer.

These replication studies will provide two kinds of important information. First, they will provide an opportunity to check the conclusions drawn from the original studies. If the earlier findings regarding such crucial issues as the negative influence of Church of England aided primary schools on pupils' attitudes towards religion are repeated there will emerge a very firm basis on which to argue for a serious evaluation of the situation. If the earlier findings are not replicated it will be necessary either to explain the discrepancy or to caveat the strategy on which the whole research exercise is being mounted. Either way the findings of the replication studies stand to be of considerable importance.

Second, the replication studies will provide a completely new dimension to the research knowledge already available. This dimension concerns the change which occurs in pupil attitude towards religion over time. The mapping of change in attitude over time can only be achieved when the same Attitude Questionnaire is applied, in the same conditions, at different points in time, to samples constituted on the same basis. The present study by Francis, Rust and Wesley will provide the first occasion that these stringent criteria will have been met among such a wide age-range of English school children.

Suggestions for future research

The exciting thing about being engaged in research is the way in which each new step taken opens up more possibilities and suggestions for further research. There are five ways in which I would like to see the use of my Attitude Scale extended.

1 Further replication studies

The 1974 and 1978 studies could now become the foundation for a continued monitoring process at four-yearly intervals. In order for this possibility to be realized two things are necessary, the continued co-operation of the schools involved and the necessary level of financial support for the research. Such a programme of replication will provide an accurate measure and sensitive indication of changes which occur in the child's attitude towards religion from one year's intake to another. Such information would also provide an indication of shifts in the attitude of society itself. I hope that such replication studies will be made possible.

2 The development of new psychometric tools

The Attitude Scale discussed in the course of this paper is able to provide a careful measurement of one dimension of the child's religion, the attitudinal dimension. Other dimensions also need to be subjected to equally exacting measurement, for example, the dimensions of belief, thinking, and the ability to use religious language. I accept that it is possible to create psychometric instruments to measure these dimensions. The task is, however, a slow and exacting one. I hope that time might be made available to tackle these issues.

3 Further survey and hypothesis testing projects

The work undertaken by Mike Stubbs, William Kay, and James Jones and Pete Meadows, demonstrates the way in which my Attitude Scale can be employed in different situations to collect information about specific groups of people and to test specific research hypotheses. I hope that more researchers might become curious about the incidence and correlates of the child's attitude towards religion, and that they will wish to employ my Attitude Scale in order to put their curiosity to the test.

4 A national survey

My own projects have been limited in their scope by the restrictions imposed by my own lack of time and lack of adequate sponsorship. For this reason my projects have been limited to schools in the three counties of Essex, Suffolk and Cambridgeshire. I would like to see my own studies adopted as the pilot project for a nationwide initiative in the assessment of the standards achieved under the provision of religious education in county, voluntary aided and voluntary controlled schools.

5 International comparisons

William Kay's study has already located my own Attitude Scale in the context of comparative education. I hope that other researchers might follow his initiative and so enable us to compare with our own children the attitude towards religion held by children in other English speaking countries.

End-piece

'Cheshire Puss', Alice began . . . 'Would you tell me, please, which way I ought to go from here?'

'That depends a good deal on where you want to get to' said the Cat.

In the course of this paper I have argued the direction in which I consider research in religious education ought to proceed. The question is no longer one of determining the direction but of canvassing the support which is necessary in order to make the journey possible. The only real answer to this need is for the Churches and Christian Youth Organizations to consider seriously the establishment of a university-based research project in the area of religious development in childhood and adolescence. The need is pressing and the answer needs to be put into operation quickly.[15]

Notes

1 Francis, L.J., 'Readiness for Research in Religion' *Learning for Living*, 16, 1977, pp. 109–114.
2 See Edwin Cox's editorial in *Learning for Living*, 17, 1977, pp. 1–2.
3 Francis, L.J., 'Attitude and Longitude: A Study in Measurement' *Character Potential: A Record of Research*, 8, 1978, pp. 119–130.
4 See, for example, the discussion in Rosenthal, R., *Experimenter effects in behavioural research* (enlarged edition) New York: Irvington Publishers Inc., 1976.
5 I review this earlier research thoroughly in Francis, L.J., 'An Enquiry into the Concept "Readiness for Religion"'. Unpublished Ph.D. dissertation. University of Cambridge, 1976.
6 Likert, R.A., 'A technique for the measurement of attitudes' *Archives of Psychology, New York*, 22, 1932, pp. 5–55.
7 See Edwards, A.L., *Techniques of Attitude Scale Construction*, New York: Appleton-Century-Crofts, Inc., 1957 and Lemon, N., *Attitudes and their Measurement*, London: B.T. Batsford Ltd., 1973.
8 See, for example, Eysenck, S.B.G., *et al.*, 'Interpretation of Children's lie scale scores' *British Journal of Educational Psychology*, 41, 1971, pp. 23–31.
9 Full details regarding the construction and psychometric properties of this scale are available in Francis, L.J., 'An Enquiry into the Concept "Readiness for Religion"'. Unpublished Ph.D. dissertation, University of Cambridge, 1976.
10 See, for example, the studies cited by Evans, K.M., *Attitudes and Interests in Education*, London: Routledge and Kegan Paul, 1965.
11 For example see Cambridgeshire and the Isle of Ely *The Cambridgeshire Syllabus of Religious Teaching*, Cambridge: University Press, 1949.
12 West Riding of Yorkshire *Suggestions for Religious Education*, Wakefield: County Education Office, 1966.
13 See Eysenck, S.B.G., *Manual of the Junior Eysenck Personality Inventory*, London: University of London Press, 1965.
14 Peatling, J.H., 'The incidence of concrete and abstract religious thinking in the interpretation of three bible stories by pupils enrolled in grades four through twelve in selected schools in the Episcopal Church in the United States of America'. Unpublished Ph.D. dissertation. University of New York, 1973.
15 On this point, see further Francis, L.J., 'Theology and Education: a Research Perspective', *Scottish Journal of Theology*, 31, 1979, pp. 61–70.

*Towards a Standardized Test of Religious Language Comprehension**

E.B. Turner

It has long been considered that vocabulary gives a good estimate of capacity for conceptual thought and, while the complexity of the language/thought relationship is very evident in relation to religious ideas, it is suggested that a carefully constructed test of religious language may be a suitable means of assessing the understanding of religious concepts. The development of such a test is described.

Introduction and rationale

The abstract nature of many religious ideas[1] and the logical features of religious language[6,27] raise complex issues concerning the nature of the relationship between language and thought. Intuitively, it seems desirable that an approach to these problems should be seen in the context of more general cognitive psychology, not least because of the conceptual and methodological weaknesses of many studies of children's religious thinking. Having said this, it must be admitted that the extensive psychological literature on concept formation is notable for its terminological relativism[26] and, clearly, it is possible to discern different emphases in discussion of the language-thought relationship. However, it seems reasonable to accept the views of those writers, from Terman[35] onwards, who assert that language is important in concept formation, representing experience and transforming it[5] and greatly expanding the scope of thought. An impressive amount of research indicates that it is by means of words that many abstract concepts are developed which can be utilized in the absence of exemplars,[3] a finding of obvious relevance to religious concepts which

*This article first appeared in *British Journal of Religious Education,* Vol. 1, No. 1, Autumn, 1978.

often have no physical referents at all and must be explicated in terms of distinctive words and phrases.[28]

Vocabulary has long been considered to give a good estimate of capacity for conceptual thought. When vocabulary tests have been used for diagnostic purposes, qualitative marking of responses under headings such as 'concrete', 'functional' and 'abstract' has proved useful[11] and there is much support for the view that vocabulary standards reflect successive stages in cognitive development,[37] with increasing numbers of abstract definitions and growing awareness of the class features of words.[25,30,44] Other workers have seen particular advantages in proverb tests.[4,9] Gorham[13] suggests that such tests, requiring a grasp of symbolic meaning, readily stimulate an abstract attitude. Tests using words in context have also been advocated;[19] sometimes these reveal illogical extension of word meaning or failure to distinguish between word and context.[45] An important aspect of vocabulary development lies in the acquisition of new meanings for words already known[29] and this is evident with religious language, where there is reason to suppose that progress depends on prior development of other concepts from which analogies are drawn.[12,21]

The Religious Language Comprehension Test described here was devised because a search of relevant literature did not disclose any comprehensive test of religious understanding which could be regarded as satisfactory for adolescents of a rather wide range of ability and which could meet the normal criteria of test construction, validity and reliability. For example, there must be many reservations about attempts to base sweeping conclusions on children's understanding of two or three biblical narratives,[12] particularly when it is not clear that any objective principle underlies their selection. More conventional tests have also been used and one or two illustrations may be appropriate to show that these, too, are rather vulnerable to criticism.

A questionnaire designed to test religious and biblical knowledge was drawn up by the University of Sheffield Institute of Education[42] and adopted, with very slight modification, by Loukes.[23] Subjects were required to place lists of biblical events in order, to name biblical personalities, and to indicate the significance of major Christian festivals but, although the question list was administered to very large numbers of children and seems to have produced similar results in both studies, no clear principle seems to underlie the selection of items and there was no serious analysis of results, so that validity and reliability have not been established. Alves[2] uses tests with multiple-choice responses to assess ability to identify and understand certain quotations from the gospels, but this very interesting idea is rather spoiled by inclusion of an insufficient number of items to ensure a statistically meaningful interpretation of results for all levels of response.

It seems that one of the best ways of assessing the understanding of religious ideas would be a carefully constructed test using biblical words.

It would not be legitimate to equate biblical language with religious concepts but it would appear reasonable to suggest that, if a good knowledge of biblical language is present, this is evidence that religious concepts are well developed. The idea of a word-list is not new: Hyde[20] employs a multiple-choice test of twenty biblical terms, with five responses for each, but, again, there is the possible objection that seven or more correct answers would be required before the possibility of answering on a chance basis could be excluded (at the five per cent level of confidence).

Selection and words

For any vocabulary test, the method of word selection is very important. Terman and Childs[36] drew up their vocabulary test by taking the last word of every sixth column in Webster's pocket dictionary, the assumption being that one hundred words selected according to some arbitrary rule would be a large enough sample to afford a reliable index of the subject's entire vocabulary.[33]

For present purposes, it would not have been satisfactory to select words at random from a biblical concordance, since this would have led to the inclusion of words having no special 'religious' meaning. It would have been equally unsatisfactory to draw up a list of words which the investigator happened to consider important. Instead, a preliminary list was made of one hundred and thirty words included by Richardson[29] and by Douglas.[8] These are biblical dictionaries which attempt the 'theological elucidation of the whole Bible'. They seek to achieve this not inconsiderable aim in articles dealing with 'such words as have acquired specific biblical-theological meaning'. It was felt: (i) that a word would have been included in the two reference books only if a consensus of opinion existed among the contributing scholars that it contained one or more ideas of theological importance and (ii) that the method of selection minimized the influence of the investigator's subjective judgment. Certain words, though common to the two dictionaries, were excluded because they seemed wholly unsuitable and here, it is admitted, an element of subjectivity is introduced. However, it would have been difficult to justify the inclusion of most proper names or of certain words used figuratively in the condemnation of idolatry. The use of one hundred and thirty words in the pilot study must be thought to have ensured the investigation of a wide range of religious ideas among the subjects interviewed.

Method of presentation

The words were presented to the subjects, in individual interviews, and they were asked for explanations as is done in, for example, the vocabulary sub-tests of the Wechsler Intelligence Scale for Children and the Stanford-Binet Intelligence Scale. This has advantages over a pencil and paper test, in that the child's spontaneous definitions often throw light on the degree of maturity of his understanding.[34]

Because context affects understanding,[45] it seemed desirable to present some words in the context of short biblical quotations and others without such explicit contexts. Four points are noteworthy: (i) Quotations were drawn from the Revised Standard Version because it was not in use in any of the schools concerned in the investigation and, being slightly unfamiliar to most subjects, its use would not give advantage to any particular group. (ii) There was often no choice in the placement of a particular word. For example, it would have been pointless to request a definition of 'bread' without placing it in a biblical context where its metaphorical significance might be clear. This is why the numbers of words in the two preliminary categories were unequal. (iii) No assumption was made about the relative difficulty of the two categories. (iv) It is accepted that, even if a biblical word is presented in isolation, it cannot be assumed to be 'context-free'; a word such as 'parable' would have too many associations in the minds of most children for such an assumption to be justified.

Scoring method

After much consideration, it was decided to adopt a dichotomous scoring method, a decision which demands some comment and illustration.

Carter and Bowles[7] and Wechsler[43] are among those who have stressed the diagnostic value of considering qualitative levels of definition. The benefits of this are widely attested[14,25] and Wechsler introduced differential scoring into the WISC so that poverty of content is penalized and vague knowledge given only half credit. Feifel and Lorge[10] used a five-fold qualitative system, feeling that qualitative patterns may illuminate conceptual levels and, perhaps, support other data concerning the child's thinking processes.

On the other hand, Terman and Merrill[37] abandoned the differential marking of the 1916 version of the Stanford-Binet Scale and introduced a strictly dichotomous, right or wrong, scoring system. They claim that this adequately reflects successive stages in the development of thinking, since the more abstract and difficult the word the more exacting is such a scoring method. Terman and Merrill cite the work of two graduate students, Marx and Green, who investigated qualitative scoring methods; they conclude that the value of the test was not greatly increased and that more subjective factors may be introduced by a complex scoring system. It has been doubted[32] whether the responses which some people classify as 'concrete' and 'functional' really represent different levels of thinking.

In dealing with religious ideas, rather than with general vocabulary, there may be even less need to make provision for such gradations. The two theological word-books from which the items had been compiled were used as a check in assessing the responses and, in practice, the dichotomous scoring system raised few problems. Some arbitrary decisions were involved but this would have been at least equally true if a more complex method of classification had been introduced. Three examples may be illuminating.

The word 'Church' may be considered first. If a child says, as many did, that 'It's a place you go to speak about God', he is, in one sense, correct. In fact, the first meaning given in the Concise Oxford Dictionary is not dissimilar. But *kuriakon* in the sense of 'the Lord's house' does not occur in the Bible. 'Church' in the New Testament translates *ecclesia* which always means an assembly or group of assemblies and cannot mean a building. Therefore, if a child gives an answer, as a smaller number did, showing some grasp of the notion of a group of people, a community existing through its unity with Christ, he must be thought to have attained a fuller understanding. As the aim, at this stage of the investigation, was to rank words according to their degree of difficulty, it seemed better to classify only this fuller type of response as 'correct'.

Similarly, 'bread' was described by many subjects as 'something you eat', while others said, 'He gives us our food and all'. Some answers indicated an understanding of Christ as the sustainer of both physical and spiritual life and noted a relevance to the Eucharist. It seemed better to accept only these insightful answers as 'correct' and to give no credit for literalism.

An example which is, perhaps, less clear-cut is the word 'Adam'. Accepting that the story was taken literally for centuries, with the idea of the sin of Adam transmitted like a physical defect, it could be said that children who define 'Adam' as 'the first man on earth' are not without knowledge. A minority gave answers suggesting that only for the purposes of the myth does 'Adam' become a proper name. This minority, who used phrases such as 'a parable for the whole of mankind' or 'our first parents' or 'a story to show how sin affects us' seemed to grasp the idea that they were dealing with a truth about the paradoxical nature of Man, with Creation as an eternal activity and the 'fall' as an ingredient of all human life. Again, only this second type of answer was regarded as 'correct'.

Choice of subjects

This stage of the investigation was confined to boys. There were two reasons for this: there is ample evidence that girls tend to have greater facility in most verbal tasks and more favourable religious attitudes. One hundred and ninety-two boys were selected from the enrolment of a local authority secondary school. Forty were taken at random from each of the first four year-groups and thirty-two from the fifth-year group. Even following the raising of the school leaving age, there are grounds for thinking that those in their fifth year of secondary schooling are not strictly comparable with younger groups and it was not intended to involve such subjects in subsequent use of the developed Religious Language Comprehension Test. They were included in the pilot study in order to give an adequate 'ceiling' to the test. The ages of the selected children are summarized in Table 1 where it will be seen that the fifth-year group shows considerable variability.

Table 1. Age-distribution for subjects in preliminary study of religious vocabulary

Year	I	II	III	IV	V
Number	40	40	40	40	32
Mean age	12.3	13.5	14.5	15.2	16.8
S.D.	0.1	0.3	0.4	0.2	0.9

Test procedure

Each boy was interviewed separately in an ordinary classroom and, after his age had been noted, he was tested on the vocabulary sub-scale of the Wechsler Intelligence Scale for Children. This seemed an excellent introduction to accustom the subjects to the procedure of giving explanations for words. Furthermore, as a vocabulary scale provides a good estimate of general intelligence, it was thought desirable to have scores on a test of established validity to which scores on the Religious Language Comprehension Test could be related. The scores on the WISC vocabulary subscale are summarized in Table 2.

Table 2. Distribution of WISC vocabulary scores

Year	I	II	III	IV	V
Number	40	40	40	40	32
Mean score	36.23	37.45	39.65	40.23	50.09
S.D.	6.71	7.13	7.02	6.90	6.67

To go through a list of one hundred and thirty words, taking an average of twenty-five minutes, is asking a great deal of boys, some of whom are only eleven years old and some from backward classes, and every effort was made to help them feel at ease by maintaining a normal conversational atmosphere. Each boy was told that he was helping to choose 'a list of Bible words which boys your age would know' and was assured (truthfully) that the list, and not himself, was being tested.

For the list of words in quotations, the subject was shown a series of cards on each of which was typed, in capital letters, the appropriate word.

Underneath was typed the quotation, with the key word underlined. The cards were presented in alphabetical order of the words under consideration. For example, a subject would be presented with the relevant card and asked, 'Bread. Jesus said: "I am the bread which came down from heaven". What does bread mean there?'

The words without explicit context were then presented, again in alphabetical order. For example, the relevant card would be shown and the subject would be asked, 'Church. What does Church mean?'

Frequently, the subject was told, 'That is very good', or, 'You are doing very well'. If he did not readily answer, he was told, 'Try. What do you think it means?' and, perhaps, 'Does it mean anything else?' This simple encouragement elicited many good answers which confirmed the opinion that the interview method, while time-consuming, is more likely to reveal the true degree of understanding than is a written test in which, either, the child may leave an unnecessarily large number of items unanswered or may be restricted by fixed-choice responses. If no answer was forthcoming, the subject was told, 'Don't worry. You are doing well', or, 'Maybe we shouldn't put that one in'.

Every reply was recorded in full.

The scores, for each age-group, on the seventy-six words in quotations are summarized in Table 3, those on the fifty-four words without such context are summarized in Table 4 and the combined scores in Table 5.

Table 3. Distribution of scores on list of seventy-six words in quotations

Year	I	II	III	IV	V
Number	40	40	40	40	32
Mean score	20.40	23.95	25.95	30.68	39.47
S.D.	9.82	10.24	12.72	11.21	10.78

Table 4. Distribution of scores on list of fifty-four words without explicit context

Year	I	II	III	IV	V
Number	40	40	40	40	32
Mean score	14.63	14.88	16.25	17.58	24.97
S.D.	6.77	6.11	7.39	6.85	7.45

Table 5. Distribution of scores on combined lists of one hundred and thirty words

Year	I	II	III	IV	V
Number	40	40	40	40	32
Mean score	35.03	38.83	42.20	48.25	64.56
S.D.	15.77	15.93	19.51	17.10	17.28

Spearman Rank-order Correlation Co-efficients[31] were computed for each year-group: (a) between scores on the 'quotations' and 'words' lists; (b) between each of these scores and the WISC vocabulary scores; (c) between scores on the combined list of one hundred and thirty items and the WISC vocabulary scores. It is noteworthy that every correlation, for each year-group, was highly significant ($p < 0.005$). Chi-square tests for goodness of fit[18] were applied to the distributions of scores, for each year-group, on 'quotations', on 'words', and on the combined items. The results indicated that none of these distributions differed significantly from normal.

Choice of scaling method

It was to be expected that subjects would find considerable variation in difficulty among the one hundred and thirty words on the preliminary lists, some being widely understood and others too difficult for the great majority. It was necessary to adopt a scaling method which would not only establish the relative difficulty of the items but also differentiate between them on the basis of their power to discriminate between high and low scorers.

Much previous research with non-quantitative date has used Guttman's[16,17] scalogram procedure to scale items for test purposes or to classify responses. The Guttman technique has the advantage of simplicity; it is neither time-consuming nor mathematically demanding. However, two points regarding it must be considered. The first is that the scales evolved have usually been based on very few items. According to Stouffer,[33] although hundreds of Guttman scales have been constructed, many of them have been reduced to four or five items on completion of the scaling procedure. Stouffer comments that 'even a ten or twelve item cumulative-type scale is easier to talk about than to accomplish', although Guttman specifies at least ten items in the completed scale if the items are dichotomous. The second point is that Guttman's 'co-efficient of reproducibility' is a highly deceptive index.[38] In general, a set of items with a co-efficient of reproducibility half-way between unity and that expected by chance is likely to be considered scalable.[15,38] Hence it seems clear that the ideal Guttman scale does not really describe empirical data very closely.

Consideration was, therefore, given to other available methods of scaling dichotomous data and that of Tucker[40,41] was selected. This rather sophisticated method is discussed by Torgerson[38] and its practical application has been demonstrated, by Tucker, in scaling vocabulary and verbal analogy items.

Final selection of items

On completion of the scaling procedure, twenty items were selected from the 'quotations' list and twenty from the 'words' list so that the entire range of scale values was evenly covered and items of low discriminative power were excluded. The number was arrived at from a consideration of the overall length of the task for the children and because it was felt that forty items should provide an adequate opportunity for most subjects to indicate their knowledge.

Table 6. Distribution of scores on scaled list of twenty words in quotations

Year	I	II	III	IV	V
Number	40	40	40	40	32
Median score	4	4	4	7	12
Range	0–9	0–13	0–13	0–15	2–16

Table 7. Distribution of scores on scaled list of twenty words without explicit context

Year	I	II	III	IV	V
Number	40	40	40	40	32
Median score	3	3	4	5	10
Range	0–11	0–8	0–12	1–15	3–17

The test was re-marked on the basis of the scaled lists and distributions of scores on the scaled 'quotations' and scaled 'words' are given in Tables 6 and 7. These distributions are slightly skewed and therefore the tables present median scores and ranges instead of means and standard deviations. The Kolmogorov-Smirnov test[31] was used to compare the distributions of scores on the scaled list of 'quotations' and the scaled list of 'words'. The result of this two-tailed test indicated no significant discrepancy between the distributions and therefore the two lists could legitimately be combined and regarded as a single test. The distribution of combined scaled scores is summarized in Table 8.

Table 8. Distribution of scores on combined scaled list of forty words

Year	I	II	III	IV	V
Number	40	40	40	40	32
Median score	6	7	10	13	22
Range	0–18	0–21	0–25	2–30	6–34

For each year-group, a matrix of twenty-one Spearman Rank-order Correlation Co-efficients[31] was computed, indicating the strength of association between every possible combination of scores on WISC vocabulary, original list of 'quotations', original list of 'words, original combined list, scaled list of 'quotations', scaled list of 'words' and scaled combined list. Although significance in such matrices must be interpreted with caution, it is interesting that every correlation, corrected for tied scores,[30] is highly significant ($p < 0.005$). Correlations between scores on the original list of one hundred and thirty items and on the final scaled list of forty items are particularly interesting: these were 0.93, 0.93, 0.95, 0.92 and 0.93 for the five year-groups and give an indication of the efficiency of Tucker's method. The uniformity of the correlations between WISC vocabulary scores and those on the final list of forty items suggests that this Religious Language Comprehension Test is a very stable measure.

Kendall's Co-efficient of Concordance[18] was calculated, for each age-group, to establish the extent of the relationship between scores on the WISC vocabulary sub-scale, the scaled 'quotations', the scaled 'words' and the scaled total. The values for Kendall's 'W' shown in Table 9 are both high and uniform, giving some further indication of the stability of the Religious Language Comprehension Test in its final form. All are highly significant ($p < 0.001$)

Table 9. Values of Kendall's Co-efficient of Concordance

Year	I	II	III	IV	V
W-value	0.77	0.84	0.82	0.84	0.84

To determine the reliability of the Religious Language Comprehension Test, Kuder-Richardson Reliability Co-efficients[22] were computed, for each of the first four year-groups, from scores on the scaled list of forty items. The results, given in Table 10, indicate that reliability is high and consistent across all year-groups.

Table 10. Kuder-Richardson Reliability Co-efficients for Religious Language Comprehension Test

Year	I	II	III	IV
r	0.84	0.84	0.75	0.82

Conclusion

It would be gratuitous to claim that a high score on the Religious Language Comprehension Test proves the existence of mature religious thinking but religious concepts, as commonly used, are highly verbal and it may be claimed that the test gives a good estimate of capacity for understanding their verbal expression. Just as a normal vocabulary test gives a good estimate of general intelligence, religious vocabulary may be considered to give a good measure of the intellectual apprehension of religious ideas.

It would seem that progression towards a standardized test of religious language comprehension is indeed a realistic aim. Already the Religious

Language Comprehension Test has been used successfully in studies involving more than seven hundred secondary schoolboys, showing significant age-related changes in the understanding of religious language and significant differences between the performance of boys attending local authority schools and those attending schools run by religious orders.[41] The use of the existing measure with girls is an obvious priority in its further development.

References

1 Allport, G.W., *The individual and his religion*, New York: Macmillan, 1950.
2 Alves, C., *Religion and the secondary school*, London: SCM Press, 1968.
3 Bourne, L.E., *Human conceptual behaviour*, Boston: Allyn and Bacon, 1966.
4 Brattemo, C.E., Differentiating borderline schizophrenics from other diagnostic groups by use of the proverbs text. *Acta Psychologica*, 20, 1962, pp. 279–284.
5 Bruner, J.S., The course of cognitive growth. *American Psychologist*, 19, 1964, pp. 1–15.
6 Bultmann, R., *Jesus Christ and mythology*, London: SCM Press, 1960.
7 Carter, J.W. and Bowles, J.W., A manual on qualitative aspects of psychological examination. *Clinical Research Monographs*, 2, 1948, pp. 25–26.
8 Douglas, J.D. (Ed.). *The new Bible dictionary*, London: Inter-Varsity Fellowship, 1965.
9 Elmore, C.M. and Gorham, D.R., Measuring the impairment of the abstracting function with the proverbs test. *Journal of Clinical Psychology*, 13, 1957, pp. 263–266.
10 Feifel, H. and Lorge, J., Qualitative differences in the vocabulary responses of children. *Journal of Educational Psychology*, 41, 1950, pp. 1–18.
11 Gerstein, R.A., A suggested method for analyzing and extending the use of the Wechsler-Bellevue vocabulary responses. *Journal of Consulting Psychology*, 13, 1949, pp. 366–370.
12 Goldman, R., *Religious thinking from childhood to adolescence*, London: Routledge and Kegan Paul, 1964.
13 Gorham, D.R., Use of the proverbs test differentiating schizophrenics from normals. *Journal of Consulting Psychology*, 20, 1956, pp. 435–440.
14 Graham, C., Differential marking of two vocabulary tests. *Psychological Reports*, 1963, pp. 421–422.
15 Green, B.F., A method of scalogram analysis using summary statistics. *Psychometrika*, 21, 1956, pp. 79–88.
16 Guttman, L., A basis for scaling qualitative data. *American Sociological Review*, 9, 1944, pp. 139–150.
17 Guttman, L., The principal components of scalable attitudes. In Lazarsfeld, P.F. (Ed.). *Mathematical thinking in the social sciences*, Glencoe: The Free Press, 1954.
18 Hays, W.L., *Statistics for the social sciences*, New York: Holt, Rinehart and Winston, 1963.
19 Heim, A., The word in context. *Bulletin of the British Psychological Society*, 21, 1968, p. 123.
20 Hyde, K.E., *A study of some factors influencing the communication of religious*

ideas and attitudes among secondary school children, University of Birmingham, Ph.D. thesis, 1959.

21 Lee, R.S., *Your growing child and religion*, Harmondsworth: Penguin, 1965.

22 Lord, F.M. and Novick, M.R., *Statistical theories of mental test scores*, Reading: Addison-Wesley, 1968.

23 Loukes, H., *New ground in Christian education*, London: SCM Press, 1965.

24 Macnamara, J., O'Cleirigh, A. and Kellaghan, T., *A developmental study of semantic structure in the English lexicon*, Dublin: St Patrick's College, Unpublished report, 1969.

25 Papania, N., A qualitative analysis of the vocabulary responses of institutionalized mentally retarded children. *Journal of Clinical Psychology*, 10, 1954, pp. 361–365.

26 Pikas, A., *Abstraction and concept formation*, Cambridge: Harvard University Press, 1966.

27 Ramsey, I., *Religious language*, London: SCM Press, 1957.

28 Reid, L.A., *Ways of knowledge and experience*, London: Allen and Unwin, 1961.

29 Richardson, A. (Ed.). *A theological word-book of the Bible*, London: SCM Press, 1950.

30 Russell, D.H. and Saadeh, I.Q., Qualitative levels in children's vocabularies. *Journal of Educational Psychology*, 53, 1962, pp. 170–174.

31 Siegel, S., *Non-parametric statistics for the behavioural sciences*, New York: McGraw-Hill, 1956.

32 Stacey, C.L. and Portnoy, B., A study of the differential responses of the vocabulary sub-test of the WISC. *Journal of Clinical Psychology*, 6, 1950, pp. 401–403.

33 Stouffer, S.A., *Measurement and prediction*, Princeton: Princeton University Press, 1950.

34 Terman, L.M., *The measurement of intelligence*, Boston: Houghton Mifflin, 1916.

35 Terman, L.M., *The vocabulary test as a measure of intelligence. Journal of Educational Psychology*, 3, 1918, pp. 198–208.

36 Terman, L.M. and Childs, H.G., A tentative revision and extension of the Binet-Simon measuring scale of intelligence. *Journal of Educational Psychology*, 3, 1912, pp. 198–208.

37 Terman, L.M. and Merrill, M.A., *Measuring intelligence*, London: Harrap, 1937.

38 Torgerson, W.S., *Theory and methods of scaling*, New York: Wiley, 1963.

39 Tucker, L.R., A method for scaling ability test items in difficulty, taking item unreliability into account. *American Psychologist*, 3, 1948, pp. 309–310.

40 Tucker, L.R., A level of proficiency scale for a unidimensional skill. *American Psychologist*, 7, 1952, p. 408.

41 Turner, E.B., Paper in preparation.

42 University of Sheffield Institute of Education. *Religious education in secondary schools*, London: Nelson, 1961.

43 Wechsler, D., *Wechsler intelligence scale for children*, New York: The Psychological Corporation, 1949.

44 Wechsler, D., *The measurement and appraisal of adult intelligence*, New York: Wilkins and Wilkins, 1958.

45 Werner, H. and Kaplan, E., Development of word meaning through verbal context. *Journal of Psychology*, 29, 1950, pp. 251–257.

RELIGIOUS LANGUAGE
COMPREHENSION TEST
Experimental Form
Items in each section in order of scale value

Section A

ALMIGHTY	And I will be a father to you, and you shall be my sons and daughters, says the Lord *Almighty.*
DEATH	Truly, truly, I say to you, if anyone keeps my word, he will never see *death.*
JUST	If we confess our sins, he is faithful and *just,* and will forgive our sins.
LIFE	In him was *life* and the *life* was the light of man.
JUDGEMENT	Jesus said, 'For *judgement* I came into this world, that those who do not see may see'.
LAMP	Thy word is a *lamp* to my feet and a light to my path.
IMMORTALITY	The King of kings who alone has *immortality* dwells in unapproachable light.
DRINK	Whoever *drinks* of the water that I shall give him, will never thirst.
BREAD	The Jews then murmured at him, because he said, 'I am the *bread* which came down from heaven'.
ADOPTION	God sent forth his Son, so that we might receive *adoption* as sons.
WITNESSES	This Jesus God raised up, and of that we are all *witnesses.*
BREATH	By the word of the Lord the heavens were made and all their host by the *breath* of his mouth.
MIND	Set your *mind* on things that are above, not on things that are on the earth.
MEDIATOR	For there is one God, and there is one *mediator* between God and man, the man Christ Jesus.
IMAGE	So God created man in his own *image.*
VINE	(Jesus said) 'I am the *vine,* you are the branches'.
RECONCILE	For in him all the fulness of God was pleased to dwell and through him to *reconcile* to himself all things.
FEAR	Now therefore *fear* the Lord and serve him in sincerity and in faithfulness.
HEIGHT	He looked down from his holy *height,* from heaven the Lord looked at the earth.
IMAGINATION	He has scattered the proud in the *imagination* of their hearts.

Section B

RESURRECTION PROPHET CONFESSION BAPTISE PARABLE COMMUNION HEAVEN WORSHIP SIN REDEEMER TEMPT ALMS REPENT SALVATION CHURCH MINISTER FAITH COVENANT ADAM GOSPEL.

2
The Nature of Religious Education: The Search for a Rationale

Introduction

Religious education has been undergoing a process of secularization. This means that when the nature and purposes of the subject are being explored and explained, the same types of arguments will be used as might be used in the case of any other subject of the curriculum. In 1944 the curriculum was conceived of as being two hemispheres. One of these was 'secular instruction' and the other was 'religious education', this being divided into 'religious instruction' (that is, classroom work) and the collective act of worship.

Religious educators today continue to value the unique public accountability and community participation which its special status offers religious education. However, it is now widely agreed that this special status must not be construed as meaning that the subject has some kind of privileged access to supernatural revelation, to which it can appeal to justify its place in the school. Religious education cannot be justified as representing the word of God spoken over and against the secular subjects; it is not 'the Gospel' witnessing to 'the world'.

The distinction between evangelism and education has been realized for many years and was certainly affecting religious teaching in county schools well before the 1944 Act. The motives behind the Act were naturally complex and diverse. But if, when it is said that religious education today ought to stand upon its own educational feet, and not be supported by compulsory clauses in the legislation, it is being implied that in 1944 there was no educational justification for the subject, that implication is certainly an over-simplification. Religious education was emphasized at that time because the educational argument for it (as well as the political necessity of it) was thought to be very strong. It is true, however, that the kinds of educational justification which were common in the 1930s and 1940s often involved appeal to theology in a more direct way than would be considered appropriate today. There is a place for a theological critique of the curriculum today, but any theological arguments will *bear upon* the educational arguments rather than taking their place. To put it in a different way, theological arguments must today be mediated by and through the educational arguments and will not often bear directly upon the rationale for any subject, even when that subject is religious education.

This is partly the result of the growth in recent years of a more specialized and disciplined philosophy of education. It is also the result of the secularization process in general, which has caused theology to find relationships with the secular disciplines (including religious education in county schools). These relationships tend to be more subtle and complex than those which prevailed when religious education was thought of as being part of Christian ministry in a direct and even naive fashion.

Another factor has been the rise of Curriculum Studies and theories of curriculum development as a branch of the study of education. If religious education were to ignore the impact of such studies, it would become a 'sacred island' in an entirely new way. For in spite of the kinds of direct theological justification which were used in earlier decades, and in spite of the 'two hemispheres' mentality of the Act, religious education was not placed in any position of remarkable isolation, partly because such direct theological arguments were used with respect to the whole curriculum and partly because educational studies themselves were not as well developed or so highly specialized.

These are the factors which lie behind the search for what Edwin Cox has called an 'educational Religious Education'. Many ways of achieving this have been put forward, and while it would suggest too great a degree of intellectual and organizational coherence to speak of 'schools of thought' within religious education, there certainly are different emphases. John Wilson has seen religion as comprising the emotions of wonder and awe which the religious believer feels with respect to the objects of religious worship. Religious education would thus be a matter of enabling pupils to share in these feelings and to develop critical understanding of their appropriateness and of the nature of the realities (or alleged realities) which evoke them. Religious education should thus promote rationality in this particular area of the emotional life. John Marvell contrasts the 'theological', the 'empirical' and the 'phenomenological' approaches. Pupils can be given experiences of the numinous, and religious education will thus be affective as well as cognitive. But these experiences will be related to the religions of the world, and will not involve a theological interpretation of ordinary life experiences, as had been suggested by Goldman and Loukes. The phenomenological method in the study of world religion is recommended for use in schools with pupils of all ages. David Attfield, on the other hand, emphasizes the centrality of concepts in the development of a religious understanding, seeing the task of the religious education teacher as selecting and elucidating basic religious concepts, which will in turn depend upon an earlier stage of more fundamental concepts. Edward Robinson places greater stress upon the evocation of direct experience of religion, but although there are links between his approach and those of Wilson and Marvell, his own writing is more intuitive and poetical.

*Educational Religious Education**

Edwin Cox

Schools are intended to provide education, and to justify its presence in them any activity must show it is contributing to the educational process. Religious education, which has often been confused with evangelism and indoctrination, has perhaps more than any other subject at present, to show that it is a worthwhile, and even necessary educational activity. The purpose of this paper is to try and show that a teacher in a secular and pluralist society can see his work in that way. This will involve discussing the manner in which our present culture is secular and pluralistic; stating what criteria a teacher can use in choosing his aims in such a setting; and trying to say what aims fit those criteria. R.S. Peters, in *Authority, Responsibility and Education*, has pointed out that to discuss the aims of a school subject is, in effect, to discuss not objectives to be attained, but 'principles of procedure' in teaching it. So I am really trying to state what sort of religious education is likely to have some hope of being understood and absorbed by pupils in the present culture, and of contributing to their educational development.

A secular and pluralistic society

When we speak of our present age as secular we do not necessarily mean it is irreligious. The antonym of secular is perhaps not religious but ecclesiastical. There have been ages in the past which might have been described with some accuracy as ecclesiastical irreligious, ages much dominated by church politics and administration, but with a cast of thought that lacked truly religious sensitivity. Our age is one that has found the ideas that the church deals with not altogether relevant to the experiences of a scientific and technological age, and so has repudiated both those ideas and the authority of church leaders, while still retaining religious sensitivity

*This article first appeared in *Learning for Living*, Vol. 10, No. 4, March, 1971.

in a changed form. Having repudiated the existing religious formulations there are no generally agreed patterns of thought by which this present religious sensitivity can be expressed. Each man has to think out his own pattern for himself. So some remain orthodox, others are agnostic in various ways, some of the young look to Indian religions and gurus and maharishis, some are materialistic. Scientology, existentialism, Becketian fatalism, Mormonism, and many others have their followers. Whatever religious stance you care to mention, you name it we have it, in our present world. The sensitivity is there, but there is no publicly agreed method of describing or expressing it, and every man's ideas are as good as the next. That is what I mean by a secular and pluralistic society.

In what way is that society religiously sensitive?

If we define religion, and there is some justification for doing so, as man's attempts to find answers to his deepest problems, and examine those problems, we find that they have changed significantly in the last hundred years, and this may explain the shift in religious sensitivity. Formerly the deepest problems facing man were:

> How was the world created and why does created matter behave as it does?
> Why is life so precarious, with death coming as frequently to the young and middle-aged as to the old?
> Why is life so unfair, with many better endowed than others with strength, acumen, wealth and opportunity?

These problems were swept aside in the East by a denial of the reality of experience, but in the West they were generally answered by postulating a creator God, who had made the world in a particular way (which is why it is here and behaves as it does), who was omnipotent and just and would therefore compensate for the precariousness and unfairness of life by redressing the balance after death. Western religion has fitted into that framework, and seemed reasonable and acceptable as long as the mythology behind it appeared consonant with experience. In the past hundred years, however, those problems have largely ceased to trouble, and when they do, we look for answers in other terms.

Creation and the interaction of matter we now try to explain in terms of astronomy, physics, anthropology and biology. Even when the very young ask 'How was the world made?', the religious answer of 'God made it' seems to them unconvincing and skipping too many intermediate steps. The problem of the precariousness of life has been largely solved by medical science. Tuberculosis, diphtheria and diabetes have within my own memory ceased to be inevitable killers. As for the unfairness of life, we hope to remedy that, not by pie in the sky, but by political and social action. So the problems that traditional religion deals with begin to look irrelevant and religion is, to many, answering problems that no longer puzzle, in terms that don't seem very practical.

Even if that is so, it does not mean that the human race has no longer any deep problems. It seems to have found itself a new crop of them which can briefly be summarized in the term living together. The population explosion means there are so many of us crowded together in a small space, the complex nature of the industrial and commercial system, which many feel controls their life and from which they can't break loose, and the pollution of environment by industry in order to provide for the crowded population (almost to the extent of endangering the continuance of the species) have brought this new set of problems. The solution of them may not be entirely in social and mechanistic terms. It involves consideration of the nature of people, the purpose of life, our responsibility for natural wealth, all of which are at bottom religious considerations. So our new problems may make us approach religion from a different angle. It may be encouraging that the young seem more alive to these problems than the older folk, as their zeal for social righteousness expressed in protests and marches, and some of the involved words of their pop songs bears witness. But this is the way in which our secular society can be called religiously sensitive.

What sort of aims can a teacher of religious education use in this situation?

If what has been already said describes accurately the existing climate of thought, what criteria can a religious education teacher use in selecting between the various aims he sets himself?

The aims should be realistic and attainable. He can set himself the aim of making all pupils believe in the complete historical veracity of all the Bible, and go to church twice on Sundays. Such an aim is possible, but I doubt if it is realizable. It seems more sensible to take notice of the situation and choose aims more likely to succeed.

They should be acceptable to the community. If the community has an agreed religious position this is easy, but in the present pluralistic society it is difficult to know what it will accept – hence the active debate about what may be taught of religion in schools.

They should seem worthwhile to the teacher, otherwise his lessons will lack conviction. One has seen lessons where one suspected the aim was to keep the beggars quiet until the bell went. The educational temperature in them was low.

They should also seem worthwhile to the pupils. If the teaching is assuming a situation that no longer exists outside the school, and dealing with ideas that are unlikely to have any practical relevance, the academically inclined may still find them interesting as an intellectual exercise,

much that is taught.

They should above all be justifiable on educational grounds and no other. Even in church schools religious education must be seen to do something more than recruit members of a church. It has to be shown contributing to the growth of the pupils' understanding and their ability to think about and deal with the secular pluralistic setting of their lives.

What aims satisfy these criteria?

What precise aims any one teacher sets himself will depend to a large extent on what sort of person he is, and how he sees religion. If he has derived personal help and peace of mind from a traditional religion he may charitably hope that he can share this with his pupils. And he will succeed with a few. If he thinks the present empirical modes of thinking and the present pre-occupation with the problems of personal relationships are a passing phase in the history of thought, and that we shall eventually return to the older religious expressions, he will try to perpetuate belief in those expressions in some of his pupils. And he will succeed with a few. He will make his faithful remnant. If he teaches in a church school he may, with some plausibility, maintain that his job is to teach the doctrines of that church, and if the customers don't like it they can go to another school. And he will succeed with some. But is there not some deeper purpose that may apply to all? I suggest there is, and that it is to help pupils to understand the nature of our present secular, pluralistic society, to help them to think rationally about the state and place of religion in it, to enable them to choose objectively and on sound criteria between the many conflicting religious statements that are made in a pluralist society, and to work out for themselves, and to be able cogently to defend, their own religious position or their rejection of the possibility of having one. This seems on examination to come down to four main aims, which seem to fit the criteria described and to be practicable.

1 To enable pupils to understand what religion has contributed to our culture. It has greatly influenced music, art, architecture, drama and literature. To understand much of these and to appreciate their effect on our lives one needs to know something of their religious inspiration and origin. And this has the advantage of being an objective study. Religion has had this influence on our culture and it is difficult to object to studying it on ideological grounds. It is therefore something all can do irrespective of their religious backgrounds.
2 The second aim is to help pupils understand what people believe and how their beliefs influence their lives. This has become all the

more urgent and accessible by the extension of travel and by immigration. We come across a far more varied section of religions nowadays, often we have to live in proximity to their adherents. Learning to understand neighbours and their motivations is a part of education and this is a contribution that religious education can make to it. Admittedly in Britain this will include a large element of study of Christianity since this is still the major religion here, but it will also include other world religions and certain religious, if non-theistic, philosophies.

3 The third aim will be helping the pupils to understand that a rational attitude to life includes making up one's mind on certain fundamental or ultimate questions of the nature of life and of human personality. This will spring to some extent from the previous aim of studying religious phenomenology, but it can also be evoked by much of modern literature, the words of protest and pop songs, and by the practical necessities of choosing a career, and so on. The way to deal with it is probably not to pose the questions directly and starkly, but by this indirect approach, and, if it is achieved, this aim will involve showing how these ultimate questions do not permit of an empirical solution, but involve, in the last resort, making a working hypothesis or an act of faith.

4 Fourthly there is the aim of helping the pupils to decide for themselves what their working hypotheses or acts of faith are going to be; that is, deciding their own religious stance. This is where RE can so easily go wrong by appearing at this stage to produce the answers out of a hat and dictating what that stance must be, so that the pupils accept it without referring to their experience, and the decision is not a genuine one and breaks down under stress. In the present pluralistic confusion it is all the more important that RE should let the pupils know what choices are available and help them to realise the implications of making any one of them, but not deprive them of their right and duty to make up their minds honestly in a decision that is all the more committing for being a genuine personal decision.

These then are the aims that seem worth attempting. They may not be all that a strongly religious person of the older type would think adequate. But it can be argued that they are morally permissible in the present situation, because they lead to a type of teaching that increases pupils' awareness and understanding. And an activity that does that can justify itself as a contribution to the educational process.

*Taking Religious Education Seriously**

John Wilson

In these brief remarks I have two quite different things to say. The first concerns the requirements of *any serious* attempt to think about (or indeed to practise) anything that could reasonably be called 'religious education' or 'education in religion'. The second concerns a few basic points which, in my opinion, seem to follow fairly obviously from any such serious attempt.

Of these, the former is both more important and (as I see it) less disputable than the latter. It is also the one thing which is least attended to in the constant flow of literature, debates, working parties and so forth which flock around 'religious education' like Homeric ghosts seeking blood; and because it is not attended to, most of what is said and written on the subject appears shadowy and bloodless.

'Religious education'

It seems incontestable that we educate people *in* various subjects, spheres of thought or activity, departments of life, or whatever terms we use to distinguish one area from another: also that the notion of education carries with it the ideas of success and failure, progress and mistakes, learning more or less, being more or less well-informed, understanding, perceptive, etc. In most subjects (areas) this is entirely clear: under such headings as 'history', 'English', 'science' and so on we have some idea both about what we are doing, and about whether we succeed or fail, in this or that case, in doing it. Not just *anything* counts as 'education in science' or 'learning history': and not just anything counts as 'being good at (well-educated in) science' or 'having learned a lot of history'.

Without some such idea of what we are doing, we could hardly educate at all: for we would not know what would count as educating. Thus

*This article first appeared in *Learning for Living*, Vol. 16, No. 1, Autumn, 1976.

without some established tradition or understanding of what science is and how to do it well, we should not know (1) what to count as 'science' (as opposed to alchemy, or magic), or (2) what to count as success and failure, mistakes and correctness, progress or backsliding, on the part of our pupils. To put this generally: without (1) a clear definition of the subject or area, and (2) clear criteria of success, we should not know whether we were *educating* pupils at all – as against merely giving them a good time, keeping them amused, telling them a few interesting facts, and so on.

Sometimes (1) and (2) are comparatively easy to state: it is not too hard to give some account both of what mathematics, science, history or Latin grammar are, and of what counts as doing them well, making a mistake in them, and so on. But sometimes they are harder: we might argue, for instance, about what is to count as 'literature' (and hence 'education in literature'), and about just what it is to be 'good at' (perceptive, understanding, well-informed, etc., about) literature. But even here, if we did not have some idea of what we were doing, we could hardly do it at all. We know, at least, that certain things do *not* count as 'literature': that it is one thing to discuss the Norman Conquest, or the cases of 'mensa', or magnetism, or the square root of 144, and another thing to try to 'appreciate' Shakespeare or Chaucer. In fact, there is a wide measure of what one might call unconscious agreement amongst English teachers: they may find it hard to put down clearly on paper just what counts as a good 'appreciation of literature', but they may well be able to recognize cases of it in practice.

However, if there is serious dispute about (1) and (2), it is clearly essential to reach agreement about these before we can proceed: for the simple reason that otherwise we do not know, in a quite literal sense, what we are doing. With religious education the situation is, in my judgment, about as bad as it can be. It would not even be quite true to say that there is serious dispute about (1) what is to count as 'religion' (and hence 'education in religion'), and (2) what is to count as progress, success, being 'better-educated', etc., in this area – not, at least, in many educational circles. My impression is that these questions have not been squarely faced at all. There are disputes, but not about these questions: most of such disputes appear to arise from certain very general 'ideas' or 'movements' which go on under the heading of 'R.E.'. Most of these I find unintelligible, since those who engage in them rarely or never give a clear account of (1) and (2): hence, since I know neither what they count as religion nor what they count as being educated in it, I am unable to know whether their remarks are sensible or not.

If a Martian were to appear and say 'My goodness, you chaps on earth are missing out on one terribly important area of education – you just don't educate your pupils in squmpery at all: yet it's a most important subject (topic, department of life, etc.), it would be difficult even for the least serious of us not to reply 'Well, that's interesting: but tell us (1) what 'squmpery' is as a subject or topic – what does the term include and what does it exclude? Perhaps we already deal with it under another name, or perhaps it overlaps with one of our existing subjects. Then we want to know (2) what counts as being good at squmpery, what makes a good or competent or perceptive squmper (?). After that, perhaps we can do business'.

With 'religion' and 'religious education' we do not adopt this procedure, or not wholeheartedly. There are a variety of reasons for this. One is that we think we know already – yet, since people give (or at least tacitly imply) such widely different accounts, we cannot all be right. Another is that we have an emotional vested interest in influencing children in certain ways (transmitting, inculcating, teaching, indoctrinating, etc., certain things), and we pursue and defend this interest without worrying much about whether it can properly be entitled 'religion' or 'religious education'. A third reason, if possible more pernicious than the previous two, is the vague idea that we cannot or ought not to get clear at all: perhaps we should not try to reach the truth – perhaps there is no truth to reach – and had better settle for what is politically acceptable, or for a 'general consensus', or for the current fashion. These and other tendencies, too numerous to mention here, are standing temptations for all of us. They are marks of not being serious about what we are doing.

Fortunately (though there is a temptation to deny this too) words do not mean just anything. If somebody taught his pupils algebra and said he was engaging in religious education, we should say that he had an insecure grasp of English: we might want to examine his dictionary, if not his head. However imprecise or plastic the term 'religion', it has some limits: so too with 'education'. So we have a starting-point, surely the only starting point for a serious person: that is, we just have to do the work of finding out what these limits are. Partly in doing this, we shall also be working at finding out the ways in which a person can be good or bad, competent or incompetent, sane or barmy, correct or incorrect in this area: to be clear about what the area is involves some clarity, as it were *en passant*, about what it is to perform well or badly in it.

It is unfortunate that contemporary philosophers of education tend to put these (very obvious) points in too restrictive a form, thereby offering many of us a (feeble) excuse for dodging them. Hirst, for instance, writes of religion as a 'form of thought' or 'form of knowledge', and seems to imply that 'religion' refers only to a particular kind of religion.[1] I want to stress that, whatever deficiencies there may be in this (or any other) account, the basic points of methodology or procedure that I have made above still stand. Exactly how we are to describe 'religion', and to describe what counts as 'performing well' or 'being educated' in it, is precisely our problem. My point is simply that it is a problem which has to be solved before we can go any farther.

The only possible way out of this, so far as I can see, would be to give some account of religion to which the whole notion of criteria of success did not apply. One might, I suppose, regard religion as something which simply overtook one, like lightning or lumbago, and about which nothing could profitably be done. There would then be no sense to be made of words like 'right', 'wrong', 'sensible', 'prejudiced', 'perceptive', 'understanding', 'correct', 'progress', 'wise' and so on in reference to this sphere – either as predicated of particular beliefs and attitudes, or of people with these beliefs and attitudes. Some religious believers occasionally talk as if they took this view, but I doubt whether anyone seriously does: we believe, surely, that religion is within the scope of reason and understanding in *some* way – that it is not wholly arbitrary, a matter of taste, or a matter of indifference, And in any case, if it is wholly outside the scope of understanding, and if no criteria of success apply, then *education* in this sphere is impossible. We could only note that various people and societies were overtaken by various beliefs and attitudes, without having anything to say (because, on this view, there could *be* nothing to say) about whether some of them were more sensible, or wiser, or truer, or more perceptive, than others.[2]

I have read with interest, and often with admiration, the writings of various *doyens* in religious education – in particular those of Goldman, Loukes and Smart; but I am bound to say that I have not found these points properly catered for. Goldman seems to interpret 'religion' along grotesquely specific lines, and takes it as equivalent to one version of Christianity. Loukes, with whose more specifically practical and educational views on religious education I have the most sympathy, interprets it on much more modern (one might say, post-Quaker) lines, and regards it as roughly coextensive with almost *any* 'outlook on life', 'ultimate commitment', 'meaning we give to the world', 'infinite dimension of experience', and so on: this hardly caters for worshippers of Baal or Poseidon, who would have found most of such talk unintelligible – one would like from him a clearer account of what attitudes, outlooks, beliefs, or psychological states did *not* count as 'religious'. Even Smart, despite his philosophical ability, seems more interested in what is found in actual *religions* than in trying to define a *sui generis* form[3], mode or area of thought and activity which may fairly be entitled 'religious': and this might lead, in practical education, to something more like a shop-window tour of various faiths than a determined attempt to educate pupils in relation to whatever criteria of success fit this *sui generis* form.

It is necessary to add, with some haste, that these cavalier remarks do not of course begin to do justice to the contribution which these thinkers have made to both the theory and the practice of religious education. But the difficulty of assessing these contributions brings us straight back to the basic questions I have been talking about. With lesser writers one has the distinct suspicion that what they really want is to get something, of which they have a fairly clear idea, done in schools: and the theoretical or philosophical backing for this is then added more or less *ad hoc*. There is perhaps a touch of this even in Goldman, who is plainly not very interested in the questions, but hurries on to the applications of Piagetian psychology as quickly as possible. But this is no way for serious educationalists to do business: we must know what we are talking about first.

As a final, if disconnected, point in this section I should like to stress the point that these questions are intellectual, not political. By this I mean that any attempt to reach a 'general consensus', or something which will embrace as many people and offend as few people as possible, is doomed to failure. For one may get a consensus but *still be wrong*: it is not a matter of determining what is acceptable to Christians of various persuasions, immigrant Sikhs, the Humanist Society and so forth, but of determining what is *reasonable*. This, I suspect, is why the constant round of conferences, agreed syllabuses, helpful remarks by religious advisers, teacher-inspired working-papers and so on are not of much use: they tend to politics, not to truth. The fact is that we are not as yet clear about what we are trying to do; but we can at least be clear about our own ignorance, and bend our efforts in the right direction.

'Religion'

How do we identify beliefs, attitudes, activities and so on as 'religious'? To give the term any clear sense at all we have to *exclude* beliefs, etc., which we already categorize under some other heading – for instance, historical, moral, scientific or aesthetic, in the case of beliefs; or, in the case of 'ideals' or 'outlooks on life', those we might call political, or moral, or aesthetic ideals. On what grounds do we classify at least some of the things people do in churches and temples under 'religion', rather than (say) 'mental health', 'moral uplift', 'music' or even 'gymnastics'?

I should like to cut a long story of conceptual analysis short here, and simply say without further argument that religion is tied pretty tightly to the notions of *awe* and *worship*. These notions themselves no doubt require further explication, which I have tried to give elsewhere; but as at least a sighting shot they seem clear enough. One may, for instance, apply the standard test of the border-line case: asking at what point (say) a man's attitude towards women could be called 'religious', we should naturally look to see at what point he ceased merely to admire, desire, respect or even wonder at them, and began to revere, be in awe of, and worship them – ending perhaps in the full-blown case in which he seriously sees and describes them as goddesses, gives them names, sacrifices to them and so forth. Similarly we should be more inclined to describe Communism or Marxism as a religion the more that Communists and Marxists saw and described Lenin (or Marx, or whoever) not just as in a high degree important or admirable or outstanding, but as some kind of *god* – and 'god' implies 'something to be worshipped'.

Whether or not particular enterprises which we *call* 'religions' always meet this criterion hardly matters: nor does it matter that religion obviously has many connections with other types of activity – notoriously, with morality. What matters is to get some tolerably clear account of a *sui generis* activity, which does the maximum justice to the word 'religion' (so that it is fair to describe it under that title) as we actually use it in normal speech, and which distinguishes it from other activities, in a way which is generally intelligible to anybody. This process has nothing to do with (1) the historical origins of religion, (2) the particular beliefs, attitudes, etc., of particular religions, (3) any questions about whether religion itself is desirable, or (4) the place religion may have in various societies or cultures. On this criterion, the account given (far too briefly) above seems to me in general satisfactory.

'Educated in religion'

On this account, the crucial question is 'What sort of mistakes or failures (good moves or successes) are possible in this area?' Plainly this question has answers: most obviously, one can be in awe of or worship the wrong things (gods, people). Somebody who worships, say, Hitler must have made some kind of *mistake*, or failed in some kind of understanding – at least, that is our view, and even if we are wrong there is something to discuss here. What sort of characteristics would a person properly educated in religion have, that would enable him to avoid failures of this kind?

Some answers are fairly easy: he would, presumably, be *well-informed* about Hitlerism (or whatever religion he was considering). He would perhaps need to know something about its history, or literature, or cultural background, and about its professed beliefs. He might with profit consider its moral code and its social consequences. But, useful though all this might be, it hardly seems central to the religion *qua* religion. Such a person might become well-educated in the history (literature, sociology, etc.) *of* religion; but he would still have to face a central question, roughly of the form 'Some people believe X to be worth worshipping: are they right?'

In other words, he would still have to make some judgment about the *attitude* or *emotional investment* which necessarily lies at the core of all religion. Only such an attitude can make sense of religious beliefs: indeed, the beliefs are largely a linguistic expression of the attitude. To *see* and feel Christ (Hitler, Poseidon, Nature, or whatever) *as god* – this element is central. That somebody called Jesus (or whoever it may be) was born on a certain date, acted in a certain way, said certain things, and so on is, so far, a matter of historical, not religious, education: it turns into religion when we are told that he is divine, worshipful, to be adored, regarded with awe, the destined leader, etc. As soon as any specifically religious term is used – 'god', 'supernatural', 'divine' and many others – we have to face the question of whether the attitude which these words incorporate is *appropriate*.

There seem to be two general types of competence here. The first, which I now feel to have underplayed in what I have written elsewhere, is that the person must be open to, or able actually to feel, the emotions and attitudes which he might then want to invest or adopt. Whether or not this kind of openness and ability to feel is sufficiently 'cognitive' to count as 'education' is an arguable point which we can perhaps leave on one side. A parallel here is with aesthetics: 'learning to appreciate' works of art is only possible at all if the pupil is capable of actually having certain feelings which can then be directed and sophisticated ('educated', if you like). If they are, as it were, emotionally blind – if they do not allow themselves to feel or to be conscious of their feelings – we cannot even start. A person who cannot feel the 'pull' of various religions or objects of worship, perhaps because he dare not, is not well placed to be educated.

The second general type of competence is to be able to identify, refine, and criticize these feelings, in relation to their objects or targets. I feel in some general way drawn towards Hitler, or Jesus, or Buddhism, or whatever: well, I have to ask myself, just what *do* I feel? What, more precisely, are my emotions in relation to this person, or other object of worship? In particular, do I see the person (object) straight – am I projecting things onto him, deceiving myself, inventing? What is he really like? Do my feelings fit their target? Am I just seeking an authority, or unconsciously rebelling against my parents, or trying to furnish the world to fit my own desires – what *am* I doing exactly?

Another parallel (besides aesthetics) which displays both these types is the case of falling or being in love. Certainly, the 'educated' person here will need to know some facts about the other person. I meet Flossie, and find myself strangely drawn towards her: no doubt I ought to know about her family background, her past history, and so forth. But in order to make right decisions and adopt appropriate attitudes, I must (1) *be able* to feel love, and (2) scrutinize my feelings and their object in order to determine their appropriateness. As we all know, this is an immensely difficult task – so difficult, indeed, that we may give it up as a bad job: and then there will be the temptation to say that 'It's just a matter of taste', 'You can't do anything about it anyway, it's a sort of compulsion', and so on. Yet we know both that we can make mistakes here, and that – with difficulty, because we know very little about how to do it – we can improve ourselves. So too with religion.

The central practical question for religious educators, then, is of the form 'Under what conditions (with what teachers, using what materials, in what social contexts or relationships) does it happen that pupils can become more able to bring their feelings to consciousness and to inspect them critically, in the area roughly bounded by "awe", "worship", and cognate terms?' If there is a discipline or enterprise which seems more nearly relevant to this than any other, I suppose it is some kind of clinical psychology or psychotherapy: and we should expect to learn a great deal from those in this field. My guess is that it happens best in non-directive relationships of trust, and that any practical advances will be made by exploring further how to set up or induce such relationships: also that we shall not get far unless we take seriously into account what various pupils actually *do* worship (revere, stand in awe of, etc.), and in general begin with the existing state of their emotions.

This is not to dismiss other types of work in religious education as useless; but almost everything depends on how it is used. To get pupils to feel, or strongly imagine, what it is like to worship (say) Jehovah would obviously be impossible without using the Bible: but this is a very different thing from simply using it as factual information, or as literature, or as 'part of our cultural heritage'. Similarly a text-book on Greek polytheism may be no more than academic: whereas to be able to feel the 'pull', the power, of those psychic forces encapsulated in Aphrodite, Apollo, Zeus and so on is likely to be much more effective. What sort of feelings about 'purity' must the authors of the food taboos in Leviticus have had? Do the pupils recognize any such feelings in themselves? What *is it about* pop stars, or football heroes, which attracts such strong emotions? Why did the Germans fall for Hitler? These are the sort of starting-points for developing the required emotional insight: I do not say 'questions to be discussed', because that is liable to turn into an unreal and well-defended set of 'opinions' or 'beliefs', which conceal (even as they unconsciously contain) the real feelings lying below the surface.

It seems to me entirely clear that this subject is in its infancy, and that there are many theoretical and practical problems to be solved. This should not deter practising teachers from doing all that they can along these lines. What it should do, surely, is to distinguish this from *other* things which are not properly described as 'religious education' or 'education in religion' at all. If we want to inculcate Christianity: to give pupils some familiarity with the facts and background of world religions: to make sure that, as members of a Christian or post-Christian culture, they are aware of the part that faith has played: to discuss moral or political problems, social welfare, or contemporary society: to talk generally about life, 'ultimate reality', 'commitment' – well, any or all of these may be justifiable enterprises. But they are not, or certainly not centrally, education in religion.

I hope that two points will emerge quite clearly in regard to these other enterprises:

1 I am not denying that some, at least, of them may in practice be coextensive with what should be done in the enterprise of religious education. To take the most obvious case: suppose a parent's or a school's aim is conceived in some such terms as 'transmitting the Christian faith', or 'bringing up their children as good Muslims'.

Much of what they did might be a useful, perhaps even an essential, basis or background for the children being educated in religion. They would at least know what a religious tradition and environment was *like* – something which seems necessary if they are to accept or reject it with any degree of rationality or understanding, just as *some* kind of clear-cut moral tradition and environment seems necessary at least as a background for moral education. So too with 'transmitting a cultural heritage': obviously it is desirable, from the strictly educational point of view, that children should be familiar with the Bible (Koran, etc.). But there is, clearly, a great difference in ultimate aims, even if some of the methods – what the child is taught, and the tradition in which he is placed – overlap.

2 Nor do I deny that these other aims may be in themselves desirable, and may sometimes be reasonably thought to take precedence over strictly educational aims. The important thing is that they should be distinguished. If parents, rightly or wrongly, insist that some aims be pursued for some of the time – for instance, that their children should receive an hour's instruction every day from a strictly Roman Catholic (Marxist, Buddhist, etc.) viewpoint – we must at least distinguish this from whatever time should be spent in more open forms of religious education: that hour's teaching followed by a genuinely 'open' hour would be infinitely better than two hours of general muddle.

An extremist might, I suppose, hold that *no* time should be spent in doing what I have called 'education in religion', on the grounds that certain beliefs, or traditions, or institutions are so important and desirable that children should be brought up wholly within them, without running any risk of 'contamination' (as such a person might call it) from an enterprise which would necessarily involve doubt, enquiry, comparison with other beliefs, and mixing with adherents of other traditions. I think it is fair to describe him as an extremist, because it is hard to see how the enterprise of education could not be regarded as *some* sort of good, at least for some people for some part of their time. One might think that it should be restricted to pupils above a certain age, level of intelligence, or level of psychological maturity. But as long as we wish people to hold (or not to hold) religious beliefs of any kind *for good reasons*, we must provide some contexts in which these reasons are examined.

It is, in any case, very difficult to see how this sort of separatism could be viable under modern conditions of communication, and especially in a 'pluralist society'. This is, of course, an empirical rather than a conceptual argument; but if we attempt to resist the empirical facts, we shall find ourselves having to resist communication in general. We – that is, any separatist partisan group – will need special schools, effective censorship of radio, television, literature, etc., and some way of preventing our children from meeting and arguing with other children or adults of a different persuasion: not a logical impossibility, but something which might well bring more loss than gain. For 'contamination' spreads not just by the existence of different *religious* persuasions, but rather by the existence of more general norms and ideas that inhere in communication: the idea that one ought to have reasons for what one believes, that evidence must be produced in argument, that one should try to understand another's point of view, and so forth. Even if this were thought, as it might in specific instances reasonably be thought, to be undesirable, the process is not easily reversible.

But be that as it may: I address myself primarily to those many people who do, in fact, feel that some more 'open' (educational) enterprise needs to be undertaken. I think this climate of opinion has been increasingly prevalent for some decades: but what has happened, as in the case of moral education, suggests chiefly something like a failure of nerve and clear-headedness. We feel uncertain about accepting past or present authorities, about 'indoctrination', about the narrowness of sticking to Christianity: well and good. But we then find a vacuum, just because we have no clear idea of what to do instead: and so we mess about, filling in the time in ways which we hope are at least 'interesting', 'stimulating', 'relevant' and so forth. I make so bold as to say that, as soon as we adopt a serious posture towards what we are doing, it does not take very long to establish (roughly) what religion is and what it is to be educated in it: our problem is not an intellectual one, requiring the endless labour of philosophers of religion, but the emotional problem of adopting the right posture. Whether or not the particular account I have given is substantially correct does not so much matter.

Notes

1 See, for example, Hirst, P.H. and Peters, R.S., *The Logic of Education* (Routledge), p. 64.
2 *Cf.* my *Education in Religion and the Emotions* (Heinemann), p. 4*ff*.
3 *Op. cit.*, pp. 21*ff*.

*Phenomenology and the Future of Religious Education**

John Marvell

The teacher's problem

Besides the normal problems which he shares with his other teaching colleagues, the teacher of religious education is faced with two particular challenges in his work. These are that he undertakes his work in an increasingly pluralistic society and in a progressively secular situation. Nicholls[1] traces the history, since the Reformation, in which the problem of speaking authoritatively concerning religious belief has become increasingly difficult and, accordingly, the maintenance of public conformity finally impossible. England has been a plural society, in religious terms, since the Reformation, and an increasingly secular one since the introduction, during the last century, of radical alternatives to religion. A number of studies[2] by sociologists confirm what everyday experience leads one to suppose, that all sections of society are affected by the secularizing trends at work in our midst. The influx, during recent years, of large numbers of Commonwealth citizens has added to the plurality of belief in English society. One study[3] has shown that the school can be the situation in which the young person can meet the modern plural and the secular world for the first time in personal terms. Many Agreed Syllabuses still instruct the teacher to put forward one religious outlook in an authoritative manner in the very place where doubts and questions, concerning such beliefs, are likely to be raised in a serious way for the first time in the pupil's life. The teacher of religious education, if he is unable to suspend his own convictions and adopt an alternative approach, is in a dilemma. Many who have entered this field from sincerely held Christian convictions experience this dilemma vividly.

Not only is the teacher in a position of *direct* disadvantage but also in a

*This article first appeared in *Learning for Living*, Vol. 16, No. 1, Autumn, 1976.

situation of *indirect* disadvantage, due to the lack of religious experience in the background of many pupils. In the past, one could assume that the majority of the children would have had some experience, in a Protestant Christian form, of what Otto[4] has called the 'numinous'. At least within their own tradition they would have gained some insight into the source of what gives *homo religiosus* his conviction and certainty. This is less and less the given situation with any particular child. In every other area of the curriculum the pupil has had some experience (for example, of time, space, social relations, etc.) on which the teacher can build the framework of rational understanding. The religious educator must not only make the bricks of reason, but also gather the straw of experience for his children. Until this latter task is successfully achieved the subject, to the student, will continue to seem at best boring and irrelevant. Before discussing ways in which the dilemma may be solved it will be useful to look at the tools that are available with which to tackle the task.

Ways of studying religion

There are three ways in which religion can be studied: the theological, the empirical and the phenomenological. The first method has been the traditional one in schools, colleges and universities. As a method, however, it demands that one make *a priori* assumptions which are largely unacceptable in a plural and secular society, and has been labelled by some as 'indoctrination'. Attempts have been made to retain this method in schools in a modified form. The 'neo-confessional' or 'open' approach[5] was the first to be tried. If this view is accepted, it is a simple step to argue that if one faith may be presented to the pupil in such a way that he can make a personal and informed choice concerning it, he should also be enabled to do the same with other beliefs, religious and non-religious. A further development, which seeks to retain something of the theological stance, is seen in the 'implicit religion' approach advocated by the Schools' Council Secondary Religious Education Project.[6] This implies that the groundroot of all life experience is, in essence, religious. This appears to be based on Tillichian theology. 'Concern' can be seen to be of the same order as 'ultimate concern' and 'being' is of the same order as 'Being', *ipso facto* anyone can accept the view that we are all religious and that all have religious experience through which we can understand the rationality of theology. The work of Loukes[7] and Goldman[8] can be seen as based on such assumptions. Later, it will be argued that religion is a *sui generis* experience and that a dichotomy exists between the sacred and the profane which cannot be bridged by such a method.

The second method, the empirical, has largely been confined to universities and similar institutions. This method asks no questions as to the truth or otherwise of religious claims; it simply examines religious behaviour scientifically. This is why it has mainly been the province of the behavioural sciences: sociology, psychology and anthropology, although historical and geographical studies of religion can be included in this category.[9] The argument has been put forward that as neither the religious nor the theological *a priori* is available there is a case, nevertheless, for young people in schools to understand the part that religion has played in their cultural inheritance. The empirical approach would provide a satisfactory vehicle for accomplishing this task. It would, however, fail to introduce the pupils to that experience which is the essence of religion.

The third method of studying religion is the phenomenological. This was developed originally in continental and Scandinavian universities and has found its basis in the work of the philosopher Husserl and his successors. It is concerned primarily with elucidating the universal essences and structures of the religious subject in 'his knowledge-of-the-object'. It seeks by way of 'bracketing out' one's own understanding and experience to enter sympathetically into the 'knowing situation' of the other person. Three key scholars, whose works illustrating the method are available in English are Kristensen,[10] van der Leeuw[11] and Eliade[12]. A recent article by Sharpe[13] describes the history and essence of the method simply and clearly. Otto[14] has argued that religious experience is unique and *sui generis*. Religion in all its forms is a response to the experience of a revelation of the 'numinous.' This is an argument with which most phenomenologists of religion would agree. A secondary textbook using the phenomenological method and based on Otto's idea is Turner's *Living Tribal Religions*.[15] In a straightforward and uncomplicated manner Turner demonstrates the universal structures and essences of primal religion in terms of the subject's experience of revelation and response.

The classroom situation

Phenomenology of religion, then, is concerned with a 'presuppositionless' approach to that which is essential and unique to the essence and manifestation of religion. Thus, unlike the empirical approach it does not avoid the central issues, nor ask, as does the theological approach, that certain *a priori* assumptions be made which are not universally acceptable. Theology, when used as the vehicle of religious education, is concerned with what Otto[16] would describe as a particular schematization of the 'holy'. It assumes a particular form of the '*sensis numinis*' as the childrens' normative experience, and the curriculum is concerned with a rational and logical exposition of the particular schematization, that is, it seeks to expound a theology which 'explains' the experience. In a pluralistic society we can neither expect a particular experience to be accepted as the normative, nor, indeed, that any one person would accept that any experience of the numinous was possible. Phenomenology, seeking that which is universal and by 'bracketing out' our own presuppositions, allows us to go back to what Otto and Turner[17] would call the raw experience of the Numinous. This raises the question as to whether children of all or any ages are able to 'do phenomenology'. Concerning the experience of the numinous Otto[18] writes:

> The reader is invited to direct his mind to a moment of deeply felt religious experience, as little as possible qualified by other forms of consciousness. Whoever cannot do this, whoever knows no such moments in his experience is requested to read no further. . . .

Otto appears to be suggesting that 'deafness' to the sense of the 'numinous' is as fatal to grasping what the reality of religion is, as deafness to pitch is for grasping the reality of musical experience. Turner[19] has questioned Otto's absolute in this instance. It would appear that the vast majority of people, and therefore children,[20] are capable of experiencing the numinous, as Otto describes it, even if they do not accept it as establishing any kind of metaphysical truth. Such ability is sufficient for the religious educator. In the past, it was assumed that the young person was connected in some way with a Christian religious body and would have had opportunities of experiencing the numinous within that framework. Educators can no longer assume that the young person will have any kind of religious experience. The task of encouraging young people to 'bracket out' their own conceptions and of entering, sympathetically, into the religious experience of others is a difficult one, within the limits of what is possible within the school. One must start with what is at hand; this will be more varied in urban areas, particularly those with multi-racial populations. If, where necessary, any prejudice on the part of the student can be overcome, it is the religion of his own culture which is the easiest for him to enter into and from that into others.

Implicit in the preceding paragraph is the idea that the central aim of religious education should be to enable the learner to understand, not only cognitively but also affectively, that which is central to religion: the essence of the experience of revelation and response, as known by the religious person. When this has been achieved the young person will be in a position not only to understand the religion of others but to make an authentic and personal decision as to his own position. The question then arises as to how this can be achieved.

The universals of religious experience

The author believes that a two dimensional approach is required. Firstly there is a horizontal dimension, which technically could be called typological phenomenology. This will be an examination of the universals of religious experience. The religious educator will no longer rely on the child coming to him with an initial understanding. He must, as was suggested earlier, gather the 'straw' of experience. It is therefore useful to begin with that which is nearest to hand and closest to the pupil. This will depend on the ethnic and cultural structure of the class and the local community. One teacher takes his first year secondary remedial class on visits to local churches of various denominations (what better place to gain a sense of the numinous?). In a multi-racial area this would include non-christian places of worship. A list of topics which would enable pupils to explore the universal experience of revelation and response in religion would include such titles as: sacred places; sacred persons ('numinous' visitors to the class?); sacred times; sacred books; prayer (one teacher has voluntary meditation in class). A perusal of the books by Kristensen, van der Leeuw and Eliade, mentioned earlier in this article, will give the class teacher many further topics to explore.

The history of religion

Secondly there is the vertical dimension, which technically can be called the history of religion. This is the study of specific religions and the forms which these have taken at particular times and places. Here again, one would start with what is at hand and nearest to the child's experience. This will obviously vary from class to class, district to district, and the teacher would be called on to exercise his professional judgment as to what is best in a particular situation. In this country some examination of Christianity in its various forms seems necessary but the emphasis on varying interpretations of Christianity would change according to location, and home backgrounds. Study of other religions, past or present, would be dictated by the ethnic origins of the class and by its interest, linked to the teacher's own expertise.

Non-religious ideologies

The Schools Council Secondary Religious Education Project[21] has adopted, in part, a type of phenomenological method. Although the project is a step in the right direction, there are certain things which one would wish to question. Firstly, the idea that ordinary experience is the right starting point for religious education. This is implied by what the project calls the 'implicit' approach to religious education. The view expressed in this article that religious experience is unique runs counter to this, and also to the view that secular ideologies can be termed 'religions', because they start from the same life experience and only differ from what is normally called religion in that they have a different rationale. This is not to say that the study of non-religious interpretations of life has no place in the school curriculum, or that this should not be taught by the staff responsible for religious education, but that a clear distinction should be made between the two forms of knowledge. It is perhaps as important as in the case of religions that non-religious ideologies should be studied phenomenologically, if their inner reality is to be understood.

The 'dimensions' of religion

Secondly, one is led to question Smart's six dimensional model for the phenomenological study of 'Explicit' religion. It has been argued earlier that the central feature of religion is revelation and response. This appears to equate with Smart's experimental dimension, which should, perhaps, be seen not as separate but as integral to every dimension. Looking at the other dimensions they seem to be nearer to a sociological analysis of religion[22] than a phenomenological. If we need to look for broad headings, the divisions of van der Leeuw or Kristensen, which could be summarized as the object of religion, the subject of religion and the object and subject in their reciprocal relations, might be more useful.

Conclusions

If the phenomenological approach is adopted for religious education, three points should be borne in mind. First, the teacher will be concerned with man's religious experience and that this is distinctive from any other form of experience. This means that he will be concerned to give even the youngest child an understanding of religion, and that life themes, as developed from the work of Goldman[23], and the life problems approach as developed from the work of Loukes[24], are unlikely to achieve this end.[25]

Secondly there is the need to develop new teaching materials. One research[26] has shown, that for one multi-racial group at least, sacred places were particularly evocative of the numinous. A whole series of phenomenological themes need to be studied and developed in relation to the English situation, and teaching materials for different ages of children developed and tested. It is most important that that which is universal in religious experience should be demonstrable from that which is to hand. Similarly, materials needs to be developed which expound particular 'schematizations'. Some of the units developed by teachers for the Schools' Council Religious Education in Secondary Schools Project form the tentative beginnings of both of these tasks. Much remains to be done, particularly in the former area with regard to scholarly research so that the basic material for the construction of curriculum content is available. Material is becoming more widely available in the latter area from publishers, at least for the secondary age range.

Lastly, teachers of religious education need to be equipped. Very few have been trained for anything but the theological approach, both in-service and initial courses, in the future, should equip the teacher to understand and be able to communicate to others that which is universal in religion and that which is particular to various times and places.

Notes and references

1 Nicholls, W., *Systematic and Philosophical Theology*, The Pelican Guide to Modern Theology, Vol. 1, Penguin. 1969.

2 Vide: Martin, D., *A Sociology of English Religion*, SCM Press, 1967.
Argyle, M., *Religious Behaviour*, Routledge and Kegan Paul,1958.
Busia, K.A., *Urban Churches in Britain*, Lutterworth, 1966.
Wilson, B., *Religion in a Secular Society*, Penguin, 1969.

3 Marvell, J., *The religious beliefs and moral values of immigrant children*, M.Ed., Thesis, University of Leicester, 1973.

4 Otto, R., *The Idea of the Holy*, Oxford University Press. 2nd ed., 1950.

5 Schools Council Working Paper No. 36. *Religious Education in Secondary Schools*, Evans/Methuen Educational, 1971, pp. 30–34.

6 *Ibid.*, pp. 34–36.

7 Loukes, H., *Teenage Religion*, SCM Press, 1961.

8 Goldman, R., *Religious Thinking from Childhood to Adolescence*, Routledge and Kegan Paul, 1964.

9 Examples of empirical studies which illustrate this point are:
Durkheim, E., *The Elementary forms of the Religious Life*, Allen and Unwin, 1915.
Douglas, M., *Natural Symbols*, Barrie and Rockliff. The Cresset Press, 1970.
Allport, G.W., *The Individual and His Religion*, Macmillan, 1960.
Thouless, R.H., *An Introduction to the Psychology of Religion*, Cambridge University Press, 1924.
Wright, D., *A review of empirical studies in the psychology of religion*, ARE 1972.
Yinger, M., *The Scientific Study of Religion*, Macmillan, 1970.

10 Kristensen, W.B., *The Meaning of Religion*, Martinus Nijhoff, 1971.

11 van der Leeuw, G., *Religion in Essence and Manifestation*, 2 vols, Harper and Row, 1963.

12 Eliade, M., *Patterns in Comparative Religion*, Sheed and Ward, 1958.

13 Sharpe, E., 'The Phenomenology of Religion', *Learning for Living*, Vol. 15, No. 1, Autumn, 1975.

14 Otto, R., *op. cit.*, passim.

15 Turner, H., *Living Tribal Religions*, Ward Lock Educational, 1973.

16 Otto, R., *op. cit.*, p. 45*ff*.

17 Turner, H., *Rudolph Otto: The Idea of the Holy – a guide for students*, obtainable from author, Aberdeen University.

18 Otto, R., *op. cit.*, p. 8.

19 Turner, H., *Rudolph Otto: The Idea of the Holy – a guide for students*, *op. cit.*, pp. 11–12.

20 Gates, B., 'Readiness for Religion' in Smart, N. and Horder, D. (eds) *New Movements in Religious Education*, Temple Smith, 1975, pp. 65–70 give an

outline of recent research in this country which gives general support to this point.

21 Schools Council Working Paper No. 36, *op. cit.*, pp. 34–42.

22 Smart' analysis may be compared with the following sociological analyses of religion. The parallels are close:

Clayton, R.D., '5D or 1', *Journal for the Scientific Study of Religion*, Vol. 10, No. 1, Spring, 1971.

Cohn, W., 'What is Religion? An analysis for cross cultural purposes', *Journal of Christian Education*, Vol. 7, Nos. 2 and 3, November, 1964.

Glock, C.Y. and Stark, R.S., *American piety and the nature of religious commitment*, University of California Press, 1968.

Yinger, J.M., 'A Structural Examination of Religion' *Journal for the Scientific Study of Religion*, Autumn, 1969.

Wach, J., *The Comparative Study of Religions*, Columbia University Press, 1958. (This is a useful comparison as it is by a scholar who straddles the two disciplines.)

23 Goldman, R., *op. cit.*

24 Loukes, H., *op. cit.*

25 Vide: Turner, H., *Rudolph Otto: The Idea of the Holy – a guide to students*, *op. cit.*, p. 28, where he discusses Otto's idea that spiritual awareness will not arise from moral failure. Similarly, if the argument in the article is correct, awareness of the sacred will not arise from experience of the profane, however 'deep'.

26 Marvell, J., Thesis *op. cit.*, N.B., pp. 137–140.

*Conceptual Research in Religious Education**

David Attfield

The purpose of this paper is to explain and clarify the nature of conceptual research in the service of religious education. Such an enquiry is essential to defining and formulating the aims and objectives of this subject. Conceptual clarity also is an aid to teaching, in that for a teacher to be clear what he is doing will greatly assist his choice of content, method and order in the presentation of material. New approaches in the classroom, imaginative techniques and research into their effectiveness are likely to be abortive if we are not sure what we want the children to grasp *as a whole* and *in the arrangement of its parts.*

What is conceptual research?

We may approach this question by beginning from the aims of religious education. If the general aim of the subject today is the open-ended exploration of the major world faiths, then a central part of teaching will have to consist in presenting their chief concepts. Should knowledge of religion, for example, be a necessary element in a liberal education, and theology be a form of knowledge in Hirst's sense,[1] or a possible candidate for such a status, the crucial concepts distinctive of a religion or the categorial concepts underpinning this whole realm of thought would have to be made clear to pupils.

For example, in a religion like Christianity, the central concept is probably that of God. God is the object of worship, faith and of religious attitudes and the central object of belief.[2] Religious language may be roughly defined as that which contains the term 'God' or which implies or presupposes a reference to God in order to be intelligible and reasonably used. Thus to

*This article first appeared in *Learning for Living*, Vol. 15, No. 3, 1976.

acquire the notion of the divine is as fundamental to religion, and so to religious education, as it is to acquire the idea of number for mathematics or of a map for geography. Further, in so far as other faiths are included in contemporary religious education – as it is widely agreed today that they should be – and in so far as these work with a similar concept of the divine to the Christian or at any rate as there is a substantial overlap with the latter notion, the argument of this paper will apply for example, to Jewish, Islamic or some Hindu ideas of deity. Also a parallel approach is doubtless possible to other key concepts in other religious traditions for example, Nirvana or Brahma.

The main claim being made for conceptual research simply amounts to saying that the central concepts involved in a school subject should receive careful and conscious attention on the part of educators, that what is implicit in having or gaining a key notion should be analysed and clarified logically and philosophically before we turn to the empirical and practical questions of teaching, its methods and content.

Controversial concepts

Conceptual research presupposes the propriety of teaching the central concepts of an area and in the case of a subject so controversial as religious education, this may seem doubtful. Is not trying seriously to present the concept of God to children indoctrination or religious proselytism of the kind which today we abhor in educational RE? In answer to this objection, it is necessary to note two things.

First, you cannot explore Christianity, for example, if you do not know what it is. This involves giving pupils a description of Christian belief. But beliefs cannot be understood, or even the fact that some people have or have held certain beliefs today or in history cannot be properly grasped, without understanding the concepts that occur in those beliefs. Reformation controversies are unintelligible, even to the modern unbelieving or detached historian, without some comprehension of what it meant to accept transubstantiation or double predestination. How can one grasp Marxism in social studies or geography or history unless one has gained concepts like surplus value or proletariat or relation of production or mode of production?

Secondly, education is not only about ideologies and belief systems as historical entities or as facts of modern society to be portrayed and understood; education also requires exploration of what may be a valuable life-option. If we grant *prima facie* that there may be some truth or value in a faith like Marxism or Christianity, we are obliged to encourage pupils to investigate, in case these worldviews should turn out acceptable to some of our children, and should become a worthwhile element in their picture of life. To explore, however, requires concepts, in order to be able to think in the area designated. Yet it is not necessary, in order to be able to discuss and reflect in a competent, informed and rational way, to accept the requisite notions as coherent or having any real reference in the world.

Before one can argue, for example, whether God exists, one has to know what this term means and that, conceptually speaking, it is impossible for space research to find or fail to find the deity on a distant planet. Indeed, some grasp of the concept of the biblical God is a precondition of any intelligible position in regard to Christianity: an atheist must know what he rejects, an agnostic what he claims cannot be known, a theist what he believes in, a logical positivist what he thinks is untestable, incoherent or vacuous. Further, a believer who prays must have some minimum idea of what he addresses, at least to know it is a 'Who' and not a 'What'. What the mystic experiences cannot even be satisfactorily identified and individuated[3] except by an appropriate concept he brings to the data. In inter-faith dialogue and in debate with unbelievers we need to know which deity we are discussing and whether a problematic object of concern and commitment may be called divine in any sense. So to equip our pupils with the concept of God is vital if they are to be placed in a position to explore a wide tract of religion. But to have the concept is not to be committed to any use or application of it whatever. This is to open the child's mind to the possibility of God, not to close it to belief or unbelief as the indoctrinator hopes.

It may, however, be contended that acquiring a particular concept of God *is* to be indoctrinated, but in a further, subtler sense. God's existence is left open, the critic objects, but not the kind of God. In order to teach a concept at all, one interpretation of it has been chosen for simplicity's sake and this alone is presented or given priority. Thus a bias is exerted, loading the pupil's mind towards accepting one particular concept of God, in an age where the theologians are uncertain and any notion of the divine is problematic. Once the child has the preferred idea, his intellect is closed to others, judges them always by an arbitrary standard of conceptual orthodoxy and is less ready to try out new notions on their merits. The question thus emerges, for conceptual research, as to which concept of God do we offer in religious education in a period (of concepts) of 'gods many and lords many'.

In respect to Christianity, there are in fact some limits set by the state of the matter in current theology. A certain range of notions for construing the divine is available today: classic theism, the new theology, process theology, existentialism.[4] Presumably we exclude (except in describing popular religion the world over) anthropomorphic crudities, ideas of demons and fairies, since we are concerned in education with possible truth and rationality and are not proposing initiation into probable superstition. There has to be some criterion of what can be permitted, perhaps a consensus within philosophy of religion as to what is *prima facie* defensible (this approach allows for the possibility that religion even in its best known and classic forms *may be* but refined superstition). Also we leave out of account the concepts of deity that went with pagan pantheons like that on Olympus or with Elijah's view of Jahweh, since it is agreed in the modern world that such divine beings do not exist and that claims about them are false and have no place in any living western faith.[5]

Granted then a range of minimally respectable notions, to avoid indoctrination several alternative conceptions can be presented. So pupils might be inducted into classic theism, new and process theology, existential ideas of God as options, as an area of divergent conceptuality to explore. Or one might choose one only of these conceptions of God as a starting point for the child's thinking. Conceptual research would then have to show how other notions could be reached from the one given priority by various logical operations and modifications of the central concept, for example, by dropping, qualifying or reinterpreting the transcendence, immutability or perfection elements in thinking of the divine. Once one version of the key idea is firmly grasped by pupils, at a later stage in education alternative versions may be investigated through ordinary teaching approaches. Special, elaborate and comprehensive procedures may be required for the basic, logical jumping-off ground to be placed in children's hands; later, straightforward instruction and exploration may suffice to capture the alternatives.[6] Such a two-stage scheme has the advantage of economy of effort and concentration, in so presenting a key idea that all the main avenues to theism are opened up for exploration.

To the extent that modern movements in theology are to be seen as protests, criticisms and as offering alternatives to classical notions, the latter have a claim to be treated as basic in education. What is objected to has to be grasped first; such grasping is a logical condition of being able effectively to assess for oneself critiques of and variants on orthodoxy. Only in this way are pupils capable of judging whether newer ideas are adequate translations of the old, better suited to modern conditions, yet at the same time do not fail to be faithful to the valuable traditions and experiences of the past. Conceptual research must map the field and find a way into the area, so that the traveller can in the short compass of his schooling see both old and new Jerusalem and decide where he prefers to live. To find for oneself how the new temple supersedes the old may be logically difficult if one so tarries in the new as to be hazy about what the first temple really was.

Key concepts

Religion is a form of life, and material from it has to be chosen to serve the ends of religious education. The object is to generate an understanding of religion, suitable for the mind of an educated person in the modern world. Given the pressures of the subjects, specialization, the 'knowledge explosion', and the vast volumes of literature on world religions – let alone upon any one faith – selection of matter must be rigorous. Far less detailed knowledge is required in the religious education of school pupils than is required in the scholarly and academic training of a professional theologian, minister or priest. Now, within this selection of basic items from a faith, certain concepts will be the central, nodal points in the logical structure of a religion as a sphere of discourse, a dimension of experience and praxis, as a way of life. The normal pupil wants key intersections on a map of religious language and cultic practice, by which he can orientate himself and find his way about in the course of his educational and possibly spiritual explorations.

Of course, some concepts are categorial to the whole sphere of a religion, they are the central rock beneath the terrain the subject maps. Such a categorial concept is that of the transcendent or sacred.[7] In western religions like Christianity this role is played by the idea of Creator God. In addition there are many other secondary concepts which depend on the categorial, and with these religious education is also concerned. Here there may well be alternatives, and teachers may choose among them. Various groups of secondary notions may be equivalent in the sense that a general grasp of a religion can be attained through the study of any of them. There are several prophets in the Old Testament from which to choose a representative prophet in the course of introducing the concept of prophecy; similarly one can select any from the several categories of parable scholars picked out[8] to teach this concept; there are many instances of any kind of sacrifice. Thus many roads lead to concepts like prophet, parable, miracle and sacrifice and the ordinary pupil who needs a general education need only travel a few of these tracks. Teachers can choose material by other, less fundamental but equally important, practical and pedagogical criteria of time, interest, convenience, etc. Where secondary concepts are concerned there may well be alternatives, both in terms of exemplary material in which these concepts are embedded and also among the concepts themselves. It is doubtful whether children, for instance, need to be acquainted with all or many of the various concepts of a minister of religion or sacred person, even within one faith. But in Christianity all relates to God, and is only intelligible through some comprehension of the category of the divine. Conceptual research thus will focus on the categorial centre, and select material from the whole Christian (or equivalent) tradition, so the pupil's mind is structured in understanding the religious dimension, and is prepared for exploration of it. With secondary notions a range of possibilities rather than unique items will be indicated and carefully studied.

The role of conceptual research

In the light of the foregoing discussion, the general task of conceptual research in connexion with religious education can be set out and systematically ordered.

1 The crucial or categorial concepts of religion have to be identified. Presumably with Christianity this would be the idea of God.
2 A range of alternative interpretations of the central concept needs specification, and the logical relations between these must be exhibited. Possible strategies of presentation have to be appraised and the merits of juxtaposition, as opposed to priority, for exploring one version through another, must be weighted.
3 With secondary concepts, conceptual research, using the criterion of what a general education in religion desiderates, will delineate acceptable alternatives among these less central concepts themselves or among the pieces of material used in presenting any one of them.
4 Once the concepts required for religious education are listed, conceptual research includes logical analysis of them, or at least of the central cases, for the purposes of teaching. The philosopher's question about how a concept or term is ever learnt[9] becomes the teacher's: he wants to know how that learning can be most efficiently and surely promoted. With an important concept, we must first give a brief statement of its main logical features, either as these have been agreed among philosophers and theologians to date, or as this part of the logical map of religious discourse can be clarified by the educationist himself for his purposes.
5 The dependence of the listed concepts on other concepts and the various prerequisites for acquiring them have to be exhibited. What a child must first know, or what cannot not be known or understood if the main ideas in a subject are to be grasped, must be made clear and emphasized. In arithmetic you need to understand addition to understand multiplication; in geography scale for map; in moral education a moral rule for the enterprise of justifying rules; in religious education earthly fatherhood for God as Father. In every case, the purely logical, as opposed to psychological, empirical or temporal claims, need very carefully sifting out: in general when A depends on B, some grasp of some element in B cannot be absent when A is known or understood. Beyond that the conceptual researcher hands over to his other colleagues in the furthering of religious education.
6 Conceptual research may very tentatively suggest how the preconditions of concept acquisition may be supplied and the minds of pupils prepared. This has to be done to make the concepts themselves clearer and to elucidate what depends on what and how. It has also to be shown, from the conceptual side of the logical/psychological frontier, just where the empirical worker takes over from the philosopher of religion in the service or religious education. A half-hidden line, difficult to discern, needs mapping from both sides: Piagetian-type researches may bring to light concealed conceptual connexions.

It is desirable to know what hinders or helps, slows or hastens the growth of mental structures as these are specified and governed by the aims of our subject. In the process of so doing, logical links need distinguishing from empirical factors, and some idea gained of what these factors may be. The job then goes to the creative teacher, to devise new approaches, to find better material and methods that take account of the conceptual liaisons that have been uncovered. Finally, the task of the researcher emerges. He evaluates the success of these new approaches and measures concept-formation in average schools, among pupils of varying cultures, in experimental and control groups where innovations are tested.

Thus the philosopher or theologian may clarify which elements in human fatherhood are necessary to the analogy used in divine paternity; to what degree this analogical base must be grasped before statements about God as Father become significant; while the empirical researcher sees how the child may better acquire this base; how he does so at present in school, at what age, how satisfactorily and so on. Then programmes of conceptual enrichment and qualification may be formulated to aid the child's discrimination between local and temporary, and essential elements in his conception of father. We may not, for instance, be anxious today for authoritarian overtones in the image of a father to be transferred to God, nor the idea of the male parent as sole bread-winner or as a non-nurturant disciplinarian. Enlightened teachers next try out the new programme and researchers evaluate it and conceivably produce material of interest to the philosopher, who can always profit by testing his analysis against other people's descriptions of concrete cases. Should it seem a child has acquired earlier what logically must come later, a problem of great philosophical interest arises, as it would were a human infant to reach formal thinking before concrete.

Conclusion

In these ways conceptual research may be placed within the spiral of curriculum development in the context of religious education. The subject's logical foundations are clarified and it is so presented as to avoid indoctrination. Considerations germane to the translation of high-level aims into detailed objectives are produced and guidance proferred in the choice of matter and method. Teachers are assisted in finding methods and procedures that are at least logically possible, and even sensible in the light of the nature of religion and its conceptual structure. A diversity of roads to Jerusalem is allowed; a few culs-de-sac, circles or crescents in the maze are excluded, and the wide range of foothills the climber must ascend, and sometimes a necessary sequence of slopes in his ascent, are mapped. The mountaineer then is at least at the foot of Everest and not lost in jungles below.

Notes and references

1 Hirst, P., *Knowledge and the Curriculum* (1974), Ch. 3 and pp. 180–189.
2 Ward, K., *The Concept of God* (1974), Chs. 1–4.
3 *Cf. ibid.*, pp. 32–35.
4 Owen, H.P., *Concepts of Deity* (1971), Ch. 1, 2(d), 3(e) (f).
5 Wisdom, J., *'Gods' in Philosophy and Psychoanalysis* (1953), p. 149; Bambrough, R., *Reason, Truth and God* (1969), Ch. 2; Nielson, K., *Scepticism* (1973), pp. 10–11, 98–92.
6 Attfield, v.D.G., 'Creed-Centred RE' in *Learning for Living*, May, 1973, p. 12.
7 Ward, *op. cit.*, Chs. 3 and 5.
8 Jeremias, J., *The Parables of Jesus* (1954), Ch. III; Dodd, C.H., *Parables of the Kingdom* (1935), Chs. V and VI.
9 Hamlyn, D.W., *The Logical and Psychological Aspects of Learning*, Ch. 2 in (ed.). Peters, R.S., *The Concept of Education* (1967).

*Religious Education: A Shocking Business**

Edward A. Robinson

In his autobiography, Sean O'Faolain writes:

> What end is there anyway to child education except to learn a few necessary things and after that to shock the intelligence, stir the sensibilities and warm the imagination into some sense of the mystery, horror and beauty of life?[1]

Children are remarkably tough: their bones are like rubber, their joints supple and elastic. I can take my five-year-old son by one arm and swing him round and round and produce nothing but delight; with an adult such games would soon produce a dislocated shoulder. He will tumble head over heels downstairs, to the alarm of his parents, and pick himself up at the bottom, after a few tears, none the worse but for a few bruises. In many ways their minds are similar: resilient, volatile, fantastic in imagination, and capable of conceiving the impossible with simple ease that is quite beyond most adults.

It is true that children are in other ways more vulnerable than adults, both in body and mind. No one should be ungrateful to the studies of child psychologists who in the last generation in particular have shown the many subtle ways in which early incidents and relationships may influence for good or ill the whole course of subsequent development. But respect for such findings may lead to a loss of nerve. Some modern religious education textbooks, for example, based upon a presumption of the 'readiness for religion' of children at this or that age, are so *jejune* in material and so banal in their treatment of it that only the most inventive of teachers could use them without boring their pupils to tears – or violence. Such unintelligent patronage is not only offensive: it is self-defeating.

'As far back as I can remember I have never had a sense of separation

*This article first appeared in *Learning for Living*, Vol. 11, No. 2, November, 1971.

from the spiritual force I now choose to call God and the natural world around me. From the age of about six to twelve in places of quiet and desolation this feeling of "oneness" often passed to a state of "listening". I mean by listening that I was suddenly alerted to something that was going to happen. What followed was a feeling of tremendous exaltation in which time stood still.'

'I had my first religious experience when I was about six and saw the whole evening sky covered by small, criss-cross, clearly defined and vividly coloured rainbow pieces. At about ten years of age I saw the entire evening sky filled with meteorites which fell like snowflakes all about me. Both sights seemed to me at the time to represent objective natural events. Only much later did I realise that they must have been purely subjective experiences. Both caused me to feel overwhelmed by an awareness of the awesome beauty of nature, as if I had been granted a glimpse of a state of absolute beauty, absolute perfection, and a meaning behind daily events which was incomprehensible to my intellect but is nevertheless deeply ingrained in my memory.'

These two accounts, as well as all subsequent passages quoted without attribution, come from the very large number of such reminiscences of childhood sent to the Religious Experience Research Unit at Manchester College, Oxford. Can we recognize these children? Their world is an alien one to most of us. What is going on behind those dreamy eyes, that attention that wanders too soon for our instruction?

'A child has no means of knowing if he feels differently from other people or not. As I grew up I was ever more perplexed to realise that many people lived in a world quite different from my own. They could kill things without hurting themselves, they could sleep without dreaming, or dream without colours. They could apparently always feel themselves to be inside their skins, and the things they saw and heard and felt seemed real and distinct realities. The objective world seemed real to most people, and the subjective world unreal or non-existent. . . . I understood without seeing, and what I saw or heard or touched seemed to be of secondary importance to what I knew. When I was a child I would experience it suddenly, and then suddenly lose it again, perhaps after only a few seconds or minutes. The awareness of unity only came over me infrequently when I was a child as far as I can remember. As I grew up it became more frequent, and nowadays it has become almost continuous when I am alone or in contemplative mood. I like this feeling, and often leave the ordinary awareness of duality and harsh definition to enter at will into the rolling awareness of the unity and edgelessness of reality.'

Such a quiet unfolding, unscarred and unaffected by the educational process, seems rare. Others have been less lucky. For them contact with adults has led to a withering, not a flowering of the spirit.

'I was brought up in the contemporary Churchianity of my childhood days, but although I was an obedient and not very clever child this kind of religion and the gloomy old Jehovah and his rather soppy son Jesus always repelled me. However, I have always been conscious of what I call cosmic experience – a feeling of being at one with some essence of the universal process. Even as a child this was so, and the personal experience clashed with the religiosity of my social background, causing considerable guilt feelings. I remember lying in my cot (they kept children in brass-railed cots until about six or seven in those days), I must have been about six, and trying to decide which kind of attitude was true and which to follow. Religion seemed horrid and anti-reality. I had already experimented by going up on the downs and shouting "Damn God", "Blast God", etc. and waiting to see if the heavens fell as I had been taught to expect. They did not, and the sheep-clipped turf remained as lovely as ever. That night I resolved to follow *my* feelings and only pay as much lip-service to Churchianity as was politic to keep out of trouble with my parents.'

In others the vision survives, in spite of the good intentions of insensitive adults:

'Always there seems to me to be a dual version of life: the one which is lived day to day, event to event, joyful or sad, while the other is portrayed by entirely spiritual participation. One's senses, one's reason guide one in the day-to-day life, the pull of ambition, the fear of pain and so on, yet in everything there is this something else, the spiritual reason for the involvement in this way of living. Someone once said that those who have this sense of duality live in two worlds really, but for myself, I think it is only one. . . . As a child I sensed this, but my parents, both good and kind, possessing simple beliefs in matters of religion were unable to understand my efforts to explain.'

It can even survive the deliberate fostering of a sense of guilt in childhood and the exploitation of that sense in adolescence by emotional pressure-groups:

'Upbringing strictly non-conformist, taken to mission halls from the age of six and put under urgent pressure to receive salvation. Salvation or hell's fire – worried about how to get saved – unable to see how it was done. Also worried by God's eye seeing me in my bath. Temper, repressed because of need to please parents (parents' will and God's now one) broke out in late adolescence in the form of bitter criticism of the bible and parents' way of life. Sexually repressed of course.

'Sudden conversion through Oxford Group – joy, joy – ending in bitter disillusionment within two years. Desolation of being alone after feeling Jesus Christ as close as a shadow.

'Eleven years of hell, a pronounced atheist, hard work smothering the still small voice which never gave up.'

Of all the early traumas from which we seek to protect children, not the least damaging may be the stunting by parental or educational repression of this intuitive feeling after the mystery of life. But O'Faolain speaks of horror as well as of beauty, of shocking the intelligence as well as of warming the imagination. I have given this article the sub-title *A Shocking Business* because I don't think it is possible to separate the horror from the beauty if the full mystery is to become apparent. The full development of the muscles involves strenuous and sometimes painful exercise. The same is true of the imagination. There are obvious dangers here. Children may have strong stomachs for the horrific; at times they seem to relish it with peculiar glee. But real terror is often just round the corner. How can we tell when excitement will turn to anxiety, or to some deep-seated disturbance whose roots we may have difficulty later in identifying?

Here I must refer to a most interesting analysis of anxiety given by Dr Richard Jones in his recent book *Fantasy and Feeling in Education.* Anxiety, he says, is compounded of three elements: imagination, loneliness and helplessness. When a child is imaginative, and lonely and helpless, he becomes anxious. Eliminate even one of these, and the situation changes. Applying this analysis to our present problem where do we start? It may seem to go without saying that we should not eliminate imagination, but all too often in today's classrooms this is the one to be kept out. Sometimes this is done in the name of some psychological theory which may seek to protect children from concepts which they are said to be unable to comprehend. At others the imagination is starved by those who wish to protect children from any aspects of reality but the nice, the comfortable: a cosy form of sentimentality which is represented in many children's hymns and in a tradition of religious art long associated with Mowbrays bookshops.

But if imagination must be encouraged at all costs, what of the other two? In the face of the unknown, the unfamiliar experience (and there can be no scope for the imagination without such) everyone, whether child or man, is momentarily helpless. The totally new sight, sound, smell, idea – they all find us for a moment at a loss, until we can relate the unknown to the known, until we can say, 'of course, I know what that is: that's a . . .', and we have fitted it into our familiar scheme, assimilated it, and cease to feel it as alien, as an intrusion or a threat. With adults the resolution of helplessness is generally quick and painless: 'funny; for a moment I never realised . . .' But for a child, so much more limited both in experience and in his means of expression, mastery of the unfamiliar is often more of a travail, an ordeal. Impossible to match with any known experience, the unfamiliar thing may hover half-forgotten on the fringes of consciousness, a vague worry, a shadow, an unformed and unrecognizable threat until it can be brought out into the light and given expression, a colour, a shape, an act or a name, so that it can be known for what it is. Helplessness is then replaced by mastery, and one source of anxiety is for the time being eliminated. Of course we cannot count on being able to help children in this process; there are no techniques to ensure it; by taking an untimely initiative we may only suggest the wrong ideas, the wrong words, and so just compound the helplessness, make the anxiety worse. Sometimes we can only wait; all we can do is just be there for when we are needed.

This is of course the cure for loneliness, or the beginning of it anyway. But the kind of presence which is the full answer to loneliness involves qualities hard to define and makes demands which are impossible to limit. I have written at greater length about this elsewhere.[2] *Disponibilite* is more than an attitude, assumed *ad hoc* or *ad hominem*; it is rather an undercurrent of the whole personality which may make itself felt in an unspoken rapport as much as in explicit expression of sympathy or support. Sympathy: the word has become somewhat devalued today, having had some of its more attractive elements transferred by psychologists to the more fashionable empathy. Thucydides could write with particular feeling for the victims of the plague which swept Athens in 429 BC: he had been there; he had had it himself, and was one of its few victims to survive. Like symbiosis, sympathy in its deepest sense implies some degree of common life, of experience or suffering actually shared alongside of others. Without such a link, expressions of sympathy, however sincere, must remain superficial. Sympathy between adult and child in this full sense is rare, perhaps impossible. But most of us can recall something of our own childhood gropings for expression, solitary little mysteries in which the suggestions of grown-ups seemed particularly silly; and so we should not forget that there is a time for speech, and also a time for silence.

Perhaps I can best illustrate this analysis of anxiety by another quotation, this time from a letter written by a profoundly religious woman who looks back from her sixties on a life that might have been enriched but in fact seems only to have been haunted by a powerful imagination, with no one to help her, either in her helplessness in face of the unknown or in her loneliness at times of crisis.

'From the time that I was a child I had occasionally what I now realize was a mystical experience. I particularly remember an occasion in my teens when I looked out of a window at a tree and knew that the tree and I were one. But instead of losing myself in the oneness (which is the usual mystical experience, isn't it?) I seemed to be reaching an apprehension of what this signified. I felt myself "going somewhere" and drew back in fear because I thought that I should not "get back" again. Was this being afraid of a mental breakdown? I often think of God telling Moses to hide his face until God had gone by, for nobody could look upon I Am's face without being destroyed.

'In 1946 I started a long breakdown caused partly by overwork, partly because I wasn't living the sort of life that suits me. I was frightened of everything, but especially of being cut off from God.

'For months I went to Dr G., a psychologist. He was an agnostic. I reached a point where I said "God, I give myself to you", though I was afraid of what that entailed – nursing lepers in Africa, perhaps.

'For several weeks (perhaps a few months) afterwards I tried to let my mind be directed as God wished though I realised it was a perilous proceeding. Then one night I knew something stupendous about God. I rang up Dr G. to pass this information on to him because I was certain I couldn't hold it any longer. He was furious with me for waking him and refused to listen to me.

'I've never been able to recapture what it was I knew. It had something to do with a pyramid – perhaps all humanity at the base and the Godhead at the top. One thing is important – what I apprehended of God was power, and not, as I should have hoped, love.

'I thought that God would not have given me such an experience without having some important work to do, but I went on and on being desperately exhausted and trembling on a razor's edge mentally. All the time I was drawn on in this search for apprehension, always pulling back when I seemed on the verge of it because the danger was so great.'

To those who feel that I am wrong in giving priority to the horror and not to the beauty of life, to 'shocking the intelligence' rather than to 'warming the imagination', I answer that this is in part because I am trying to redress a long established imbalance. I am not saying that the last writer was right in apprehending God as power and not as love; but simply that the traditional type of religious education that merely represents him to children as love leaves them inadequately equipped to cope with him as power. The spirit takes a terrible revenge, says Mauriac, in a powerful passage quoted by O'Faolain:

> L'esprit terriblement se venge à l'heure où la vie soudain attaque l'homme né, tard, de l'adolescent veule. Quel secours trouvera-t-il dans cette religion qui ne lui fût jamais qu'une source de faibles delices? . . . Malheur au garçon dont les clous, l'éponge de fiel, la couronne d'épines fûrent les premiers jouets.[3]

Life is waiting round the corner to attack the man for whom the symbols of redemptive suffering have become trivialized, turned into objects of sentimental piety.

'Spiritual experiences . . . I think they do not occur without some form of death as a prelude, whether of the body, emotions or thoughts and their appetites, though this may be voluntary or involuntary.'

We may have our doubts about the place of spiritual experiences as part of the educational process, but if we cannot teach children to recognize such experiences in others or, what is even more vital, to cope with them in themselves, we shall not have done much. What 'form of death' they are first to be brought to face must depend on the experience of their guide and how far he is able to go with them into that 'Savage and Beautiful Country'. That it should be voluntary is essential; for upon that first acceptance (or refusal) must depend the whole possibility of later spiritual growth, evolving as it must by a growing readiness to accept death in ever more deeply involving forms. 'I seemed to be reaching an apprehension of what this signified. I felt myself "going somewhere" and drew back in fear because I thought I should not "get back" again. . . . All the time I was drawn on in this search for apprehension, always pulling back when I seemed on the verge of it because the danger was so great.' 'Religion', said Adolf Keller, 'rests on one's capacity to let oneself be profoundly affected by powers that transcend consciousness'.[4] To 'let oneself be profoundly affected', voluntarily to face a 'form of death', may demand a courage which is too much for the unassisted individual, a decision which he cannot face alone, without the support of someone who has been some part at least of this way before.

Whatever practical aims any particular programme of religious education may put before us, then, it will achieve little unless we can help young people, through the growth of imagination, the mastery of expression and the breakdown of isolation, to some sense of that form of death that is the necessary prelude to any awareness of 'the mystery, horror and beauty of life'.

Notes and references

1 O'Faolain, S., *Vive Moi*, Rupert Hart-Davis, London, 1965, p. 45.
2 For example in 'Communication and contact in religious studies' in Learning for Living, March, 1971; also in 'Parousia' in *New Fire*, No. 7, 1971.
3 O'Faolain, *op. cit.*, p. 21.
4 Quoted by Spinks, G.S., in *Psychology and Religion*, p. 96.

3
The Social Context: Religious Pluralism in School and Society

Introduction

Every school subject is an expression of an intention on the part of the educating society. If the church is conceived of as having the right to educate, and as being the educational society, religious education is likely to take a form different from that which it will assume when it is granted that the State has the right to educate and that, in a democracy, society as a whole is the educator. School subjects will also differ in the extent to which they feel themselves required to be open and susceptible to changes and ambiguities in the social intention. One would expect that subjects like mathematics with a well developed linear and hierarchical structure of knowledge would (granted their value) be less subject to social pressure for change, whereas subjects like Development Education or Political Education would be more dependent not only upon the national mood for their emergence at all in the curriculum, but would also draw their content from the changing political and social context, national and international. As the right and the duty to religiously educate all its children has passed increasingly to the State both centrally and locally, religious education has found itself contextualized in an increasingly complex society.

The 1975 Birmingham Agreed Syllabus provides for a critical and descriptive education in a variety of world religions and secular ways of life. When the controversies about this syllabus were at their height in 1974–1976, it became clear that although the professional debate centred on questions of educational theory, the public debate was about the nature of British society. Is this a Christian country? Is it a secular country? Is it a pluralist country? Bishop Lesslie Newbigin offers a critique of the liberal critical stance in religious education, which he finds in the Birmingham Syllabus. This stance is itself, he suggests, an alternative ideology, all the more threatening because its relativity is implicitly denied: it is the stance which judges all others. Although Newbigin's approach is not exactly a theological estimation of religious education, it represents one kind of possible reaction from the theologian. Without denying that religious education must be based on educational grounds, the theologian is well placed to scrutinize the values and commitments of the educational grounds themselves, which he sees expressed in the religious education. One must, of course, ask whether Newbigin's criticisms of the liberal stance are valid, whether he is justified in seeing the Birmingham Syllabus as an exemplification of this stance, and whether, even if in its actual form it is an expression of the liberal critical stance, the Birmingham Syllabus approach might nevertheless be made compatible with Newbigin's suggestion as to how religion should be taught.

The most striking change which has taken place in the adaptation of religious education to the social environment is the shift in content from Christian Studies to the study of world religions. This does not mean that Christianity is dropping out of the curriculum; on the contrary, Christianity is often being tackled in a much richer and fuller way in the context of world religions than in the days when below the Sixth Form it was mainly confined to the study of Christian origins, without much reference to Christian faith today, in spite of the declared intention to foster such faith in the pupils. But what is the effect upon Christianity of teaching it alongside other religions? Indeed, will not any religion lose something of its seriousness when it is so obviously but one amongst many? Is this not to relativize each religion? But how, in that case, can a teaching of several religions be faithful to any of them? Many religions are highly self-conscious about their uniqueness, their finality and their absolute character.

Daniel Hardy criticizes one of the most common responses which religious education teachers make when confronted with this dilemma. Instead of being regarded as 'truth-tellers', religious believers are regarded as being 'truth-claimers'. But this is to 'flatten' religions and non-religions, presenting them as 'ways people have of looking at the world', and to distance the truth which they present by turning it into a 'truth for somebody else'. Hardy suggests that the religions and the non-religions must be presented in open communication, as participants in truth, which is thus with the pupil and the teacher in the classroom.

*Teaching Religion in a Secular Plural Society**

Lesslie Newbigin

The subject given to me, with which this paper tries to come to grips, raises very difficult issues in the fields of theology, politics and education. Although I have tried to reflect on these issues my experience is obviously limited. I have taught Christianity in an Indian High School and I am now teaching Hinduism in an English Training College. I have been involved in some of the discussions surrounding the recent Birmingham Syllabus, to which I shall make some reference. Though I shall be making some criticisms of it, I recognize that it is a very able and courageous attempt to deal with a quite new situation, and that it is very difficult to propose anything which would be an improvement on it.

I will say what I have to say by taking the three key words of my title in turn: religion, secularity, teaching.

I – Religion

What is meant by 'religion'? This has been a notorious crux in the debate surrounding the Birmingham syllabus, which uses such phrases as 'religious and moral dimensions of human experience' and 'stances for living'. Under the latter Humanism and Marxism have been included. In my opinion this is correct, for Marxism does take the place in Marxist societies which religion has taken in earlier societies. Yet Marxism clearly does not accept the 'religious' interpretation of those elements in human experience which the Syllabus wants to deal with.

In the 1944 Act religious instruction meant instruction in the Christian religion. This was understood to be the officially accepted 'stance for living' inherited from the centuries of the 'Christendom era' – even though

*This article first appeared in *Learning for Living*, Vol. 17, No. 2, Winter, 1977.

in 1944 only a minority of the population were practising Christians. There was no alternative 'stance for living' sufficiently influential to merit consideration. Even those who made no personal profession of Christian belief accepted this as the proper 'stance' and expected their children to be trained in it.

When the word 'religion' is used in a religiously plural society, it has changed its meaning. A 'religion' which is simply one of a class, is no longer an ultimate commitment, a stance for living. The committed adherent of a universal faith such as Islam cannot, while remaining a faithful Muslim, regard Islam as one of a class called 'religions'. God has sent many messengers – including Moses and Jesus. But Muhammad is the final Messenger, and to include the Qu'ran as simply one among the religious books of mankind is to deny Islam. The Hindu acknowledges many ways to salvation – Saivism, Vaishnavism, Buddhist, Christianity, etc. – but he understands them from the standpoint of the *Sanatanadharma,* the eternal order to which the ultimate key is found in the Upanishads. To suggest that the *Sanatanadharma* is itself just one of the possible ways of looking at things would be to cease to be a Hindu. So also Marxism has a highly developed interpretation of 'the religious dimension of human experience'; it claims to have unmasked the real character and origin of this experience. To say that this interpretation is merely one among the variety of experiences which it claims to interpret would be to cease to be a Marxist. So also the Christian sees the Gospel as the end of religion. God has spoken his word in Jesus Christ and whatever echoes of that word are to be found in the religions and cultures of mankind can be heard as echoes, not as parallel and independent messages.

What meaning can the word 'religion' have in a religiously plural society? Three types of answer can be distinguished.

The first looks at the religions from a standpoint outside of any one of them. This has been the characteristic approach to the 'comparative study of religions' in Europe since the age of the Enlightenment. The age which interpreted human experience by means of the models provided by Descartes, Newton, Leibnitz and Kant required that religion, in order to be acceptable, must be 'within the limits of pure reason'. What fell outside of those limits was 'superstition'. The ultimate 'stance for living' was provided not by any of the religions, but by a commitment to the methods of mathematical reasoning and experimental science. Religions could be classified in a variety of ways within this overall world view, but it was 'reason' not religion which provided the ultimate 'stance for living'.

A second way of looking at the religions (plural) is from the point of view of their social function. While religion can be an explosive and revolutionary force, the phenomena known as 'religions' have functioned during most of history as forces for conservation and cohesion among the groups which professed them. Rulers, especially imperial rulers who aspire to weld together many peoples into one political unit, are therefore bound to look at the usefulness or otherwise of religion for their purpose. The Emperor Akhbar promoted religious dialogue with this in view, and it is with the same purpose that the Government of India today has a 'Committee on National Integration' composed of representatives of the religions. During the 1960s many Christians believed that world development was the most pressing need of mankind and therefore evaluated religions, including Christian missions, on the basis of their contribution to development. Much of the emotion surrounding the question of religious education in British Schools, even among those who are not practising Christians, arises from the belief that 'religion' helps to keep the social fabric from splitting. The furore over the inclusion of Marxism in the Birmingham Syllabus arises largely (one suspects) from this way of looking at 'religion'.

A third possibility is that religions may be understood as varied manifestations of one common experience. Naturally different thinkers define this common experience in different ways – sometimes in terms of mysticism, sometimes in terms of belief in God or of the soul, or of life after death. 'God' in this case is conceived in unitarian rather than trinitarian terms. In any case the formulation of the 'essence of religion' by which all the varieties of 'religion' are brought into a single class is that of the individual thinker, and will always contain elements which are vehemently denied by other people claiming to be religious.

A little reflection on the current debate about religious education in schools will show that all the above three ways of understanding 'religion' are operative, often with no attempt to distinguish them. The first two represent a 'stance' outside of religion from which the religions are understood and evaluated; the third represents a stance within the religious experience. What they all have in common is that they represent one particular stance among the many which are available. In every case the way 'religion' is understood is governed by the prior commitment of the one who is trying to understand. There is no standpoint which is above all standpoints! The eighteenth century rationalist or the twentieth century humanist who claims to observe all the phenomena of religion impartially is also under an obligation to expose for examination the fundamental axioms, the prior decisions about what is allowed to count as evidence, which underlie his way of understanding. Equally the man who claims to have found the 'essence of religion' which entitles him to regard all religions as members of a class, is under obligation to expose for examination his understanding of religion and his claim that this is in fact the truth about all religion.

The Birmingham Syllabus insists that religions are not to be studied with the idea that one is superior to the rest, but 'objectively and for their own sake'. Plainly there is illusion here. The Syllabus itself rests upon one particular view in which religions should be regarded. But this view is necessarily concealed from view. If 'objectively' in this context means without any presuppositions about what counts as evidence and what makes sense', then it is impossible. If it does not mean this, then it means that all 'stances' are open for examination except the 'stance' of the Syllabus itself.

I am at present engaged in teaching the Bhagavadgita to a very intelligent group of students. I do not try to teach it as just one of the peculiar varieties of religious experience. I try to teach it, so to speak, from the inside. I try to help the students to read it as a Hindu reads it, to feel the force of it, to see the perplexities (common human perplexities) with which it is wrestling, and to see why it has come to mean so much to men like Mahatma Gandhi and Vinobha Bhave in the India of today. But at the end of the exercise, I cannot stop the students from asking me: 'Do you believe that this is true?' I am no proper teacher if I try to evade that question. If I answer Yes, I should be a Hindu. If I answer No, I should still have some answer to the question about the hundreds of millions of devout and godly people who do believe it to be true. If, on the other hand, I try to study Hinduism and all the other religions from – so to speak – an equal distance, as this Syllabus suggests, then I must also undertake the study of the ideology which underlies this Syllabus, and must answer the question: 'What are the grounds for believing that this way of looking at Hinduism is true, as against the Hindu way of looking at Hinduism?'

What is meant by saying that all religions are to be studied 'objectively'? I do not understand anything except when I have related it somehow to the rest of my experience, and therefore to the models in which I have (provisionally) grasped my experience up to now. One can 'understand' Christianity from the point of view of the Marxist model, and one can understand Hinduism from the point of view of the Christian model. One can also understand all religions and ideologies from the point of view of this Syllabus, which is the point of view of a secular, liberal inhabitant of the Western capitalist post-Christian world. This point of view is naturally accepted by the majority of the inhabitants of this corner of the world as being simply 'how things really are'. This is the character of all myths. Those who inhabit them do not 'see' them, because they are the framework, the model by means of which they see. But this 'myth' is very recognizable by the inhabitants of other parts of the world as our particular cultural model. It is also, incidentally, a model which seems at this time to be disintegrating. (One could cite, for example, the revolt of the 'counter-culture' against the claims of 'scientific objectivity', the way in which students in the western world are voting with their feet against science and technology and in favour of the humanities, the fact that astrology is now very big business in all the 'developed' countries and the popularity of such works as *Zen and the Art of Motor-cycle Maintenance*!)

With the insistence upon 'objectivity' the Syllabus protests that 'there can be no question of making it an aim of religious education to convert pupils to any particular religion or ideology'. I am afraid that at this point the framers of the Syllabus are too innocent. Assuming that the effect of the programme of religious education is not to be a totally vacant mind, what will in fact be communicated will be the ideology which informs this Syllabus, which is as much one of the possible 'stances for living' as Marxism or Christianity. It will not do to say that it is simply the 'right approach', for in that case the pretence of neutrality has been dropped. Nor will it do to say that this is not done by indoctrination or brain-washing after the manner of an evangelist, for my whole point is that this ideology is *not* exposed for critical examination; it is simply taken for granted.

II – Secular

We come, secondly, to the word 'secular'. What is meant by calling a society secular? And what would the implications of this be for the practice of religious education? There is, of course, a large literature on the subject. T.S. Eliot's *The Idea of a Christian Society*, and the reply by Denis Munby entitled *The Idea of a Secular Society*, pose the questions sharply. Owen Chadwick's recent book on *The Secularisation of the European Mind* shows how extremely subtle and complex the issues are. I find myself compelled to ask the question: 'Can there be a secular society in the sense of a society which does not use pressure to bring about conformity to certain shared convictions and norms?' We in this part of the world have been living for so long on the inherited capital of a thousand years of Christendom that we do not really know, and can hardly imagine what would happen if the process of burning this up was carried right through to its logical conclusion, if we had a society which did not accept any of the values which we have inherited from this past. I am haunted by a paragraph from Michael Polanyi which I think has much relevance to our subject.

> The critical movement, which seems to be nearing the end of its course today, was perhaps the most fruitful effort ever sustained by the human mind. The past four or five centuries, which have gradually destroyed or overshadowed the whole mediaeval cosmos, have enriched us mentally and morally to an extent unrivalled in any period of similar duration. But its incandescence has fed on the combustion of Christian heritage in the oxygen of Greek rationalism, and when this fuel was exhausted the critical framework itself burnt away. *Personal Knowledge*, pp. 265–6

'Secular' is a notoriously slippery word, but I would like to suggest that in the context of this discussion we must distinguish two ways of defining secularity. There is, on the one hand, the idea that every form of study and action should be developed on its own, on the basis of the data – and 'data' in this context is held to mean 'valuefree facts' which are simply 'there' apart from their place in a larger context of meaning. I believe that is simply illusion, and that modern scientists recognize it as such. Even in physics there are no 'value-free facts'. The physicist works by means of models which are valued not merely because they 'explain' the facts, but because they do so with greater 'simplicity', 'elegance' or even 'beauty' than other possible models. The student of physics begins to 'understand' by means of these models. This is even more true of the study of history. If you read histories of nineteenth century England by – for example – A.L. Rowse and E.P. Thompson, you will soon find that totally different pictures emerge, because the data are being interpreted through different frameworks of meaning, and there is no way of teaching history which does not involve the (provisional) acceptance of some such framework. All knowing, of whatever kind, is an activity which is part of a commitment to some way of valuing things. It is a heuristic activity directed towards something which is valued. It develops through the use of a common language which expresses a set of shared values. No society could exist without such a set of shared values. It would simply disintegrate.

But there is a second, and more promising way of understanding secularity – and here the word 'plural' in my title is important. There can be a society which is secular in the sense that it holds together a plurality of different groups each of which has a set of shared values which is – to some extent – distinctive. If these different groups were totally self-enclosed, such a plural secular society would be impossible. But, provided there is *some* body of shared values (and I shall come to this) there can be a secular plural society in the sense that many different groups each held together by a body of shared values can co-exist and fruitfully interact. In this sense we may speak of contemporary English society as a secular plural society.

But the secularity cannot be unlimited. Here let me make three points very briefly – recognizing that I am only pointing to enormous areas of debate.

(a) We have to ask about the organs of government which will enable this plural society to function. Do they operate outside any accepted system of values? Is Government above any moral law? Are the actions of governments immune to criticism on ethical grounds? If no, then the state is but the resultant of forces and society must be dominated by the most powerful of the groups which compose it. If yes, then the state is not wholly secular.

(b) If society is to be democratically ordered, then all the separate groups will have to accept some norms of behaviour which are applied even when it is to the disadvantage of the sectional interest of the group. Otherwise a plural society cannot function in freedom.

(c) In fact, even the most secular societies acknowledge some limits to pluralism. Let me take two examples from the contemporary British situation. Among the 'stances for living' available in our society, racism has powerful attractions. The National Front can poll more votes than the Communist Party. Indeed the appeal to ethnic identity is a powerful one for all societies undergoing rapid change. But our 'secular' society has (rightly) made the practice of racism in public affairs a criminal offence. A second obvious contender among the stances for living is hedonism. The view that whatever creates erotic stimulation is good and should be available to all is widely held and propagated in accepted organs of opinion. But there are serious doubts even in our secular society about whether total free trade in pornography would not be so corrupting as to destroy society. And so we have the endless debates about the laws governing obscenity. Why do we not include racism and hedonism among the possible 'stances for living' in a syllabus of religious education? I have read attempts to answer this question on allegedly 'objective' grounds, that is without making value judgments on them. I am totally unconvinced. There are certainly more racists and hedonists in England than there are Marxists and humanists. The fact is that we do not include these in the Syllabus because we know that it would be *wrong* to offer these as stances for living to children – even though we could doubtless find some pretty stories about the personal behaviour of Adolf Hitler at home to go beside those about Lenin in the Birmingham Handbook.

I conclude this section by expressing the opinion that there are limits to the possibilities of a secular society even in the pluralist sense which I have discussed. No society, and certainly no democratic society can cohere without some common values which are shared and therefore – to some degree – enforced. If education does not have the effect of transmitting these values to the coming generation, then it can only have a socially disintegrating effect. This means, surely, that the teacher cannot be totally neutral as between the various possible 'stances for living' which are on offer. In spite of all the warnings in the Syllabus against seeking to influence children in the direction of any particular religion or ideology, I would have to insist that the teacher has a *duty* to encourage children to adopt some kinds of 'stances for living' and to avoid others.

This brings me to the third of the three key words, and to the question of thc manner of teaching.

III – Teaching

How is 'religion' to be taught? The answer of the Birmingham Syllabus is 'subject to the same disciplines as other areas of study'. I fully agree, but I am not sure whether the authors of the Syllabus do.

How does a teacher of physics set about teaching Boyle's Law to his students? He does not take a non-committal attitude to its truth. He does not expound it in the manner of a teacher of 'world religions' expounding the views about creation held by some tribe in Papua. He does not portray it as one of the possible views of the subject. He believes it to represent what is the case, and he hopes that his pupils will come also to *understand* that it is so. He does not try to brain-wash them into a blind and unquestioning acceptance of it. Nor does he offer it as one among a number of options. He tries to get the pupils to see the evidence for it in such a way that they will come to hold it as true, and yet to be open to further evidence (if such should appear) which might enable them to amend this belief. He does not teach it as an aspect of the 'scientific dimension of human experience', but as a way of stating what is the case which he hopes they will accept because they understand.

A teacher of history who is trying to take his class through the history of England in the nineteenth century will be aware of the many different ways in which it can be viewed. He will – it is to be hoped – do something to make his pupils aware of them. But he cannot help communicating to them the picture that *he* has of the story. If he does not do that he will be a very dull teacher. But his purpose should be that the pupils should look at the facts, become interested in them, and grasp them for themselves.

In both cases the purpose is to enable the pupils to begin to grasp for themselves what is really the case, and not just what are the various possible ways of looking at it. I do not think that you can really teach without wanting the pupils to see what is really there, and this means that there is a certain amount of excitement about the subject. A teacher who, in a detached spirit, merely surveys the various possible points of view on the matter, without trying to communicate what he himself sees, is likely to communicate only his own attitude. In fact he will communicate the typical 'stance for living' (or shall we say 'for dying') of our rather tired culture: 'Taste everything, but don't be committed to anything'.

The Birmingham Syllabus affirms that religious education should be 'directed towards developing a critical understanding of the religious and moral dimensions of human experience and away from attempting to foster the claims of particular religious standpoints'. The word 'critical' is repeated at every important point in this section, and evidently the framers of the Syllabus attach great importance to it. I would like to propose a small critique of the use of the word 'critical'. Criticism is an activity in which, on the basis of one set of beliefs (A) you examine another set of beliefs (B). No critical activity is possible except on the basis of some way of understanding experience which is (for the moment) assumed. While you are examining A, you accept B uncritically. No advance in knowledge is possible which does not begin by the uncritical acceptance of something which is given. The pupil's capacity for critical reflection on a proposition can only be developed on the basis of what he is ready in the first place to accept on the authority of the teacher. Religious education will have to be subject to the same discipline. Human understanding has to begin by the provisional uncritical acceptance of experience. One may compare the development of understanding with the way in which a climber advances up a crag. He can only advance by letting go of one of his hand-holds or foot-holds and feeling round for a secure one further up. While he does so, he must accept the other holds he has. A climber who tries to let go of all his four holds at the same time will not advance.

Religion, like science and history, is an expression of the human attempt to understand and respond to what is really the case. A pupil will advance in this understanding, and will develop the proper critical faculties in the field, by a process which must begin with the uncritical acceptance of models which are part of the culture and experience into which the pupil is growing up. A study of the eye is useful in its proper place, but it cannot replace the use of the eye for seeing what is to be seen. Religious education is self-defeating if it is only concerned with the study of 'the religious dimension of human experience' and not with the realities which religious experience tries to grasp and respond to.

The Syllabus seeks to develop a 'critical understanding' of the varieties of religious experience precisely by its uncritical acceptance of a particular 'stance for living'. To the framers of the Syllabus this stance is obviously simply 'what is right'. To an observer from another culture it is easily recognizable as a particular stance characteristic of the present phase of Western middle-class culture – a culture which has ceased to believe that the Christian faith is the truth about how things really are. The Syllabus does not offer the possibility that the critical faculties of the children might be employed in examining *this* stance, because in order to do so they would have to accept uncritically (though provisionally) one of the other stances reviewed.

The point that I am trying to make is no mere quibble about words but goes to the heart of the contemporary cultural situation in the Western world. We are heirs of the movement of radical criticism of all traditional beliefs which surfaced in eighteenth century Europe. We can now see that this movement was sustained by the enormously powerful current of belief which Europe had come to accept uncritically. At this point another quotation from Polanyi seems to me relevant.

> In propagating their own beliefs the early rationalists were opposing traditional authority on so wide a front that they could well regard themselves as radical sceptics. But the beliefs of rationalism have since been effectively called in question by the revolutionary doctrines of Marxism and Nazism. It is absurd to oppose such doctrines now on the ground of scepticism. For they gained their present ascendency only recently by a sweeping rejection of Western tradition, and it is rationalism which today relies on

> tradition – the tradition of the eighteenth and nineteenth centuries – against them. It should also have become clear by this time that the beliefs transmitted by this now imperilled tradition are by no means self-evident. Modern fanaticism is rooted in an extreme scepticism which can only be strengthened, not shaken, by further doses of universal doubt.'
>
> *Personal Knowledge*, p. 298

The critical faculty is not self-sustaining. It can only develop on the basis of beliefs which are accepted – in the first instance – uncritically. If the capacity to believe is not developed along with the capacity to criticize, the result can only be fanaticism or nihilism.

Religious education must surely take as its first aim the awakening of the pupils' understanding of the realities to which religious experience is a human response.

IV – How can this be accomplished?

How is this to be done in our religiously plural society? I confess that the answers I try to give are hesitant and stumbling, but I try to sketch them because failure to make the attempt would be cowardly evasion.

1 I believe that religious education is an essential part of any real education because religion is concerned with realities, because every human being must come to terms in one way or another with these realities, and because the greatest of human minds have wrestled with them.

2 I believe that religion must be taught in the context of a real concern for, a real passion for the truth. We are not operating in the spirit of a travel agency which offers a rich variety of exotic beliefs and practices for those who care to take a world cruise. We are not inviting the students to look at stuffed birds in a museum. We will approach the subject as those who are deeply concerned about what is really the case about the human situation, and we will recognize the adherents of the various religious and ideological systems as men and women who share one world with us and who – like us – live at the meeting point between ancient traditions and the demands of modern life.

3 We will try to help our pupils to understand the different answers which are given in our society to the ultimate questions about the meaning of human life. In doing this the teacher will (a) help the pupils to understand other faiths as their adherents would wish them to be understood, to feel their power and beauty; (b) not conceal his own commitment or pretend that he is above commitment; (c) welcome and encourage difficult and searching questions. The purpose all the time will be to direct the minds of the students not

just to the varieties of religious experience, but to the realities with which the religions are seeking to come to terms. It is only thus that we shall be taking the subject seriously in the same sense that we take other subjects in the curriculum seriously.

4 The religious pluralism of our society must, it seems to me, be reflected in a plurality of solutions for the problem we are discussing. This pluralism may well be represented in a single school where members of the staff have differing commitments. These must be openly faced and accepted. Pluralism may also mean that there is a variety of different solutions in different parts of the country. What is suitable for Cumbria will not be suitable for Birmingham. Pluralism should also mean, I think, the possibility of schools conducted by (but not exclusively for) distinct religious communities, or that – where desired – provision should be made for the authorized teachers of a religion from outside the school being invited to teach pupils their own faith. It does not seem to me necessary that the same solution should be found in every place.

5 The central matter is surely the commitment of the teacher. We must reject the illusion of non-commitment. Every teacher is committed to something – even if it were only to the earning of his salary with a minimum expenditure of energy. He should not be asked to pretend that he is above all commitments, that he has a stance above all stances from which he can 'critically' assess them all. What will ultimately be communicated to the pupils is the commitment of the teacher, and therefore this must be open and explicit. Only so will it be open for criticism and revision in the light of rational discussion.

*Truth in Religious Education: Further Reflections on the Implications of Pluralism**

Daniel W. Hardy

Introduction

Exceedingly important issues, both for the religions and for education, intersect in religious education. The serious exploration of them can only benefit all who are concerned, whether as religionist, educator or student. The issues are as much religious and theoretical as educational and practical, and to begin in any one is quickly to become involved in all the rest. They have to do with such matters as: What the religions are, How they are (or are not) true, How they are to be presented and understood severally and together, How these compare with other subject-matter and its presentation and understanding, How these function in the personal lives of teachers and students who may be sympathetic or hostile to the religions, and How religion is involved in the ideals and practice of the educational process as a whole. There is little in the world, human life and society upon which they do not touch in some way: that is why the exploration of these issues can make a significant contribution to human understanding and the educational process.

It is quite natural to want these issues resolved, for example so that one can go on to the practical business of living – as a student of religion or as an educator. But *wanting* them resolved does not make them so; indeed it may block the valuable continuing critical reflection upon these issues by producing a premature answering of the questions. There is a good deal of evidence that just this has happened in current discussions of religion in and outside of religious education circles. Much of the research into the nature of religion, into historical aspects and texts of religions,

*This article first appeared in *British Journal of Religious Education*, Vol. 1, No. 3, Spring, 1979.

and into beliefs and religious doctrines and practices has been based on certain suppositions, for example that they are ways of interpreting and living in the world. These suppositions form a kind of critical orthodoxy which produces a certain view of the religions but also, in doing so, domesticates them. To take this view of religions is also thought to be necessary for 'the enterprise of religious education', which itself is conceived according to the same set of suppositions – as enabling the imaginative participation by students in religious practices and views. But this view of religions and religious education is what is the problem, because it answers those basic issues mentioned at the outset prematurely – thereby prejudging the outcome of a continuing discussion and importing preconceived notions about religions into the study of them.

Perhaps we can free ourselves of this premature resolution of issues by looking at a number of basic questions which affect religious education, education and the religions.

Religious traditions as truth

It would seem incontestable that one should, in religious education, be presenting religious traditions in a fashion which accords with their nature – in a way which actually will be helpful to students who may number themselves in the particular traditions. Yet here is where the most acute problem begins. Each religious tradition is, according to its nature, the vehicle for truth: and its truth is not dependent on the claims of its adherents that it is true *for* them – its truth does not rest on a truth-claim, nor does it rely on the quality of arguments its adherents may advance for it. In fairness to its nature, and to its adherents, can it then be presented as a truth-*claim*, as truth *for* its adherents?

It has become commonplace, in a secularized situation, and also in a multi-religious one, to translate religious truth into a religious truth-claim. Religious truth is taken as equivalent to intersubjectively shared truth-claims which have the force *for* their adherents of truth. This is, apparently, an instantaneous translation made by those reared in certain self-conscious traditions in some modern western and some eastern understanding, now widely adopted because it accounts rather easily for divergences in religious truth and between religious truth and secular, non-religious truth. The translation, however, reduces religious (indeed, *all*) truth into truth-claims.

It is frequently assumed that this makes little difference to the religious traditions, in that it allows the adherent of the tradition to suppose the truth of which the tradition is the vehicle; after all, is not its truth precisely what he affirms when he claims that it is true? But the matter is not so simple. What the translation of truth into truth-claims does is to open up a gap between the truth and a claimant whereby he must begin from his own *disqualification*, his own inadequacy to know the truth. The truth which had previously qualified him to receive it recedes into the distance, leaving him to claim it insofar as he can sustain the claim: the truth of the religious tradition becomes dependent on the claim made for it by the claimant.

Of course, many people are content with this situation. As in the case of Hans Küng's recent book, *On Being a Christian*, religion becomes a matter of what you decide or claim to believe in the face of alternative possibilities – or possibly a long questioning or searching process. But the fact is that this ignores the religious supposition that in religion one begins not at a distance from the truth, disqualified from it, but in the presence of the truth which is qualifying the knowing of the truth – even if one has a long way to go before achieving a full knowing of the truth. In other words, the truth makes itself true for me, and makes me adequate for it; any reversal of the process, by which the truth is established by my claiming it, is seriously misleading.

Truths alongside each other

What happens when several religious traditions presenting themselves as truth are to be presented alongside each other? Of course, within the truth presented in a particular tradition another religious tradition has to be seen as less than what it presents itself to be: within the truth of religious tradition (a) religious tradition (b) will be seen as less than the truth it claims. There is a legitimate issue between them, for religious tradition (b) will take the same view of (a). But the important point is this: do *we*, in a supposedly neutral position, then present the two traditions as (rival) '*claims*'? If we do, we actually abandon our neutrality, and present the two as views sponsored by their respective adherents. This distances both from the truth, and assumes that the adherents are disqualified from the truth. More important, it prejudges the question which (if either) is *true*, and says that both are *claims*.

Does the teaching process require this judgment of the religious traditions to be made? One can understand the teacher's desire to avoid 'indoctrinating' students with the teachings of a particular religious tradition, and for that reason to avoid presenting a particular tradition as 'absolutely true'. In this case, the teacher avoids the prejudgment of a particular tradition as true, a truth into which the student is to be inducted. But the alternative is surely not to suppose that all religions are claims, for that is to engage in a prejudgment of another kind, that they are claims made by their adherents. This is not a neutral judgment, but one which prejudges the question of truth by calling the traditions 'claims'.

Another good reason for the teacher to wish to avoid presenting a particular tradition as 'absolutely true' arises in a multi-religious situation, or in one where the tradition is challenged by disbelief. In such circumstances, presentation of a tradition as 'absolutely true' prejudges other religious, or non-religious views, as false or defective. Here again, however, the alternative is not to prejudge the question of which is true by asserting that all are alike claims, for that is unfair to the truth which comes to believer or disbeliever.

Why cannot religious traditions be presented alongside each other and with non-religious ones, without engaging in these prejudgments? Even beyond this, why can they not be presented in such a way that they can be seen to engage in real dialogue and mutual understanding without the initial supposition that each is less than the presentation of truth? That, it would seem, is the precondition for a positive approach to the pluralism of a multi-religious and multi-cultural situation, one which takes it seriously and values it in its own right, rather than as the embarrassment which it often now seems to be. As I have said in a previous article, 'pluralism' has so far produced only the presentation of religions severally, plurally – as though they were 'eggs' in a 'basket' of 'religions'. We need to see pluralism more positively, and use it more positively.

Teaching traditions without prejudging them

Where do we begin in this? There are many who would begin with human questing and concern, and with the answers which human beings have constructed; despite wide differences, due to different cultural situations and developments, they find an essential commonness in this 'religion'. There have been skilful expositions of this view, and much interesting work has been done to chart basic dimensions of 'religions' as thus seen, the shared insights and practices by which religious traditions are similar despite other differences. Amongst other things, these approaches suppose the possibility of, and enable, an imaginative and sympathetic approach to religious understanding and practice which had been previously unfamiliar.

This beginning-place is very different from the old comparative religion approach, because no particular religion is taken as the point of reference or standard of measurement. But a notion of human questing and religious conceptualizing has taken the place of a particular religious tradition, and this has become the reference-point in terms of which particular religious traditions are seen as similar. All religious traditions are seen as 'what humans do', and the truth they may bear is seen as the truth *claimed* by their adherents, probably different from that claimed by other religionists only because of cultural differences.

Though this approach avoids judging a particular religious tradition as absolutely true, thereby prejudging other traditions, it is not neutral as its proponents claim, for it translates truth into truth-claims, prejudging the truth (so far as it may be) of each particular tradition. Furthermore, it prejudges that there are similarities between religious traditions, primarily by placing the different traditions under a matrix of 'dimensions' which identifies aspects in which there are alleged to be similarities. Why is this a prejudgment rather than a legitimate generalization of manifest similarities? There are two reasons: (1) the matrix affirms similarities before they are found, setting up a system of categories which are affirmed not simply as *aids* to *seeing* what is there in the religions (which is probably unexceptionable) but as *what is there* in the religions; in other and more technical words, a phenomenological construction has become an ontological statement. (2) If what occurs in one (or more) particular religious tradition is true, even if it bears a similarity to what occurs elsewhere, the fact of its truth makes it dissimilar to what otherwise 'looks the same' in other religious traditions. A religious practice or concept, for example a ritual meal or the notion of king, may appear in several religious traditions, and so similar between them; but if it is true in one religion, the fact of its truth makes it dissimilar there from its use in other religious traditions. But precisely this is prejudged: this dissimilarity disappears in the claims that the religious practices and concepts are similar.

Again we may ask: must we begin with such prejudgments? Why not present religious traditions alongside each other, without applying pre-established similarities between them – either from a matrix of dimensions or from the similarities discerned by a comparer standing over them? Instead, let the particular practices and ideas of different religions emerge with full clarity and without prejudgment of their truth or dissimilarity.

Where is the truth?

This raises another difficult and crucial question. We have been trying to safeguard the truth and dissimilarity (or uniqueness) of the truth in religious traditions. There is then the question of the 'locality' of this truth. For example, when given a class whose members are drawn from various religious traditions, do we talk about the traditions as though they existed somewhere else than in the class – as true for '*them*' ('those people over there') rather than true for some of *us*? In other words, do we place the truth 'somewhere else' than where we are, at a distance from us?

One can see advantages in this. (1) In a situation where a number of religious traditions are represented, to place the truth somewhere else – outside of the class – creates a 'cool zone' in the class where discussion can go on which does not favour particular claims for particular traditions. This neutral situation is not only valuable for discussion, stopping bids from those who claim to possess the truth with authority, and therefore allowing sympathetic appreciation of unfamiliar views. (2) In an important sense, it expresses the situation of human beings in relation to the truth. It is surely the case that human beings do not wholly possess the truth. Even where religious traditions are vehicles of truth, their adherents are not considered adequate to this task: their situation is the complex one of being in and yet not in the truth. The 'neutral situation' expresses well the being 'not in the truth'.

But this is by no means the whole story. Neutrality and independence are not the only things important in a classroom. Perhaps religious education is still too much reacting against authority-sponsored indoctrination to see this. Just as important is the capacity of human beings to be found by, and to share, the truth. The long-term objective of all education is to foster the obligation to seek and submit to the truth by creating and becoming a community which accepts this obligation. While neutrality is important to this, so also is the truth which may be present for us.

Where, then, is the truth? All religious, and also non-religious views, believe that the truth of which they are vehicles is not 'for them' – outside the classroom and suspended in the neutral classroom zone – but for *us* to share and be in, because it cannot be suspended in a neutral zone. The different religious traditions are not true for some distant group, but are true for us here and now. And when various religious and non-religious traditions are present in a class, the truth of which each tradition may be a vehicle is the truth present particularly in its adherent; we should not engage in the pretence that we are talking of it somewhere else, and thus disinherit its adherent. Should we do so, we would be at fault in two ways: (1) We would be de-universalizing this truth by shutting it out of our neutral zone, and (2) we would be de-personalizing the adherent in whom this truth was present, expecting him to suppress the ways in which the truth had become interwoven with his personality.

Sharing the truth

It is often claimed that distancing religious truth as truth for some distant group preserves the freedom of students. As already mentioned, a neutral zone does stop the bids of those who claim to possess the truth with authority; in other words, it does protect the freedom of students from domination and indoctrination. But this should not go so far as to produce a detachment from the truth of the religious traditions, nor from the shared task of being in the truth which is already present for us. For that detachment would surely be to encourage wrong ideas of freedom and personhood. For example, the impression would be given that freedom and personality development occur primarily in the *autonomy* of human beings. Religious traditions, as well as non-religious ones, suggest the reverse – that freedom and personality are to be found in discovering the truth about ourselves as present already in these traditions.

If the truth is not somewhere else, but here with us in the material we study and in the others we know, how is it that we become open to it and share it? How do we do this, furthermore, without glossing over the uniqueness and dissimilarities of the vehicles of this truth, religious and non-religious, and the personal adherence of various members of the class to these vehicles of truth?

Perhaps the key question is what is the nature of this truth and of the vehicles in which it is present. Even to use the word 'truth' often leads people to suppose that truth is the truth of *ideas* or that of propositions or assertions, a truth whose conditions can be defined. But truth, in whatever sphere it appears, cannot be given a concrete definition; it is rather what people at work in these spheres are striving together to delineate. And it is certainly not so narrow as to be a characteristic of assertions; it also has to do with the world, behaviour, life, personality, etc. What we have in religious and non-religious traditions is long-term and unfinished attempts, varying in character, emphasis and coherence, to find and live in truth – to correspond to its character.

Because truth and its vehicles are so broadly conceived, becoming open to it and sharing it must be multi-dimensional – involving ventures of many kinds, each of which brings its own pitfalls – antiquarianism, ideocentricism, etc. (see my earlier article in *Learning for Living*, Winter 1976). Certainly, this openness cannot suppose that stories, myths or symbol systems are the *prime locus* of the truth in religious traditions, and so give most attention to literary-historical or cultural interpretation. Nor can we suppose that the attitudes which religious people express in doctrine, worship, contemplation, or action are the main thing, and so give most attention to imaginative participation in these attitudes. These have their place, but despite their current popularity in certain circles of western theology, they are far too narrow a way of becoming open to others, especially where symbol systems and attitudes are not so primary. The truth of religious traditions is present for us interwoven with the whole personal and societal life in the world of their adherents as well as in their understanding, and so must be approached by all the means appropriate to such interweavings. Finding the appropriate approaches is, one would think, especially important for education in a multi-religious situation if the truth which is here within the traditions is to emerge fully.

The truth and practice

Clearly we are pressing here for ways of approaching the religious traditions which go beyond interpretation and imagination as those are ordinarily understood, or the acquisition of insights and skills, and into the realms of reason and practice and personal contact. In that, it is as well that we keep before us the model of learning in (say) the sciences, because that is not easily assimilated – despite some widely publicized philosophies of science – to the idea that interpretation and imagination are the main objects. But, on the other hand, since the truth evident in religious traditions is more complex and multifarious than that of sciences, reason and practice and personal contact will have a broader use in relation to it.

What form should these take in a class in which various religious and non-religious traditions are represented? First, let it be said that approaching the religious traditions through reason and practice and personal contact is not the same as 'practising religion' or engaging in religious practices employed in different traditions, though as a matter of fact, the open-cast form of Quaker meetings might not be problematic in a multi-religious situation. The practice of religion in this case is the establishing of real communication between religious traditions as mediations of truth, as carried on by the shared activity of students and teachers – in all the dimensions in which the traditions do operate.

A great deal happens when such communication is begun. Far from threatening the individual freedom of the student, this real communication involves a careful and rational listening to his position and to him as a person; and his effort to communicate his position causes him reflectively to become critical about it, and about himself as a person. If the listening is as it should be – and the teacher particularly must ensure that it grows towards this – it will give new dignity and integrity to the particular student, while at the same time enhancing his life in and representation of the truth in which he participates. In other words, it aids him to participate in the truth so far as it (the truth) enables him to do so – and not simply to stay in a neutral position and imagine what the religious tradition does for 'those' people somewhere else. This is precisely to assist the student's quest for meaning.

The emergence of comparabilities between traditions

But there are no pre-established common denominators between religious traditions or in the 'religious experience' which the educator tries to assist. As our previous comments should indicate, the truth present in different traditions is so varied and complex that suggesting 'common denominators' is simplistic and also avoids the dissimilarity of *true* religious beliefs and practices from others. The only commonness between religious traditions in our view is the mutual opening and questioning which goes on between them. From this, there may emerge some comparabilities between traditions, but these are emergent, not pre-established, and depend on the care and fullness of our listening. They are also spontaneous, comparable 'from the bottom up', achieved through full interaction of people, rather than imposed by a matrix.

What then of the avowedly non-religious person? Of course, in the view which we have been presenting, a well diversified group – fully representing the plurality present in the world – enriches religious education and makes the communicational process more productive by requiring greater listening and communicative (hence more critical) skills. In this respect, the non-religious person further enhances the group, and certainly does not lose his freedom – so long as he shares the fundamental commitment of being open to the truth present in religious and non-religious traditions and thereby being open to those who live in these traditions. There is an important sense in which he is fellow to the religious person, not because there is a 'common denominator' between them but because he operates toward the world and toward them in a way which to some extent he shares with them. He knows and behaves by a complex process of integrating many clues and thereby attending to the thing to which they point; so do they. And the means by which they may know each other is similar to this process; they integrate the clues to each other's mind and dwell in that to which the clues point from the outside (*cf.* M. Polanyi, *Meaning*, Chapter 2, Chicago University Press 1975). In other words, they share no common denominator of religion or meaning, only the means by which they establish meanings. This enables them to be open to each other without sacrificing their representation of truth.

Religious education as open communication

What we have been arguing for is a view of religious education which does not suspend the truth presented in religious traditions by creating a neutral zone within whose safety things 'outside' (what is 'true for those people over there') can be studied. But, on the other hand, we have argued that religious education should not encourage wrong ideas of individual independence and autonomy. These arguments are not offered in order to restore indoctrination by authoritative traditions or to nurture people specifically within religious traditions. The choice is not between current procedures and old-style indoctrination and nurture.

The view for which we have been arguing is that religious education should be a struggle to enable an open communication between religious traditions and between these and non-religious traditions in classroom situations. According to this view, religious education takes place as much as possible without prejudgments of the kinds we have been outlining, and therefore allows that the truth is at issue between these traditions and that it is that truth which is interwoven with the personal lives and views and actions of its adherents in the classroom. Hence religious education tries to foster open communication between truth-tellers in an atmosphere of mutual respect and trust. The supposition is that the truth is in such discussion and will emerge through this open communication.

In the course of this communication, it will become evident – especially as the participants in the discussion develop in their understanding – that religious traditions manifest very different aspects of truth, and do so very differently. How then are they to be seen in relation to each other: what order emerges between them? The first answer is: *none in advance*. It cannot be said in advance whether all are different and equivalent, or if some are more developed, and if so in what respects, etc. Furthermore, such statements are prejudgments, and ought not to be employed. The spirit of tolerance (or of intolerance) in which they are spoken ought to be manifested (or corrected) in the willingness to hear the other religion in its truth-teller, rather than in a polemic directed toward oneself or toward the other. The right ordering of the religious traditions will emerge from the communication between them; it should not be imported into the communication to form it in advance.

Secondly, the order which emerges between the religious traditions should not be seen as a matter of opinion. Seeing the place of the traditions relative to each other may be limited by the ignorance of those who are participating in the discussion, or by the inadequacies of the discussion. But, subject to these deficiencies, the ordering which emerges should reflect the order in which they 'really' stand relative to each other.

Thirdly, the means by which we understand their order relative to each other as truth-telling will not be simple (at least not in a low sense of that word). For example, their ordering will be at least as complex as that which pertains between physics, biology and moral behaviour, and probably much more complex because of their multifaceted presentation of truth. Recognizing this should make clear the naiveté of those views of religion which 'flatten' them all into culturally-conditioned human 'ways' or symbol-systems. It is precisely the complexity of the religious traditions, and of the order in which they stand relative to each other as mediations of truth, that make religious education the fascinating sphere of communication and humanity which it is – and also make it highly relevant to the whole educational process.

Notes

1 Hardy, D., 'Teaching religion: a theological critique', in *Learning for Living*, Vol. 15, No. 1, Autumn, 1975, pp. 10–16.

4
Designing the Curriculum in Religious Education

Introduction

The task facing religious education in developing its curriculum today demands that the psychology of religious development, the philosophical and theological problems, and the pluralistic context should be taken into account. In addition, the history of the subject in moving into the educational area, and in distinguishing itself more clearly from the faith-fostering activities of the religious communities themselves, needs to be studied seriously.

It is not surprising that these various ingredients are being assembled today in many different ways. Some suggest a 'meaning (or meanings) of life' approach in which the questions posed by human experience are explored in relation to the various 'answers' offered by religions and non-religious belief systems. Others suggest a 'field study' approach in which the teeming religious life of the modern industrial city is studied through first-hand experience. Some emphasize cognitive development, adopting a 'basic concepts' analysis of religions; others emphasize a more concrete study of the practices, festivals, stories and artifacts of religion. Some teachers present religion in a sort of evolutionary pattern, from folk-religion and tribal religions through the classical world faiths and on to contemporary religious movements. Some see religion as a matter of acquiring certain skills necessary for the interpretation, understanding and practice of the religious life, and, while it is still common for leaders of religious communities to press the case for the inclusion of their own faith, some religious educators are experimenting with syllabuses which for considerable sections or even years of study make little or no reference to any religion as a coherent tradition, but concentrate upon 'dimensions' or aspects common to or typical of religion as a whole. Another type of religious education curriculum development seeks to integrate it with one or more of the other subjects, thus producing a historical kind of religious education, or a moral kind, or a sociology-based variety, or one in which religious education is associated mainly with music, dance and poetry.

John Elliott emphasizes the importance of the controversial context for teaching religion, not in a 'world religions' sense but in the 'questions about religion' sense whereby the controversial character of religion as a whole (exemplified by Christianity) is exposed. H.E. Lupton gathers from the literature a wide variety of aims which religious education teachers profess, arranging them into categories and showing the difficulty which religious education has had in emerging from religious idealism into educational professionalism. David Gooderham brings many of the major emphases together in setting out the various dimensions which religious education exhibits today and shows the different kinds of curriculum which would flow from each set of assumptions.

*Problems of RE Syllabus Construction in a Democracy**

John Elliott

What sorts of questions ought a religious education syllabus to deal with in a pluralistic democracy?

The problem of how the christian religion can be handled in schools without negating democratic and educational values can be articulated as the problem any democracy faces when reflecting on how its educational institutions can make curricular provisions in the interests of the general public rather than a section of that public.

Christianity no longer has a monopoly

The christian vision of the good life can no longer claim to be the only source of belief and value in our society. A democratic form of life presupposes some consensus by the citizens who embrace it on how the phenomenon of pluralism is to be viewed. Part of this consensus will be the right of citizens to exercise their own responsibility and judgment with respect to alternative visions of the good life. Any attempt by educational institutions to transmit a sectional view *as if it were the only publicly defensible one* would contradict the value a democracy ascribes to individual judgement and responsibility. Such a policy could not be in the public interest of citizens in a democracy.

Should Christianity be excluded from the curriculum?

This argument in no way supports the view that the christian religion

*This article first appeared in *Learning for Living*, Vol. 11, No. 1, November, 1971.

ought to be abolished from the school curriculum. It merely limits the way controversial views of the good life ought to be handled in an educational context. I believe it is possible to argue that some form of religious education is desirable and in the interests of citizens in a democracy. If it is in the public interest that citizens should be allowed to exercise responsibility and judgment in relation to visions of the good life then surely it is the task of educational institutions to develop the individual's capacity to accept responsibility for his beliefs and actions and to make judgments on the basis of a critical and reflective scrutiny of alternative viewpoints. Educational values will emphasize the importance of judgments based on reason rather than authority and the belief that no other person can be held to be ultimately responsible for the beliefs and values an individual accepts. If the christian religion were taken off the school curriculum this could constitute a concession to a particular sectional interest in society, for example, all those who deny the validity of the christian way of life. It would exclude a particular alternative from being accessible to the reflection and scrutiny that an educational situation can provide. In restricting students' opportunities for enlarging their awareness and understanding of alternatives, and consequently in restricting their capacity to make autonomous and responsible judgments, a preference is implied which contradicts educational values in a democracy. Excluding a consideration of the christian religion from the curriculum is therefore open to the same objections as treating it as if it were the *only* publicly warranted definition of the good life.

The 1944 education act, in making religious instruction compulsory, was based on two assumptions. First, it assumed that we lived at that time in a christian society. Second, it assumed that the main criterion for the selection of content ought to be its suitability for inspiring and developing faith rather than its suitability for reasoned and informed judgment.

The rest of this article is based on the contrary assumptions that pluralism is a matter of empirical fact to-day and that consequently democratic values necessitate an educational context in which teaching has to substitute the criterion of impartiality, based on rational standards accessible to all for the criterion of faith, based on a *particular* vision of the good life.

I am not asserting that judgments about Christianity ought to rest exclusively on reason or that reason and faith are incompatible. I am positing that a religious education teacher's authority in a pluralistic democracy ought to be circumscribed by impartial standards of reasoning which are publicly accessible inasmuch as they might be acknowledged standards from the standpoint of a variety of 'faiths', secular as well as religious.

What kind of religious education?

Given the acceptability of these assumptions what kind of religious instruction should be taught in our schools? It should no longer be based on the assumption that we teach in the context of a christian society where there is some consensus about how the human situation is to be ultimately defined. Aims which express the intention of preparing students to participate in the life of the christian church, and content which is selected with these confessional aims in mind, place the religious education teacher in a position where he is in danger of using his authority within a public institution to promote controversial beliefs and values *as if they were publicly acknowledged truths*. This is not only an infringement of the obligations a teacher has towards those who do not share his religious convictions but also a denial of those educational values within our democracy which emphasize the importance of respecting and encouraging the development of the autonomous and critical judgment of the student. Such judgment has to be exercised today in a context where alternative systems of belief and value impinge upon the individual.

If the reader accepts the view that students in our schools ought to be prepared to make judgments about Christianity based on a critical awareness of the alternative conceptions of the human situation open to him then he has a criterion for the selection of religious education curriculum content which is very different from the more traditional and confessional aim. This criterion not only commits him to selecting content which places Christianity in a publicly controversial context but to methods which emphasize the importance of judgment rather than authority. There are no finally conclusive tests for the truth or falsity of christian beliefs and values which all thoughtful and reflective men would share. The judgments as to what reasons finally count for or against Christianity can only be left to the student. But this does not mean that the teacher has no educational function. All judgments must conform to such standards of reasoning as logical consistency and an understanding of the evidence that differing points of view would regard as counting for and against the truth of a particular judgment. The religious education teacher has therefore a tremendous responsibility for helping students to use critical standards.

CSE religious syllabuses

Since CSE syllabuses are increasingly influential in determining the kind of religious education most of our students will get in secondary schools I decided to examine the syllabuses of a random selection of boards with a view to discovering the aims their selection of syllabus content implied. I studied the North-Western, East Midland, East Anglia and Southern board syllabuses for 1970. The last two boards had North and South syllabuses, so the total sample was six syllabuses in all. Two syllabuses (NW and SS) explicitly stated confessional aims:

'The syllabus is concerned with the whole child and its aim is to bring into an encounter with Jesus Christ.' (NW)

'The purpose of the main study should be . . . partly to introduce more definitely the fundamental truths about God as revealed continuously throughout the Old Testament, and New Testament . . . . By the time a child reaches the end of his school life he should have some idea of the gradual revelation of God to Man, and have presented to him the challenge of Christianity with its moral and spiritual demands on life.' (SS)

Two syllabuses (SN and EAS) explicitly stated aims which looked more impartial:

'The syllabus is intended to foster an understanding of the spirit of christian living, but no attempt will be made to test convictions.' (SN)

'The purpose of this syllabus is to give the student a general knowledge and appreciation of the development of religion with particular reference to contemporary life.' (EAS)

The East Anglican Board (N) and the East Midland Board did not make any over-all statement of aim.

I find it difficult to see how public examination boards in a pluralistic democracy can defend the kind of statements made by the NW and SS syllabuses. However, although in isolation the aims of SN and EAS look more impartial, they raise problems. Understanding or having a general knowledge of Christianity does not entail a particular evaluation of it. Indeed understanding is essential for making an informed judgment either for or against it. At first sight these seem defensible educational aims. However, in a pluralistic democracy educational values demand that judgments about a controversial conception of the human situation should be based on an understanding of the alternatives that its acceptance would rule out. For example, arguments against the existence of God are frequently made from the standpoint of differing conceptions. But looking at Christianity in its controversial aspects the teacher can help students explore arguments against as well as for, thus making them aware of a wider range of considerations as a basis for judgment.

If the reason for stating aims of the kind suggested by SN and EAS is to give students a basis for making informed judgments, then they are inadequate, since they do not incorporate any reference to alternative conceptions. One could suspect the syllabus constructors of intending to get students to imaginatively project themselves into the christian point of view, to the exclusion of others, to such an extent that they eventually come to identify with it and accept it. Such an approach would perhaps be more open than denying students the right to choose between alternatives (a position implied by NW and SS), but it would still imply bias and be indoctrinatory, inasmuch as it made little attempt to open up the range of considerations on which judgments could be based. However, such suspicions could not be substantiated without further evidence of the nature of the content stated in the syllabuses.

Content of CSE syllabuses

Explicit statements are not the only way of getting at the aims of syllabus constructors. They can be induced from a scrutiny of the content to be learned or understood, since aims provide general criteria for the selection of content. Differences in kind of content will reflect differences of aim.

I was able to classify most of the content of the six syllabuses in categories which I think give some indications of the sort of considerations the syllabus-makers had in mind. I did this by looking at the headings and sub-headings under which syllabus content was arranged.

(a) *Doctrinal.* Statements of doctrinal 'truths': formulated propositions to be learned and accepted.

(b) *Chronological.* Content arranged around the idea of the progressive revelation through history of theological 'truths'.

(c) *Ethical.* Statements of christian values and virtues formulated in a way which took for granted their desirability.

(d) *Life situations.* Content arranged around human situations like 'work', 'family', 'friendship'. These are controversial situations which are defined differently within a pluralistic society.

(e) *Problems of meaning.* Content organized in terms of its relevance to problems individuals experience in relation to fundamental conceptions of human experience, for example, suffering, death, the nature of man. These problems are most likely to arise in a pluralistic context between the boundaries of different belief systems.

The first three categories would reflect confessional aims, since the criterion for the selection of content implied would seem to be its relevance for people being initiated into, and sustained within, the belief and practice of the christian church.

The last two categories are more open inasmuch as they focus on areas of human experience common to all men in our society. These areas are problematic in a pluralistic society since they are defined and interpreted from the standpoint of different beliefs and values. Informed judgments about them would involve an understanding of alternative conceptions. They could operate as categories for the selection of religious education syllabus content which is educationally more defensible and appropriate in a democratic and pluralist society than categories a, b and c. 'Life situations' could involve an impartial inquiry into the ethical dimension of Christianity, inasmuch as it was relevant to these situations, and a critique of that dimension in the light of alternative ethical perspectives. It would be a more appropriate category for the organization of ethical content than c because it allows a study of christian ethics to be placed in a pluralistic rather than confessional context. Similarly, 'problems of meaning' could involve an impartial inquiry into the doctrinal dimension of Christianity, inasmuch as it was relevant to fundamental human experiences and a critique of this dimension in the light of alternative beliefs. This would be a more appropriate category for organizing the theological content than a or b, placing it again in a pluralistic rather than confessional context.

Open ended religious syllabuses?

However, syllabus content can fall under headings like d or e without being very open-ended. These categories can serve as centres for organizing content which asserts the christian point of view to the exclusion of all others. Such a syllabus would still be more open than one exclusively organised under a, b or c. It would imply an admission of the seriousness and importance of the challenge of rival beliefs and values. It would acknowledge the pluralistic context in which judgments have to be made, and therefore imply some respect for alternative views, even if it did not explicitly consider them. *But it would not be open enough for educational purposes.* Its content would serve the purposes of christian apologetics inasmuch as students were encouraged to understand and defend the christian position, and not encouraged to explore rival conceptions.

Examination questions like: 'Give two examples of occasions today when Christians should be prepared to make a stand for their beliefs' (Examination paper SN 1970) suggest that the purpose of selecting content under these categories is to get students to adopt and defend the christian standpoint against all opposition.

The following conclusions could reasonably be drawn from my analysis of the six syllabuses.

1 Only two (EAS and EAN) had parts of the syllabus organized under 'problems of meaning'. However, this content was highly biased in favour of the christian position and only constituted a small non-compulsory part of the total syllabus.

2 All the syllabuses except two had substantial sections organized under 'life situations'. The exceptions were the NW and SS syllabuses that had explicitly expressed confessional aims. Only SN made this part compulsory (one third of the total). However, the other three permitted the teachers the option of having this part as 50 per cent of the syllabus.

   The content of all those parts of the syllabuses organized under 'life situations' was highly biased in favour of the christian position.

3 Only two syllabuses were organized to any substantial degree around doctrinal headings. They were NW and SS, which were also the two explicitly stating confessional aims and ignoring both 'life situations' and 'problems of meaning'.

4 All the syllabuses except one (SN) organized at least 50 per cent of content, particularly with regard to compulsory sections, along chronological lines, although SS had an alternative syllabus organized

largely under doctrinal headings, and the NW syllabus mixed the chronological with the doctrinal approach.

5 Only two syllabuses contained content organized around christian values and virtues (NW and EM). The others, with the exception of SS, which organized exclusively under either chronological or doctrinal headings, preferred to organize ethical content, under 'life situations' exclusively.

The NW and SS syllabuses were the most closed to the idea that Christianity should be treated impartially in the context of alternative conceptions held in our society. The SN and East Anglian syllabuses seemed to be the most open to the pluralistic context in which judgments about Christianity have to be made. However, none of them went beyond a biased selection of content. This confirmed my suspicion that the explicit aims stated by SN and EAS are not sufficient articulations of student achievements for religious education in a pluralistic democracy.

The content of the CSE syllabuses studied seems to have been selected with the needs of future confessional members of the church in mind. They largely contain theological and value judgments that have become acceptable truths within the christian orthodox tradition. The chronological and doctrinal patterns of syllabus organization into which half the content of most fall are peculiarly appropriate for the development of, and instruction in, the orthodox faith. Even the 'life situations' content is composed of christian values and virtues selected to help people understand and apply the christian ethic. CSE content is largely selected then from within the framework of theological judgments and christian values which define Christianity as a distinct way of life. But if the aim of religious education ought rather to be developing students' understanding of the christian religion from its controversial aspects what differences would this make to the content of the religious education syllabus?

First, content will be stated as 'beliefs about', to explore and understand, rather than 'truths' to learn and accept.

Secondly, content will be selected, not according to its appropriateness for instruction in and defence of the belief and practice of the christian faith, but according to its relevance to inquiries into controversial problems.

Controversial Christianity

Christianity can be controversial and problematic in three different contexts:

1 Christians may debate the relative importance of different kinds of religious authority – bible, church or individual experience – or different doctrines. They will segregate into denominations which

endorse their preference. But these controversies will only emerge within an orthodox tradition of doctrines. In fact without a consensus on fundamental doctrines such as the divinity of Christ there would be no problem about where the authority of Christ as God's word is to be located. Such controversies are internal to the orthodox christian tradition. I will call these *christian problems*.

The CSE syllabuses follow the Agreed Syllabuses in not touching these christian problems. This is the product of an agreement by the state not to promote a partisan denominational line. It reveals two basic assumptions. First, that if teachers are to take a non-partisan line, they must avoid the controversial issues here. Second, that England is, or ought to be, a christian rather than pluralistic society. If CSE boards had questioned these assumptions they might have understood the true extent of the divergence of belief and value in our society and the possibility that teachers could profitably help students explore differences without adopting a partisan line.

2 Christianity can be controversial in the context of disagreements between members of distinct religious traditions. Jews and Christians can debate whether Jesus was the Son of God. Christians and Moslems can debate whether the divinity is knowable or not. Although some doctrines are controversial and therefore define the boundaries between the two traditions, others will be held in common and are a necessary condition of controversy arising. For example, the debate between the Christian and Jew only takes place because there is close agreement on their doctrine of God.

These controversies I will call *religious problems*. They arise on a basis of shared religious assumptions. The CSE syllabuses are very much concerned with this area. But they do not provide content which enables teachers to help students explore the differences and similarities between different religions' conceptions of life. Instead they adopt a partisan line in relation to unorthodox sects and non-christian religions, although they are rarely mentioned. Content takes the form of christian answers to religious problems. Is this justified in a society where non-christian religions have considerable following?

I am not advocating a stale presentation of the doctrines and values of each religion in turn. Since christian presuppositions are so deeply rooted in our society, even in non-christian perspectives like atheistic humanism, existentialism and marxism, I feel there is some justification for focussing religious education on Christianity. For the same reason I do not think a study of christian beliefs and values should be absorbed totally into moral or social education. The religious dimension is logically separable from both and should be explored in its own right.

Although I am arguing for Christianity to be studied as an educationally worthwhile topic in its own right, I am objecting to the perspective from which it is treated by teachers and educators. I am suggesting that Christianity ought to be studied at the points where it is controversial for other religious traditions. These differences ought to be treated impartially by the teacher. If not we would get Christianity being taught as the truth and other religious traditions as having only some of the truth. But even an impartial treatment of these religious problems cannot be the main area for the selection of content. Religious problems do not locate the deepest points at which Christianity is controversial in our society.

3 Christianity can be controversial in the context of disagreements with non-religious conceptions of life. I will call these *problems about religion* since they could arise either at the boundaries of controversy between a particular religious tradition and a non-religious view, or at the boundaries of a religious conception of life shared by more than one religious tradition. Let me give some examples of problems about religion.
   (a) Why do some people find it necessary to believe in a purpose to life?
   (b) Does belief in an after-life arise out of a fear of life?
   (c) Doesn't suffering prove a loving God can't exist?
   (d) Does the christian sexual ethic impose inhuman demands on people?
   (e) Is the christian commandment to honour and obey parents an obstacle to the development of human freedom and autonomy?

Let's take (c). A non-christian view could be explored which asserts that the reality of suffering counts against the existence of a loving God. A christian view could then be explained which attempts to make the fact of human suffering compatible with belief in a loving God. Neither viewpoint questions the reality of human suffering. But the introduction of a buddhist point of view would suggest that suffering is an illusion from which men can free themselves. It would also question the Christian's belief in a personal and loving God. So we find that such a problem can be explored not only at the boundaries of a christian and non-religious view of life, but also at the boundaries of Christianity and Buddhism, and Buddhism and a non-religious view.

This kind of inquiry can reveal unexpected similarities between points of view. It can reveal hidden assumptions which, in spite of differences, two points of view have in common. Students can become aware of a greater range of considerations to be borne in mind when making judgments about the problem.

Only two CSE syllabuses (EAN and EAS) were concerned with those problems about religion which could be described as problems of meaning, that is, a, b, c. However, their selection of content was biased in favour of the christian solution. An impartial study of these could operate as a principle for the selection of doctrines, beliefs and theological concepts. As we have seen this would place the study of christian beliefs within a pluralistic context but the CSE boards seem to select content for its appropriateness for instruction in christian orthodoxy. Four CSE syllabuses (NW and SC were the exceptions) did select substantial content which in another form would be relevant for exploring problems about religion arising in life situations, that is, d and e. However, the content selected was highly substantive providing the christian answers to problems about religion without reference to alternative conceptions.

The content of religious education in a pluralistic society has to be selected for its relevance to problems about religion which arise at the boundaries of belief and unbelief. If they are pushed far and wide enough they will incorporate religious problems in a way which will ensure, not only the exploration of differences, but the questioning of shared assumptions.

*Checklists for Study of the Religious Education Syllabus**

H.E. Lupton

Continuing controversy, such as the legal wrangle over Birmingham's new syllabus, gives emphasis to the fact that one still cannot find an unequivocal answer to the question, 'What are the purposes and contents proper to religious education in county schools?' even though the subject has had the attention of various high-level researches, projects and reports in recent years.[1] Further, there is no account in the literature of the customary and traditional purposes and contents which relates these to the aims and subject-matter of other areas of the school curriculum or analyses them in the kind of terms now commonly used to discuss the merits and deficiencies of other school subjects. With this second problem in mind, that is with the aim of specifying what one might reasonably expect a county school to mean by 'religious education', a search was made of most of the books, syllabuses, examination material, and more important articles published in religious education during the last thirty years, and the lists which are detailed in this paper make an attempt at such a minimal specification.

Three preliminary remarks need to be made. From articles and books published on religious education within the past five years, and from some of the energetic conference and project work which has been undertaken, one might gain the impression that the subject had been wholly given over to an amalgam of quasi-political social studies and oriental mysticism. But such appears to be the case in very few places. Even today, in the colleges of education which provide most specialist teachers of the subject, the main-studies in religion are largely (and in some places wholly) given over to a remarkably conservative and Christian biblical studies syllabus.[2] And the non-specialist teachers of the subject, particularly those in primary schools, seem likely to depend greatly in planning their

*This article first appeared in *Learning for Living*, Vol. 14, No. 4, March, 1975.

work upon its customary purposes and subject-matter.

An explanation must also be given about the form in which the checklists are cast. It was thought that the analysis would be strengthened if a referent framework neutral with respect to religion were to be adopted, and one that would be defensible if subjected to criteria commonly applied by philosophers of education: so the structure within which the analysis was made was one suggested by the taxonomy (or hierarchic structure) of educational objectives devised by Bloom, Krathwohl and their colleagues (1956, 1964), one which has often been utilized by educational writers during the past decade.[3] Some practising teachers may deny the feasibility of such an analysis in religious education, but the writer has taken a psychological orientation to the analysis of both the subject-matter and the purposes of the subject, and would deny the right of its teachers to hold aims and objectives which are seriously incongruent with those of the general education of pupils in county schools.[4] He has also assumed 'religious awareness' to be the behavioural end to which religious education is directed, and he would define religious awareness as a cultural aspect of human sensitivity, which is learned, and which has both cognitive and affective components, the components being conceptually rather than empirically distinct.

The third preliminary remark to make before presenting the checklists is to say that the analysis merely represents the impression left upon one reader by a literature-search, although some statistics were gathered in the process.[5]

Consider first the broad aims to which religious education in county schools has been directed during the past thirty years. These might be expressed in some such terms as the following:

> To put children in a position to appreciate the Judaeo-Christian heritage and to inform them about the life and teaching of Christ and the growth of the church to modern times.
>
> To give children the experiences and opportunities through which they can face the claim of Christianity and make a free and responsible decision about it for themselves.
>
> To give children a feeling for an understanding of the religious dimension of life and its interpretation.
>
> To help provide children with an understanding of religious symbols and language so as to enable them to reformulate a faith for the future.
>
> To help children to develop good relations with other people and the world around them and be capable of responding to God.
>
> To help children and young people to grow into whole and mature people with understanding of themselves.

These aims are (almost verbatim) quotations from the Christian Education Movement's evidence submitted to the Durham Commission, and they are valuable in providing a general specification. This list certainly represents the customary purposes adopted by teachers and writers, but it must be admitted that the past literature of religious education has been notably vague in its description of the aims of the subject, for the reader often finds direction lost in an over-use of such common yet diffuse educational terms as 'interest', 'understand', 'appreciate', 'values', 'attitude'.

Yet aims must be subject to considerable elaboration if they are to be of application to the work of a practising teacher, and unfortunately authoritative writers (such as the preface-writers to agreed syllabuses) have never attempted to do this. What the agreed syllabuses and related documents could have done of real help to teachers was to have extended what they had to say about aims by identifying various consequent behavioural objectives and the learning experiences by means of which such objectives might be attained. But it is the working teacher who has been given the difficult task of reducing such aims to the practicalities of classroom activities.

Consider next how the first aim in the CEM list seems to be related to the subject-matter customary to religious education. This aim is largely one which implies cognitive objectives: that is, in order to realize the aims, the teachers will concern themselves chiefly with giving instruction about things religious (rather than with developing attitudes or emotions), and such work will be very similar to work in history, geography, and other informational school activities. Seven cognitive objectives relating to the customary content of religious education were identified during the literature search[6] as follows, the general aim of the teacher in this category being to promote knowledge of the various elements:

Cognitive objectives, the teacher aiming to promote knowledge of:

- Facts about Christianity, bible, church history.
- Key concepts in the teaching of Christianity.
- Religious symbols and language.
- Facts about religion(s) in the local environment.
- Living (non-Christian) religions in the world today.
- Religious controversies, especially in relation to their historical or political significance.
- Important religio-intellectual problems, such as those of suffering or of the fact of death.

This category of objectives in religious education is largely intellectual in its emphasis, and it includes activities which promote problem-solving, knowing, and thinking: that is, the kind of activities we normally consider when using the terms 'teaching' and 'learning' in the context of school.

Religious education must, however, be more than a collection of facts, descriptions, and propositions. At least two of the great religions have at root the concept of revelation; in all religions, non-material and spiritual aspects of life tend to be given emphasis; and in most religions, supernatural and transcendental aspects are vital. Such provides an awkward universe of subject-matter for any attempt to apply to religious education a behavioural-objectives approach to syllabus-writing and the making of schemes of work. The curriculum theorist must acknowledge the fact that religious people tend to become highly irritated by those who attempt to reduce their faith and beliefs to a single cognitive system.[7] So it was to be expected that the literature-search would reveal a great deal of subject-matter directed to the development in pupils of religious 'sensitivity' or 'awareness', and such educational objectives are implied by each one of the aims in the CEM list, including the first. But such affective (emotional) objectives are not all of one kind, so two separate categories were made in the analysis, as follows:

Affective objectives, the teacher aiming to develop sensitivity to:
- Personal relationships.
- Self development.
- The natural world.
- Christianity's personal demands.
- Specifically Christian affective experiences, as in acts of worship or music or art.

The general educational purpose here is the development of attitudes, values, interests, and appreciation.[8] The first four are not specifically Christian, and are also the concern of teachers who have 'maturity' or 'good citizenship' as aims in other school subjects. This set of five affective objectives is the one which is least cognitive in its nature, and it seems to be an area of the subject in which teachers are least confident of their purposes.

Affective objectives, the teacher aiming to encourage willingness to:
- Relate religious teaching to daily life.
- Respect and seriously consider the character and achievements of Jesus and other religious leaders.
- Consider and value conflicting philosophies of life.
- Develop generalized attitudes with a religious basis.

Most teachers would distinguish between 'encourage willingness to' and 'indoctrinate', because to teach at all is to influence in some degree, and curriculum theorists do not hesitate to define teaching in terms of behavioural and attitudinal change. The existence of this set of objectives within the analysis does, however, emphasize the involvement which religious education teachers have in value-loaded activities, and there is no easy escape from this situation.[9] The word 'encourage' governs the four objectives listed in this category.

The sets of objectives which have now been listed are not empirically distinct one from another, and one could further the analysis by abstracting a set of general objectives, as follows:

1 Appreciation of the Judaeo-Christian heritage.
2 Information about the life and teaching of Jesus.
3 Knowledge about the growth of the church to modern times.
4 The ability to develop good relations with other people.
5 The capability of responding to God.
6 A feeling for an understanding of the religious dimension of life and its interpretation.
7 An understanding of religious symbols and language as a means whereby faith might be reformulated for the future.
8 Experiences and opportunities through which the claims of Christianity might be faced and a free and responsible decision made.
9 Mature and whole growth with self-understanding.

As with the components previously analysed, this list does not form a hierarchy but indicates the type of end-behaviour which most religious education teachers seem to have looked for in their pupils when the teaching has been successful.

This list of general objectives may be reduced again by isolating within it various general processes in the expected behaviour of the pupil, as follows:

to appreciate = (1) above
to be informed = (2) above
to have knowledge = (3) above
to understand = (6b) (7) (9) above
to decide = (8) above

But this list is rather too general and too abstract to be useful, so it would be better written in curriculum-theory terminology, when it would take some such form as:

(i) Learning sets of facts.
(ii) Learning the inter-relationship and wider significance of the facts.
(iii) Developing a sympathetic and favourable attitude towards the sets of facts, their interrelationship and wider significance.
(iv) Developing willingness to relate what has been learned to personal growth, circumstances and choices in daily life (=8 above).
(v) Learning socially-approved manners (=4 and 9 above).
(vi) Learning attitudes and behaviours which would make possible sympathetic participation in religious activities (=5 above).

An abstraction of this kind tends to appear rather dry and wooden, even foolish in its results; but its purpose is that of gaining a better understanding of the instructional processes that religious education teachers seem to have tried to achieve in their work. It reveals that a great deal of the activity of religious education is not peculiar to the subject, but is the kind of work undertaken by most teachers, of whatever subject.

The first process, (i) above, must clearly include the objectives placed in the cognitive category listed earlier. But something more than a gathering of facts is demanded by the broader educational aims of the school, so *Learning sets of facts* must extend also into the affective categories of the analysis previously presented.

At first sight this proposition seems to be incorrect, because affective objectives refer to things to be done: things to be shown by example or discovered by experience rather than things which can be verbalized. But a dichotomy of fact-learning and activity-learning is, like most dichotomies, too simple. The tripartite nature of the categorized objectives which have been presented is valuable in that it allows place to a type of learning which, without being completely different from the cognitive learning of knowledge, yet is distinct by its emphasis. The working teacher will find that some of his most successful work has been that which has allowed pupils not only a gain in (cognitive) *knowledge of* some of the factual contents of religion, but the cultivation of (an affective) *sensitivity to* religion,[10] and a *willingness to* participation of some sort.

Some sort of commitment appears to be a necessary condition of successful work not only in religious education, but in most school subjects, even if it is only a commitment to what a phenomenologist would call 'epoche': that is, a bracketing-out of questions of truth and falsehood; a laying on one side of difficulties that would hinder the growth of knowledge necessary to understanding so that later, some understanding having been achieved, the questions could be taken up again. Such understanding is chiefly an intellectual process, and religious education teachers are doing no more than other teachers when they encourage the pupil to develop a receptive and sympathetic attitude to the subject-matter as a means of furthering his knowledge and skills, both cognitive and affective.

It may be questioned whether

(v) Learning socially-approved manners

is a fair behavioural translation of

4 The ability to develop good relations with other people.

But objectives of type (4) are commonly found in the literature of religious education, making moral and philosophical assumptions so great that 'learning socially-approved manners' is probably a fair description of their core-process. Very seldom in the literature of the subject is any clear dynamic concept of the relationships described, most writers never going beyond a conventional exposition of such biblical texts as 'love your neighbour' or 'forgive until seventy times seven'.

We commonly think that sympathetic and favourable attitudes (process iii in the list above) are things to be won and attributes of a personal relationship rather than components of a learning-situation which the teacher may engineer as a means of furthering knowledge. Many of the books and articles which have been influential in religious education have been written in such a vein, suggesting or assuming that the teacher should be essentially a guide, comforter and friend to the child's spiritual and personal development. It must readily be admitted that inadequate personal qualities in a teacher can spoil his work, but the writer would suggest that the teacher should be very careful not to make disciples for himself, but rather to concentrate on the business of learning which he has in common with his pupils. In some of the literature of religious education, a confusion of teacher with subject seems to be evident.

An underlying implication of all the writing of Harold Loukes (1961, 1965, etc.) is that the personality and attitudes of the teacher are vital in religious education, and his description of the type of teacher required is cast in terms of 'personal maturity'.[11] Loukes seems to have been unable to give a description of the distinctive qualities required by the religious education teacher. He rejected such categories as 'Christian' and 'reverent agnostic'; but it is significant that his list of desirable qualities in fact is a list of the qualities demanded *generally* in schoolteaching, rather than any specific to the subject. One might claim that he ends his discussion rather lamely by merely suggesting various spiritual synonyms for these qualities (spontaneous life; humility; acceptance; outgoing love and concern; a faith to live by; encounter with the Spirit of God), and by asserting that the general qualities required of an effective schoolteacher . . . 'are Christian qualities, not in the sense that they are exclusive to Christians, but in the sense that they are part of the Christian intention.[12]

A mischievous critic could invert Loukes' argument, use non-religious synonyms, and claim that such are atheistic humanist qualities, being part of the humanist intention. But both arguments are irrelevant, being rooted in ideological intentions rather than a defensible educational policy. Sympathetic and favourable attitudes are important in learning because (to use the terms of the lists presented earlier) they extend cognitive study towards the *sensitivity to* . . . and *willingness to* . . . which in any individual provide a mastery of self and environment: a mastery which gives value to the learning of sets of facts and their interrelationship. Facts alone are of little value until they can be placed within an organizational scheme or structure which is, at least partly, the creation of the individual: so that motivational and emotional factors in the personality of both pupil and teacher are enabled to operate and give the possibility of realization to the fourth process in the list detailed previously, and perhaps also the fifth and the sixth processes.

Notes

1 Such as Alves' research (1968); the Durham Report (1970); and the Schools Council secondary project (1971).

2 Naylor's (1970) unpublished dissertation made a study of the teaching of main-course Divinity in colleges, and showed the situation indicated in this paragraph to be normal for teachers in training.

3 In a previous article (Lupton 1971a), the writer has indicated the value of this type of objectives approach for planning in religious education.
4 Such a denial could be justified, but it would be inappropriate to include the argument within the present article.
5 Some of these statistics were given in (Lupton 1971b), a paper which gave a critical account of the various Mode One CSE examinations in Religious Education offered by the fourteen examinations boards in England and Wales.
6 It should be noted that the various elements are not wholly distinct within each list, but indicate differing emphases. Likewise the threefold categorization of cognitive and affective objectives is one of overlapping sets rather than of exclusive categories.
7 The suggestion here is that common usage of the term 'religion' must be given adequate place in the curriculum theorist's working definition and proposals, whatever its philosophic difficulties.
8 The writer does not intend to imply here that such are general abilities. A weakness of much educational writing is the tendency to wrench such behaviours away from their specific contexts in the real world and to pretend that they can be developed as skills distinct from their subject-matter.
9 It is notable that humanists and secularists fall into the same difficulty when they consider the principles of education. See, for example, H.L. Elvin's essay (in Huxley 1961 p. 279) where he rejects religion but advocates '. . . a framework of leading ideas that will help young people to see life steadily and see it whole.'
10 Such curriculum theorists as Philip H. Phenix (1964) would at this point call religion a 'realm of meaning'.
11 See chapter 13 of Loukes, 1965.
12 Loukes (1965) p. 178.

References

Alves, Colin, 1968. *Religion and the Secondary School,* SCM Press.

Association of College and University Examiners, 1956 and 1964. *Taxonomy of Educational Objectives: the classification of educational goals.*
Handbook 1: *Cognitive Domain,* 1956.
Handbook 2: *Affective Domain,* 1964.

Christian Education Movement, 1968. Evidence submitted to the Bishop of Durham's Commission on Religious Education. *Learning for Living* 8, No. 2, November, 1968, pp. 25–27.

Huxley, J. (ed.), 1961. *The Humanist Frame of Mind,* London.

Loukes, H., 1961. *Teenage Religion: an enquiry into attitudes and possibilities amongst British boys and girls in secondary modern schools,* SCM Press.

Loukes, H., 1965. *New Ground in Christian Education,* SCM Press.

Lupton, H.E., 1971a. 'Curriculum Theory and Religious Education'. *Learning for Living* 11, No. 1, September, 1971, pp. 29–32.

Lupton, H.E., 1971b. *Religious Education in the Certificate of Secondary Education,* CEM Teachers' Department Paper.

National Society and Church of England Board of Education, 1970. *The Fourth R.* SPCK.

Naylor, D., 1970. *An inquiry into the content of Education Main Courses in Divinity.* Unpublished MA (Educ) dissertation, University of Lancaster.
Phenix, P.H., 1964. *Realms of Meaning,* McGraw Hill.
Schools Council, 1971. *Working Paper 36: Religious Education in Secondary Schools,* Evans/Methuen.

*Discussing Religious Education: A Conceptual Framework for the Consideration of Curricular Issues**

David Gooderham

How do you discuss RE in a primary school curriculum review? How do you discuss its place in a secondary school humanities programme? The range of contentious issues and possible misunderstandings is legion.

A member of staff with special responsibility or concern for RE in contexts of this kind has open to him a number of possible strategies. As a result of developments in the past twelve or fifteen years there are now available in RE not only a range of materials, revised Agreed Syllabuses and projects, but, more importantly, several different and now well-developed 'approaches'. The specialist may, therefore, if he seeks a clearly-defined stance with regard to RE in the school, advocate those materials and syllabuses congruous with such a stance. He may, if he seeks consensus, advocate some recent version of what RE 'really' is, inviting staff to join him in abandoning the out-of-date and implementing the new. He may, if he seeks considered judgments on the part of other members of staff, attempt to distinguish major approaches now available, with a view to their consideration and appraisal.

The last of these strategies expresses a view of the role of the specialist teacher, not as advocate for one particular approach, but as mediator of the range of approaches possible in the subject. Such a view, appropriate in general to contexts of curriculum review and planning, may be regarded as essential in contexts where RE is under consideration. Without an appreciation of such possibilities and the decisions that can be made on the basis of such appreciation, there is little hope of dealing with misconceptions which cloud RE in the school curriculum.

There is, further, little hope of dealing with the ironic tolerance which,

*This article first appeared in *British Journal of Religious Education*, Vol. 3, No. 2, Winter, 1980.

more seriously, vitiates RE in the school curriculum. Not only do misconceptions exist, but, in a plural society, teachers have differing religious, secular, humanist and other ideological stances. Such stances involve differing assumptions, interpretations and evaluations. It is largely because such stances are neither clarified nor seriously taken into account that ironic tolerance develops. It will, therefore, be an important feature of any effective mediation that such stances *are* taken account of. If an adequate basis for rational decision-making is to be provided, it must involve the appreciation not only of differing 'approaches', but also understanding of the relationship between such approaches and teachers' personal stances. The task of mediation, then, is a complex one. It requires, for the explication of this relationship, the clarification of the theoretical groundings of differing approaches in RE.

Here a conceptual framework is outlined for the purpose of such clarification. Initially it has to be presented at a level of some theoretical abstraction. Subsequently it will be employed to identify and distinguish relationships in several aspects of RE curriculum. Finally it will be employed with regard to teachers' stances.

Constructing a framework

Both problems in, and new approaches to, RE spring ultimately from the secularization of thinking which has taken place in the West in the last two – and more – centuries.

Two intimately related aspects of the secularization process may be distinguished. The first is the shift in the Western mind away from a world-view in which God looms large to one where man himself assumes such dimensions. The second is the concomitant differentiation and development of the disciplines of history, science, moral philosophy and the like, in their own right, distinct from theology.

These two profound changes in human thinking and feeling involve changes in the way in which questions about the character, purposes and value of human existence in the world are conceived – what Radnitzky[1] identifies as a cognitive interest in improving reflection on ontological and existential themes. With the shift, in the first place, from God to man as object of attention, questions of meaning and value may now be handled by ideas which cluster about the latter conceptualizations of man rather than the former conceptualizations of God. With the shift, in the second place, from theology, as 'queen of the sciences', to pre-occupation with the human and natural sciences, modes of enquiry may now be informed by intellectual standards and values independent of the attitudes of reverence and awe regarded as proper to faith.

Questions about human existence in the world have traditionally been handled by the use of religious concepts and theologically-oriented modes of enquiry. The development of secular thought now, however, offers a range of concepts and modes of enquiry which extend beyond the theological. These extended ranges are, perhaps, best conceived as continua along which specific conceptions may be plotted.

(i) The religious-humanistic continuum

The first of the two continua extends from the traditional symbols of religion, amongst which the concept 'God' (or, perhaps, 'the transcendent') is central, through to the concepts of Philosophical Anthropology, where the concept 'Man' is central; from a God-created and sustained cosmos to a socially-constructed reality; from the spirit 'moving on the face of the waters' to 'the spirit of man' disclosed through his own handiwork. The continuum may be fleshed out by reference to major twentieth century thinkers. It extends from an uncompromising assertion of the 'otherness' of God like that of Karl Barth at one pole, through systems like those of Teilhard de Chardin and the Christian Existentialists which, though differing widely nevertheless display what Ong[2] identifies as a common 'anthropologizing' tendency, to systems at the other pole like the monumental attempt of Ernst Cassirer to present the human spirit as the measure of all things.

The continuum of conceptual systems which enables us to handle questions about human existence in the world extends, therefore, from what may be designated 'religious' interpretations of life, where the concept of God is central, to philosophical anthropological or – more succinctly, if crudely – 'humanistic' interpretations of life, where the concept of man is central. The religious systems embrace the concept of man up to the point where the nature and destiny of man begin to assume an increasingly central place; the 'humanist' systems embrace the concept of religion up to the point where man's activities as myth-maker or as spiritual being begin to imply religion as the prime human activity.

(ii) The confessional–academic continuum

The second continuum, relating to modes of enquiry, extends from traditional conceptions of enquiry, as in the 'confessional' activities of theologians, apologists and exegetes, to the 'objective' enquiry of the human sciences and related academic disciplines. In the former case the exercise of reason and the development of understanding are conceived as being at the service of faith; in the latter all forms of personal prejudice and interest are to be rigorously controlled in the process of enquiry. In the former, understanding is ultimately subordinated to commitment; in the latter, commitment is subordinated to understanding.

Whilst the 'objective' conception of enquiry has been assumed to be the more valid, recent hermeneutic theorizing,[3] in its insistence on the historical-rootedness of the enquirer and its problematizing of the 'objective', has called in question such assumptions. In this reappraisal, the concept 'ideology' has been retrieved from its pejorative use (denoting a *false* system of ideas); it may now be employed with a positive connotation. 'In short, each ideology presents a map of 'what is' in society; a 'report' of how it is working, how it is failing and also of how it could be changed. Ideology thus is the call to action – a 'command' grounded in social theory . . .'[4]

The implications of this kind of thinking are of importance for our purpose. No longer can the ideologically or theologically-grounded enquiry be dismissed as inferior to that characterized by scientific objectivity. Such 'objectivity' may itself be seen as grounded in particular human interests; whilst the active exercise of reason in an acknowledged ideologically or theoretically-oriented enquiry may be seen to deploy certain important kinds of knowledge for action.

The second continuum extends from what will be designated the 'Confessional' (denoting religiously- or ideologically-oriented knowledge) at one pole, to the 'Academic' (objectively-oriented) at the other. In the case of the former, understanding, gained through the disciplined exercise of reason, is ultimately at the service of the 'call to action' – the ideological or religious call to response, commitment, faith; in the case of the latter, whilst understanding is always acknowledged as being historically rooted, the thrust of intellectual activity is always towards unrestricted enquiry and criticism, wherever that may lead. 'Confessional' enquiry retains this character up to the point where the intellect begins to range untrammelled by questions of response, commitment and faith; 'academic' enquiry retains this character up to the point where interests and commitments begin to restrict its freedom.

The conceptual framework expressed as a matrix

The two conceptual continua, when brought into relationship, provide a framework which enables relationships within the field of religion and relationships between this and other fields of experience and understanding to be distinguished. The related continua 'Religious-Humanistic' and 'Confessional-Academic' may be figuratively represented as the axes of a matrix. For purposes of clarity in discussion, four principal segments in the matrix will be distinguished: (Fig. 1).

The matrix may be employed to identify and distinguish relationships in several aspects of RE curriculum:

(i) to identify relationships between the different knowledge and values which differing approaches pick out for the curriculum;
(ii) to distinguish the distinctive features of major 'approaches' (cur-

	RELIGIOUS		
	1 'Theological study of Religion (in GB the Christian Religion).	2 Academic study of Religion	
CONFESSIONAL			ACADEMIC
	3 'Ideological' study of Man	4 Academic study of Man	
	HUMANISTIC		

Figure 1

riculum strategies based on explicit rationales) and syllabuses presently available to teachers;

(iii) to select subject matter for course planning;

(iv) to identify teachers' personal stances and to suggest appropriate forms of development both for individuals and in schools or departments/faculties.

(i) Knowledge and values

A first use of the matrix enables the identification of relationships between the different knowledge and values which differing approaches to religious and 'existential' themes pick out for the curriculum: (Fig. 2).

In Segment 1, the object of attention (however much preparatory 'experiential' work may be undertaken in pedagogical practice) is religion, its beliefs and practices. There is, in principle, a complete identity of subject matter in Segments 1 and 2; they are, however, differentiated by the

	RELIGIOUS		
	1 Study of one's 'own' religion as 'true'; other faiths seen in relation to one's own religion.	2 Open Enquiry into world faiths, treated impartially.	
CONFESSIONAL	Faith Commitment	Intellectual Virtues	ACADEMIC
	3 Study of one's 'own' way of life: other faiths/world views seen in relation to one's own.	4 Open Enquiry into 'Man' through a range of inter-related disciplines.	
	HUMANISTIC		

Figure 2

mode of study. In Segment 2 all world faiths are treated with equal regard; in Segment 1, however, other faiths and ways of life are seen ultimately in a subordinate relationship where they serve to point up features in and values of the 'confessed' religion.

The same relationship obtains between the subject matter and modes of study in Segments 3 and 4. Whilst in Segment 4 the concept 'Man' is an 'essentially contested' one, open to whichever direction the academic disciplines lead, in Segment 3 'Man' will be found as conceived by Christian Humanists or by those of another ideology – whichever is adopted – with other conceptions of man playing subordinate roles in relation to the 'confessed' concept.

With regard to modes of study, Segments 2 and 4, as has been implied, share in a primary emphasis on the intellectual virtues: 'clarity, coherence, consistency, relevance, non-arbitrariness, humility, accuracy, precision, truthfulness, sincerity, perceptiveness and so on'.[5] In Segments 1 and 3, whilst these values are rated highly, they are regarded as incomplete without the development of feelings, attitudes and values which belong to religious faith or ideological commitment. These include awe, reverence, faith, whether directed to God or secularized in 'reverence for the Body of a Man'.[6]

(ii) 'Approaches' to religious education

A second use of the matrix enables teachers to gain an overview of what recent developments have taken place in RE, what major alternatives exist for teachers in state and other schools, what the character of each of these alternatives is and how they are inter-related.

For this purpose the three major 'Approaches' identified in Schools Council Working Paper 36[7] may be presented, along with typical Agreed Syllabuses and projects in closely related areas. Names of curricular theorists and developers may also be presented. (In each case it must be noted, however, the matrix will only enable the presentation of the main thrust of the work.) (Fig. 3).

The matrix directs attention to the close relationship of the traditional 'Scripture' and 'Neo-confessional' approaches. It points up the fact that 'Existential'/'Experiential'/'Implicit' approaches – often in practice taking a thematic form – must, in most cases, be categorized as 'confessional', since they, along with Segment 1 approaches, are clearly ideologically-grounded. The matrix, interestingly, enables Integrated/Interdisciplinary Humanities work to be related to explicitly RE work. It must be acknowledged that both the Stenhouse Humanities Curriculum Project and 'Man, a course of study' are characterized by discernible ideological under-currents; their main thrust, however, is free enquiry through intellectual and social disciplines.

The possibility of seeing major approaches to RE in this kind of relation-

RELIGIOUS

CONFESSIONAL	1 Traditional 'Scripture' Agree Syllabuses 'Neo-confessional' Approaches: W Riding and ILEA Agreed Syllabuses (Ronald Goldman)	2 City of Birmingham Agreed Syllabus 'Phenomenological'/ 'Explicit'/'Objective' Approaches. (Ninian Smart)	ACADEMIC
	3 'Existential'/ 'Experiential'/ 'Implicit' Approaches (Harold Loukes)	4 Integrated/ Interdisciplinary Humanities (Stenhouse Humanities, 'Man, a course of study')	

HUMANISTIC

Figure 3

ship is of value to teachers, not merely because it presents them with a guide through the plethora of syllabuses and materials available, but because it breaks down the assumption that the most recent is the most valuable. Through the delineation of relationships it opens up questions about *educational* validity in a way which facilitates the serious consideration of approaches which might be dismissed as 'old fashioned' or as '*outré*'.

The underlining of the close relationship between traditional 'Scripture' and 'Neo-confessional' approaches is important for teachers. Attention is often drawn to the difference which is apparent when they are considered from the perspectives of pedagogical psychology and methodology. Without a clear acknowledgement of their common confessional grounding, however, the teacher may be left uncertain and dissatisfied – and consequently suspicious of all new approaches to RE which do not 'come clean' about such grounding.

The disclosure of the Humanities – RE relationship is a valuable one. It clarifies ways in which the two may be appropriately and productively co-ordinated. Where the philosophical underpinning of the curriculum is explicitely academic a valid relationship may be established between Segments 2 and 4; where 'Man' is employed as a central organizing concept a valid relationship may be established between Segments 3 and 4. A warning note, however, is struck with regard to 1 and 4 where there is no congruity with regard either to objects of attention or modes of study.

(iii) Selection of subject matter

The matrix may be employed not merely in general terms to distinguish and relate knowledge and values, projects, syllabuses and the like, but also to pick out, in very specific terms, what might be undertaken with regard to any given topic or theme selected as a basis for a unit of work in the classroom. This is of particular importance for primary school teachers and for secondary teachers involved in interdisciplinary and integrated

RELIGIOUS

CONFESSIONAL — ACADEMIC

1 (Christian Confessional Approach) Symbolism of Christian Initiation (Exodus and Baptism)	2 Water as a symbol employed in world religions
3 Water in human experiences of physical need and its satisfaction. Human activity in using, storing water . . . Irrigation/Power schemes. Appreciation of the beauty, threat of water . . . in literature and the arts.	4

HUMANISTIC

Figure 4 (a)Water

RELIGIOUS

CONFESSIONAL — ACADEMIC

1 (Christian Confessional Approach) Biblical understanding of suffering, with particular reference to Christ. Christians and suffering.	2 Suffering as understood in world religions.
3 Personal experience of suffering: pain, injury, bereavement . . . in biography, poetry Suffering arising from want, injustice, violence . . . Alleviation of suffering	4 Analyses of social, psychological, political features.

HUMANISTIC

Figure 4(b) Suffering

programmes, since it is in these areas that thematic approaches are often – and often badly[8] – employed. In order to avoid intellectual sterility in the use of themes there must be a clear appreciation of the distinctive kinds of knowledge and feeling that may be picked out from a theme or subject matter by a particular approach. For such identification the matrix may be employed.

Two examples are offered of such a practical application, the first with regard to a theme characteristically employed in teaching younger children, the second one for older pupils. (Fig. 4).

(iv) Personal and professional teacher stances

As has been argued earlier one of the most important matters which has to be addressed in discussions about RE in the curriculum is that of the personal stance of the teacher. This stance needs to be seen in relation both to the kinds of professional approach that are possible in the area and to the stances of colleagues. The distinguishing of the former relationship will enable the teacher to make judgments about the adoption of an appropriate personal style; the latter will enable him to see his own as one of a number of differing contributions to the experience of children growing up in the school.

The matrix can be employed both for clarification of what currently obtains and for the identification of educationally valid and productive developments. (Fig. 5).

The matrix directs attention to the range of possible stances between traditional Christian and explicitly humanist.

There are, of course, problems with regard to the educational validity of the approach to RE in any one of these segments. With regard to Segments 1 and 3 questions of indoctrination arise; with regard to Segments 2 and 4 questions about whether *religious* education is going on when the experiences of faith and commitment are either evaded or attempted only in imaginative simulation.

The matrix suggests possible approaches to such problems. Since Segments 1 and 2 both have religion as their object of attention, the believing teacher, worried about the problem of indoctrination, might well develop a personally coherent and satisfying style by adopting a professional stance on the verge of Segment 2. Since Segments 1 and 3 present a continuum along which the stances of teachers in a primary school or secondary school department/faculty may be ranged, a staff, concerned that RE should not be attenuated into the purely academic, might agree to organize their work in a confessional style where each teacher's distinctive input is seen as complementary to others. The first approach would tend to foster academic impartiality, the latter, a form of 'multi-cultural' awareness.

RELIGIOUS

	1 The religious believer, through understanding, wishes to evoke faith.	2 The academic (who may, or may not, be a believer) is primarily interested in the study of religion.	
CONFESSIONAL	1/3 The 'ethnic Christian', the transmitter of 'our heritage', the Christian humanist, through understanding, wish to evoke personal response to certain traditional values.		ACADEMIC
	3 The humanist through understanding wishes to evoke commitment.	4 The academic is primarily interested in an inter-disciplinary exploration of 'Man'.	

HUMANISTIC

Figure 5

The framework and curriculum innovation

In conclusion certain assumptions underlying such a framework must be exposed. Obviously it is held that there are educationally valid approaches to the teaching of RE and that recent curriculum developments begin to offer strategies and materials appropriate for a range of contexts and needs.

It has, however, been increasingly recognized that innovation, through the use of such strategies and materials, often fails just at the point of their implementation in school syllabus and classroom practice. The problem is not so much neglect, as disabling syncretism: the new is assimilated into established course structures at the cost of distortion – perhaps, indeed, neutralization.[9] Important among the reasons for problems of this kind is the fact that whilst materials find their way into school, too little attention is given to the need for or to the character of negotiations which must be pursued if new strategies and methods are to be sensitively and effectively related to particular contexts.

In addition, therefore, to the dissemination of information about developments in RE two further prerequisites are required for effective innovation. One is the attention to interrelationships of the kind considered through the use of the framework presented here. The second is the establishing, in school or department/faculty, of an approach to discussion and decision making in curricular issues sufficiently open to make the consideration of such interrelationships both effective and profitable.

These two prerequisites – a common framework of understanding and an open enough *milieu* for its use and development – are basic elements in the securing of rational discourse.

Nowhere in the curriculum is such discourse more obviously required than with regard to RE. The development, however, of 'communicative competence'[10] here, may not merely be an end in itself, but may offer a significant model for discussion in other curricular areas where questions about understanding and ideological grounding are now also beginning to be acknowledged – and where languages and procedures will be required for their consideration and resolution.

References

1 Radnitzky, G., *Contemporary Schools of Metascience*, Vol. 2, (2nd Edition), Göteberg, Akademi-förlaget, 1968.
2 Ong, W., 'Crisis and understanding in the humanities', in *Daedalus*, Summer, 1969.
3 Giddens, A., *New Rules of Sociological Method*, London: Hutchinson, 1976. p. 54*f*.
4 Gouldner, A., *The Dialectic of Ideology and Technology*, London: Macmillan, 1976, p. 30.
5 Peters, R.S., 'Subjectivity and standards', in Niblett, R.W., *The Sciences, The Humanities and the Technological Threat*, London: University of London Press, 1975.
6 Carlyle, T., *Past and Present*, University of Oxford Press, 1960.
7 Schools Council Working Paper 36, *Religious Education in Secondary Schools*, Evans/Methuen, 1971.
8 Sockett, H., *Knowledge and Schooling*, London: Open Books, 1975.
9 Elliott, J., 'Some key concepts underlying teachers' evaluations of innovation', unpublished conference paper, 1977.
10 Gouldner, A., *op. cit.*, p. 142*f*.

5
Methods in Teaching Religion Today

Introduction

Pupils are not being stimulated to think. This situation is by no means unique to the teaching of religion, but it is particularly unfortunate for a subject which sets itself the task of exploring basic questions, which depends upon the acquisition of conceptual and abstract thinking, and which must make greater efforts to arouse the curiosity of children and young people if it is to be a worthwhile learning experience. Trevor Kerry's investigation of the methods used by a small group of religious education teachers confirms a widely-held belief: too much religious education teaching remains at the level of information giving.

If Kerry's work documents the problem, the remaining articles in this section offer some glimpses of answers. Owen Cole shows the demand upon methods made by the expanded world religions content of the 1970s, and his approach finds an interesting contrast in that of Robin Minney. Whereas Cole emphasizes the concrete and the appeal to sense experience, advancing to abstract beliefs in later years, Minney emphasizes an approach through myth and art towards the longings and fears of mankind, with a greater stress on feeling and awareness.

It is entirely appropriate that a collection of articles dealing mainly with English religious education should open with an American contribution and should close with one from continental Europe. Paul Fueter describes a range of methods in teaching the Bible today.

The problems of method illustrated in this section raise the question of whether religious education is making progress. The historical perspective, from John Stuart Mill, with which this collection of essays is introduced, raises a similar problem. Can one speak of a religious education in Britain characteristic of the 1870s, the 1920s, and the 1970s? Is it possible to make lists of the emphases of each decade? The 1960s, we might think, were the period of experiential Christian education, the 1970s the period of world religions, and so on.

If it is possible to describe religious education (or any other social phenomenon) in this way, further interesting questions emerge. What is the relationship between the religious education of one decade and that of the previous decade, and the next? Are we dealing here with a succession of fashions, even of fads, or do we see a process of development, in which each phase is related to the previous and following stages in an evolutionary or organic manner? Moreover, if there is an organic development and not a mere succession of fashions, does it amount to a growth, an improvement in some way, so that we could speak of *progress* in religious education?

If the relationship between the religious education of the past years and that of the next few years is arbitrary, whimsical, the product of mere fashion, then there is no rational or moral ground for keeping up with it all. If the relationship between one period of religious education and the next is rational but a certain teacher or lecturer keeps up with it merely to show that he is up-to-date, but does not really understand the principles of the development, we may describe him as being 'trendy'. But if there *are* no principles of development within the subject, then anyone who tries to keep up with it *can* be nothing but trendy. The cynical observation that if you continue to do and believe just exactly what you do and believe now you will, with the passage of time, once again find yourself in the forefront, springs from the belief that one stage of religious education passes into the next without principle, and that in effect we do not learn from the experience of the last decade so as to carry forward with us into the next decade what we have acquired. And if that really is our situation, there is no longer much point in trying to think hard and clearly about our work, since we will never be able to improve it. All we can hope to create is yet another random craze, which, like the others, will fade without trace.

How would we tell if progress was being made in religious education? If philosophers of science find difficulty in stating the conditions for recognizing progress in science, there need be no embarrassment amongst religious educators about the same problem. Let us put the question more carefully. What are the marks which any religious education of the 1980s would have to show, in order to defend itself against the charge that it will be nothing but a series of fads and fashions?

We may list four marks of progressive development.

First mark: differentiation

A subject makes progress if its concepts become increasingly differentiated. First there are only trees. Then there are oaks and cedars. Then there are kinds of cedar. So a botanical taxonomy will be developed, which will be progress; because there really are so many kinds of trees, the words and descriptions which enable us to speak and think of the differences will bring us that much closer to the real world. This is certainly taking place in religious education. We distinguished in the 1930s between preaching and teaching. In the 1960s this became a difference between open-ended and closed teaching, and in the early 1970s between confessional and professional teaching. Now we distinguish between religious education, religious nurture or faith, religious instruction, and a start is being made in further developing the features of these as being different subjects. Examining this process closely, we see not merely changes in vocabulary in which certain expressions were 'in', but a closer and more discriminating examination of what takes place between teacher and pupil, which brings our thinking closer to reality, and so constitutes progress.

Second mark: integration

Once features of reality have been noticed, the next step is to bring them together again so as to regard the world as one. Progress is made when the plurality and unity of the world are rediscovered, and seen more tightly and more richly. So within religious education, first we distinguish, as the Schools Council Groundplan did, between religious concepts, feelings and actions. Then we bring all three together, making our presentation of the diverse but unitary religious world that much more realistic. Or we distinguish between several ways of evaluating religion, such as the historical (did it happen?), the philosophical (does it make sense?), the ethical (is it good?) and the psychological (does it build up personhood?). Then in our teaching we bring these various ways of responding to religion together again.

Third mark: verification

If the first two marks are present, or seem to be present, in a development of religious education, we must next ask if there is any way of verifying the claimed progress towards reality. Here some traces of progress can be seen but in other areas it is hard to be sure. We distinguished between religions and between cultural groups (Mark One), and then, through a theory of pluralism and pluralistic teaching, we advanced to unity (Mark Two) but can we verify the results? Do we know whether teaching world religion is more 'educational' than teaching the Bible only? Do we know what effect it has upon the faith and religious attitudes of the young when they are placed in pluralistic schools? On the other hand, the Piaget – Goldman psychology enabled us to distinguish certain kinds of thinking about religion (First Mark), and the methods of the late 1960s (life themes, problem-centred method, etc.) brought these insights together (Second Mark). The more recent psychological work, illustrated in this collection, probably enables us to assess and to diagnose individual learning in religion more realistically. Surely this is progress.

Fourth mark: criticism

In the last resort, a free exchange of rational criticism is the feature of a subject which enables us to distinguish progress from a series of fashions.

Are debates in religious education marked by mere assertion, by reiteration of preconceived positions, by the use of slogans, by exaggerated claims in which the research evidence is ignored? Then we have fashions. Or is discussion of religious education marked by clarification of ideas, by the encouragement of unusual points of view, in which the evidence is considered, and the arguments from previous generations kept in mind? Then there is a sign of progress.

*The Demands Made by RE on Pupils' Thinking**

Trevor Kerry

This paper examines the teaching modes employed, and the cognitive demands made on pupils, during eighteen RE lessons given by three teachers in one school. Verbal transactions, written and practical tasks are analysed. The suggestion is offered that teachers could make more opportunities to improve the quality of pupils' thinking during verbal transactions in lessons and that the nature of tasks set should be examined more closely from the standpoint of cognitive demand.

Justifying RE

A common justification for teaching RE in schools is the claim that as a discipline it is more demanding than many other curriculum areas. Presumably the ground of this assertion is that the subject matter of religion deals not merely with data (religious knowledge), but with the conceptual framework supporting the data (definitions, individual articles of faith, specific dogmas) and the over-arching systems into which religious events, phenomena, ideas and concepts fit (abstract systems and generalization).

If one accepts the crude but useful hierarchical categorization of thought into data, concept and abstraction then, in theory, it would be possible to teach history at the first level, at least to GCE standard. Indeed, history is often so taught, and is then characterized by lists of dates, information about housing conditions and pictures of Roman centurions for pupils to colour. History does not *have* to be taught like this and such teaching is arid: but it is possible.

*This article first appeared in *British Journal of Religious Education*, Vol. 3, No. 2, Winter, 1980.

Genuine RE cannot be taught wholly on the data level because it embraces belief and value systems which in turn depend upon abstract notions like 'God', 'Trinity', 'sacrifice'. So one might expect RE lessons to make cognitive demands on pupils at a higher level and more consistently than other subjects.

Investigating thinking skills

The Teacher Education Project, a four-year research and development project based at the universities of Nottingham, Leicester and Exeter, and financed by the Department of Education and Science, to innovate training materials for initial and in-service teacher education, has been investigating the cognitive demands made by teachers on their pupils. The major purpose of the study was to gauge the amount and nature of cognitive stimulus experienced by bright pupils during their classroom lessons. A special study was undertaken of cognitive demand made on pupils of all abilities in science and RE lessons. As part of this study eighteen RE lessons given by three teachers to pupils in years one to three of a mixed comprehensive school were observed in detail. A trained observer used the categories indicated in Figure 1 to record each segment of teacher and pupil talk during the lesson. The segments falling to each category were then totalled – and from the relative proportions of each kind of transaction it was possible to draw a 'cognitive map' of the lesson (for an example see Fig. 2).

Before proceeding to discuss the findings from the research it is appropriate to examine the underlying assumptions and procedures in a little more detail.

The purpose of school is to help pupils to learn. Learning is not the acquisi-

Figure 1.

Categories for coding verbal transactions

The following categories were used:

T0	Teacher talk – management, demonstration, administration.
T1	Teacher talk – data level.
T2	Teacher talk – concept level.
T3	Teacher talk – abstract level.
Q0	Teachers' questions – management level.
Q1	Teachers' questions – recall level.
Q2	Teachers' questions – comprehension level.
Q3	Teachers' questions – application level.
Q4	Teachers' questions – analysis level.
Q5	Teachers' questions – synthesis level.
Q6	Teachers' questions – evaluation level.
C	Contacts with pupils – brief and of no learning significance.
R0	Pupils' responses – management level.
R1	Pupils' responses – data level.
R2	Pupils' responses – concept level.
R3	Pupils' responses – abstract level.
RW	Pupils' responses – incorrect answers.

Figure 2. A cognitive map of one lesson (given by Mrs A to a third year slow band class) in the form of a block graph.

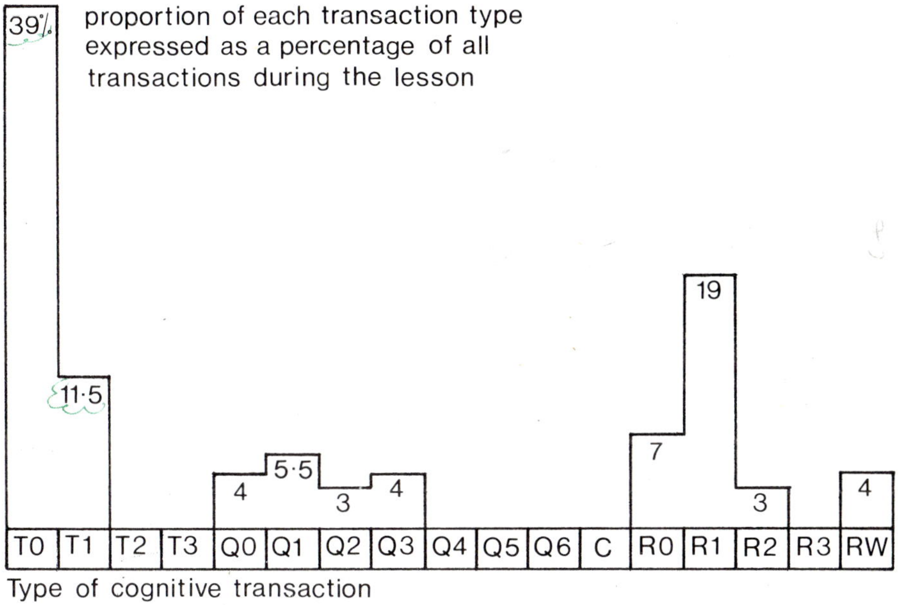

tion of facts alone, but the ability to collect facts, to sequence them, to observe or perceive relationships, to ask questions, to construct hypotheses, to sift and evaluate evidence, to conduct experiments, to draw conclusions and acquire and apply skills. These intellectual processes form as thoughts. But thoughts are invisible. They can be quantified and examined only in so far as they issue in words (spoken or written). In the classroom, evidence for cognitive processes comes most often in the words spoken by teachers and pupils. Tasks set and the ways in which these are carried out also give evidence of the cognitive expectations of teachers and the pupils' readiness and competence in responding. In this study we concentrated on collecting the evidence of classroom cognitive processes available from the spoken words of teachers and pupils. Tasks were also recorded and analysed, but this process has reached a less advanced stage of analysis as yet.

King John School was selected for study because it was felt that there would be few discipline problems, teachers were known to be well regarded by colleagues in other schools and, as far as RE was concerned, the subject had a history of innovation at the school. The researchers would thus be free to concentrate on cognitive transactions in classes which were orderly and generally well motivated. Conditions of study were chosen, then, to be favourable to effective teaching rather than hostile to it.

Findings from the research can be summarized under three main headings: the context of teaching, the cognitive level of lessons and the nature of tasks.

The context of teaching

The data sheets compiled for each lesson gave the observer scope to record the teaching mode(s) used and to record the amount of time spent on each of these. As well as whole class teaching and individualized learning, a record was made of teachers' use of groups. Group work was divided into two kinds:

G1 represented those situations when each group had a discrete learning task for the success of which members of the groups had each to perform an integral role.

G2 represented groups used merely as organizational devices (so that pupils sat with friends but worked individually on identical tasks, or where pupils worked together solely to share equipment).

The pie diagram shown as Figure 3 indicates the proportions of the eighteen lessons spent on each of the four categories of teaching mode.

The cognitive level of lessons

Each segment of teacher talk was coded by the observer using the codes

Figure 3. Proportions of time spent on whole class teaching, group work and individualized learning by three teachers during eighteen RE lessons at King John school expressed as percentages of total teaching time.

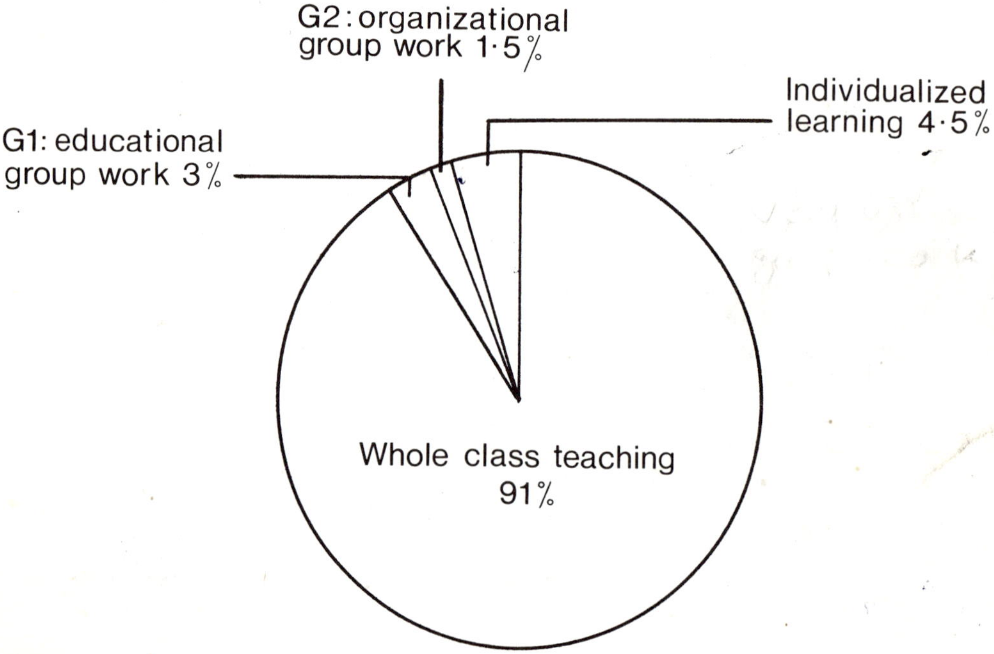

shown in Figure 1. To discover something of the cognitive level of a lesson it is necessary to consider these codes in a little more detail.

The talk coded TO represents no cognitive demand – it accounts for all management and organization carried out in the classroom ('put that coat away', 'move the chairs back', 'stop talking'). T1, T2 and T3 represent data, conceptual and abstract levels of thought and thus form a hierarchy of cognitive demand.

As well as talking or lecturing teachers ask questions. Some questions (QO) are designed to produce management ends ('Will you close that door?'). These make no cognitive demand. Questions of the first and second types (Q1, Q2) are lower order questions demanding only recall to test understanding at the minimal level. Questions of a higher order (labelled Q3, Q4, Q5 and Q6) do not necessarily form a hierarchy, but these categories in lessons should be examined both individually and collectively in order to assess cognitive demand made by teachers' questions.

Pupil responses help both to indicate how pupils interpret teacher expectations and also to act as a barometer of the thinking level at which pupils are functioning. Responses to teachers can be purely at a management level (RO) for example, 'I've checked with the librarian and there isn't a copy available'. Or they can be related again to data, conceptual or abstract levels of thought (R1, R2, R3). Incorrect responses by pupils were recorded (RW) for the sake of completeness.

Taken together, measures of teacher talk, teachers' questions and pupils' responses help to paint a picture of the cognitive demand made in lessons.

In addition to these categories we found that, especially when pupils are working in groups, teachers make fleeting contacts with individuals. These are not usually of the kind which make intellectual demands (where they are we recorded them as T or Q categories); but they 'oil the works of classroom life'. Such contacts were recorded by the code C.

Figure 4 sets out the cognitive demands made upon pupils at King John School during the observation period. The observer watched lessons taken by the head of department (Mrs A) and by two assistants, Mr B (a specialist) and Mrs C (a non-specialist). The school divides pupils into three bands, and classes in each were observed, as were pupils in years 1, 2 and 3. In all, eighteen lessons were recorded over a three week period in mid-term.

The results shown in Figure 4 are discussed in a later section of this paper.

The nature of tasks set to pupils

While the techniques for coding the cognitive demands made by teacher talk, questions and pupils' responses are relatively well-tried, it is harder to code tasks as effectively. Consequently a more qualitative approach was adopted: the observer described the task, often in detail, and a qualitative analysis was then made at a later stage based on these observations. Any

Figure 4. Transactions falling to each category indicated in Figure 1 for each class observed. (Percentages represent an average for three lessons).

Mrs A. Yr 3 Slow group

TO	T1	T2	T3	Q0	Q1	Q2	Q3	Q4	Q5	Q6	C	R0	R1	R2	R3	RW	Total
17·5	14·5	0·5	0	2	21·5	3	2·5	1	0	0	0	3·75	25	5·75	0·5	2·5	100%

Mrs A. Yr 3 Fast group (a)

TO	T1	T2	T3	Q0	Q1	Q2	Q3	Q4	Q5	Q6	C	R0	R1	R2	R3	RW	Total
11	17	1·5	0	4·75	22	2	2·5	4·25	0	2	1	1	24	5	0	2	100%

Mrs A. Yr 3 Fast group (b)

TO	T1	T2	T3	Q0	Q1	Q2	Q3	Q4	Q5	Q6	C	R0	R1	R2	R3	RW	Total
7	16·5	1	0	0	21	3·5	4·5	4	1	0	2·5	0·5	27	7·5	2	2	100%

Mr B. Yr 1 Middle group

TO	T1	T2	T3	Q0	Q1	Q2	Q3	Q4	Q5	Q6	C	R0	R1	R2	R3	RW	Total
14	31	1	0	1	15	2	0	1	0	0	20	0	13	0	0	2	100%

Mr B. Yr 2 Middle group

TO	T1	T2	T3	Q0	Q1	Q2	Q3	Q4	Q5	Q6	C	R0	R1	R2	R3	RW	Total
20	22	1·5	0	1	3·25	3	0	1	0	0	27	10	8	0	0	3·25	100%

Mrs C. Yr 2 Fast group

TO	T1	T2	T3	Q0	Q1	Q2	Q3	Q4	Q5	Q6	C	R0	R1	R2	R3	RW	Total
25	11	1	0	5·5	13	2	1	1	0·5	2	5	13	13·5	2	2	2·5	100%

snap decision made during a lesson about the cognitive demand of a task may prove erroneous when viewing pupils' work later. For example, a teacher may set an open-ended task such as 'Write about the events of Pentecost'. Classroom tradition in that teacher's class may be such that the pupils copy or paraphrase Bible or textbook – a low level operation. Alternatively, the tradition may be that pupils make up their own headings and then describe imaginatively what it may have been like to be Peter on the day of Pentecost or they may speculate about exactly what phenomena took place. The identical task can be interpreted by pupils as more or less demanding. Some hint of pupil response is often (not always) necessary before final judgments can be made about the nature of the task set.

The tasks set by each of the three teachers in the sample are described in Figure 5, along with a brief comment on the task and a fairly crude

Figure 5. Tasks set by three RE teachers at King John School.

Mrs A.

Write down 10 Christian beliefs which affect everyday living in GB (Homework)	H
Look for evidence in Bibles to prove Jesus existed (Homework)	H
Pupils answer question, each from separate workcard (Class)	H
List 5 statements which describe what Christianity is (Homework)	H
Write down any incident which takes place outside church which exemplifies Christianity at work (Homework)	H
Find 3 biblical references to show that Christians should love and care for one another (Class)	L
Give 3 examples of how we in this country show that the Christian principles illustrated affect our everyday lives	H
Write in exercise book a sentence to the effect that we live in a caring society (Class)	L
Listen to recording of 'Day by Day' (Class)	L
Think about this question: Is there a difference between Christianity and churchianity? (Homework)	H
Listen to teacher reading aloud (Class)	L
Pupils write answers to: Who am I? What am I doing here? (Class)	H

Mr B.

Write about changes between schools of 100 years ago and those of today (based on slides viewed). (Class)	L
Write the story of David and Jonathan (Class)	L
Visit local church and find answers to questions on worksheet (Class)	L
Write in style of newspaper report about one of plagues in Egypt (just read about). (Class)	L
Write about the job of seers as healers (using information supplied in textbook). (Class)	L

Mrs C.

Pupils read aloud round class (Class)	L
Pupils answer questions from textbook (8 at comprehension level) (2 at data level) (Class)	L
Pupils read aloud around class (Class)	I
Groups prepare and perform 5 minute playlet (Class)	H

Total tasks: 21
Total at higher level: 9
Total at lower level: 12

division of the tasks into low level (L) and higher level (H).

Discussion

Great care must be taken in discussing the findings from this research. Simple quantitative measures of classroom events can be misleading if divorced from the social flesh and blood context. There is little or no evidence for asserting that a specific quantity of cognitive demand is 'average' or 'below average' for a subject – still less can one as yet assert what is an 'optimum' level of higher level talk or questioning for any given lesson. Presumably higher level thinking depends upon knowing information (data) and having the ability to recall this as well as upon the ability to manipulate the data into concepts and abstractions. The amount of higher level thinking apparent in a lesson may depend upon whether a class is mixed ability, banded, setted or streamed, and upon the age of the pupils. No doubt the kinds and quantities of teacher talk and questions, of pupil responses and the nature of tasks set (for example, whether pupils learn mostly by listening or by researching alone) are a function of teaching style. With all these queries unresolved it is, however, interesting to examine the data in Figures 3, 4 and 5.

Figure 3 would appear to explode the myth that teaching in the 1980s has moved away from the whole class mode. All three teachers used whole class methods predominantly, and it was clear from pupils' reactions and seating patterns that pupils expected to be taught in this way. The lesson of groupwork used by Mrs C was nicely handled; but one group failed to fulfil its task (to produce and put on a playlet). This was obviously due to lack of practice in organizing themselves and embarrassment at being 'on show'. In other words, naïveté about how to handle this informal groupwork situation militated against success in learning for some pupils.

A glance at the percentages in Figure 4 suggests that the most common type of cognitive transaction has to do with handling data. Thus teacher talk (T1), teachers' questions (Q1) and pupils' responses (R1) when taken together make up 61 per cent of transactions in the lessons with yr 3 slow, 63 per cent with yr 3 top (a), 64·5 per cent, with yr 3 top (b), 59 per cent, with yr 1 middle, 33·25 per cent, with yr 2 middle, 37·5 per cent, with yr 2 fast.

By contrast, stimulus from the teachers at a cognitive level (T2, Q2) is fairly unusual; and this is mirrored by the pupil responses at level 2. At an abstract level teacher talk at level 3 is non-existent. However, stimulus is partly maintained by higher order questions in the Q3, Q4, Q5 or Q6 categories. Out of exactly 400 questions asked in eighteen periods 85 (21 per cent) were higher order questions in the categories indicated.

In addition to transactions at a data level, the other common kind of transaction is that dealing with management of the class (T0, Q0, R0).

Here it is noteworthy that management makes up a greater proportion of transactions for the less experienced teachers, and is less obtrusive in the head of department's performance.

In the life of many classes there are numerous contacts (C) with individual pupils. The context in which these take place is that of the teacher monitoring work in progress. Typically, when the class is set a task or when self-directed groups are operating the teacher circulates to check on performance and discipline. In the present study the monitoring contacts were usually in the whole-class context (the opposite was true for science lessons in the same school). These contacts are normally made privately with a single pupil, of brief duration, and concerned not with learning but with organization. For example, a teacher may glance down and say: 'Margin, Johnny'; or she may ask 'Are you stuck?' and receive a negative response to end the exchange. These contacts could legitimately be described as 'oiling the wheels of classroom life'.

From the percentages in Figure 4 it will be seen that the proportion of contact transactions in a lesson was one of the features which distinguished the head of department's style from that of her less experienced colleagues. Mr B made many individual pupil contacts; and these were an extension of his class management. As a response to minor disruption he tended to set the class work and walk around to check on individuals. Mrs C's contact transactions tended to be concerned with the organization of her playlets in the third lesson observed. Mrs A's style was predominantly whole class teaching in which all transactions were public and furthered the progress of the class as a unit.

The picture which emerges from Figure 4 is one in which the weighting of verbal transactions in lessons is seen to be towards management of the class and information giving. A surprisingly small amount of thinking at a conceptual level is evidenced. Beyond this, at an abstract level, there is stimulus from teacher questions but very little response from pupils.

In examining written or performance tasks set by the teachers a clear distinction of approach emerges between the head of department on the one hand and her two young colleagues on the other. In Figure 5 a breakdown of tasks shows that twenty-one tasks were at a higher level. Of the nine higher level tasks all but one were set by the head of department while only one task is set at a higher level by the two younger teachers. The head of department's tasks are often set as homework between lessons, and form the most demanding part of the lesson. They provoke the pupils to apply knowledge and to think out issues. Those tasks set by Mr B and Mrs C usually related to collecting information by recourse to a textbook or biblical source.

Though the classification of tasks is crude, it is clear that (a) some tasks are more demanding in cognitive terms than others and (b) more cognitive demand is made on pupils in the tasks set than during oral exchanges in lessons (contrast Fig. 3).

Conclusion

This research would appear to demonstrate that much of the content, even of a cognitively demanding subject such as RE, is reduced by teachers to an informational level in the classroom. Between the ages of 11 + and 14 (the age-group covered by this study) pupils ought to be developing higher level thinking skills.[1] Yet only limited progress towards this end is made during lessons themselves. The findings suggest that, even in streamed situations, important concepts and abstract ideas are often either omitted or watered down in verbal transactions; and it is reasonable to suggest that teachers might take a new look at their syllabuses and their longer-term lesson planning to discover how more opportunities can be made for work involving higher level thinking skills when they talk to classes face to face.[2] There are implications here, too, for task analysis and evaluation of learning.[3] Nor are RE teachers alone in this, since comparative studies in other curriculum areas have painted a similar picture.[4]

Further work in progress suggests that the situation may be worse in mixed ability classes, a finding implied also by HM Inspectorate,[5] because of the tendency of teachers to aim lessons below the middle of the ability range. For bright pupils the dilemma is that they are simply not being stimulated to think and the resultant boredom is itself causing teachers some difficulties.[6]

References

1 Goldman, R. (1965). *Readiness for religion*, Routledge and Kegan Paul.
2 Kerry, T. and Dennison, A.R. (1980). *Teaching religious education*, Teacher Education Project, Nottingham University.
3 Kerry, T. (1979). 'Evaluating learning in RE: some possible approaches, *BJRE*, Vol. 2, No. 2.
4 Kerry, T., 'Pupils' thinking in science lessons', *School Science Review*, (forthcoming).
5 HM Inspectorate (1978). *Matters for discussion no 6: mixed ability teaching in comprehensive schools*, HMSO.
6 Kerry, T., 'Overcoming boredom for bright pupils in the classroom', *Journal of the Gifted Child*, (forthcoming).

*Religion in the Multi-Faith School**

W. Owen Cole

I wish to begin by stating that the multi-religious society which exists in Britain highlights certain needs in the area of religion in schools and perhaps makes decisions and responses urgent – but also by emphasizing the point that these decisions needed to be made anyway.[1]

The new settlers from Asia and the Caribbean have made us aware of the bad housing conditions in many of our large cities, they have made us recognize the inadequate provision which has been made for children from educational priority areas as they are now called and they remind us that our school curriculum is geared to the production of white Anglo-Saxon Protestants, *but*, and this is very important, they have not caused bad housing and they have not created educational priority areas. Cultural pluralism existed in Britain before they came and Asians made us aware of it, and they are not responsible for the movement from christian education to religious studies, which is our concern at this conference. In fact, such evidence of which I am aware – from the West Riding and, I am told, the East Midlands – suggests that those schools with Asian children in them are the very ones in which no movement from christian education to religious studies has taken place. If a shift can be seen in these schools it is, not surprisingly, from christian education to nothing!

There are reasons for this to which I hope to return later. However, before I can really settle to my subject I must put the multi-faith school into its wider context and suggest that religious studies in such a school must have the same philosophical base as that in Penzance, Alnwick or Dolgellau.

*This article first appeared in *Learning for Living*, Vol. 12, No. 2, November, 1972.

Understanding religion

The philosophical base must be religion, or religions, not Christianity – or for that matter Islam or Judaism.

In my view the aims must have to do with the understanding of religion rather than with conversion to any particular faith or even to a religious view of life. By the time he has left school we shall hope that the student will have some knowledge and understanding of the function of religion, of the questions it is appropriate to ask of religion (or the questions to which religions provide answers) and will have examined some of the answers which religions give.

Religion in schools will not, therefore, be an induction into belief. It is very important that we should recognize this, that we *all* should, Christian and Muslim. Until we do agree on this, progress in terms of curriculum development is impossible and the subject can only become a battleground. The suspicion and hostility engendered will result in its disappearance from the curriculum. The alternative to this is in our hands – but it demands two things.

Devotion and learning

First, that the traditional ambivalence – clearly demonstrated in such terms as RI or RE and in the persistent support for the retention of an act of worship (however modified), an ambivalence between wanting students to understand and wanting them to believe, must be ended. There is a difference between devotion and learning which must be respected once it has been recognized.

Secondly, at the same time Muslims, Jews, Sikhs and Hindus must understand what we in England mean by education, and must attempt to appreciate its aims. The concept of education which I have is very different from that of the average settler from Pakistan. It is no longer primarily an induction into a culture. To meet this need for understanding, permanent opportunities for meeting, as we are doing today, need to be provided. Is this week the end, an end of the beginning, or what?

I would ask you not to assume that the alternative to inducting children into religious belief is the type of arid religious studies which is a mere naming of the parts, a kind of RK – of catechism – but on a world scale! Neither is it a technique for eliminating Christianity from the syllabus! An objective study does not preclude reference to the faith being studied, whether humanism or Judaism, being seen to be vital and meaningful.

The teacher in the multi-faith school

Perhaps it is possible, now, to become more specific and examine the multi-faith school, beginning with the teacher. The teacher must be aware of the need for radical curriculum reappraisal. The changing world and the knowledge explosion – in my subject especially the awareness that at least five major religions exist besides Christianity – makes the task of handing on a body of knowledge impossible. Yet in spite of this one finds little response in history (the story of Britain's expansion and, less frequently, contraction) or geography (anchored fast to Greenwich) or religious studies – (the story of white Christianity).

The teacher must be aware of what concepts of school and religion the children (Muslims, etc.) possess. The teacher must also be aware of the needs of every child – including Christians and not forgetting the West Indians. Not long ago I heard a headmaster describing his grief in discovering that the many West Indians in his school were ashamed of their colour. The reason it seems, was that in history, religious studies, literature – and everything else that they learned – the black man existed only to be on the receiving end of white charity or white brutality. There is a need for black examples of caring, forgiveness, courage – Christian as well as Muslim, Hindu or Sikh.

The omission of Muslim, Jewish, Sikh or Hindu content in religious studies is a way of slapping the child on the face. It is a silent but real way of saying his beliefs are primitive or unimportant. Why are kind teachers guilty of creating prejudice by neglect? Why is Christianity or nothing the religion taught in multi-faith schools?

One reason is clearly lack of awareness. The multi-cultural factor has yet to be taken seriously in curriculum development – in any subject. No RE syllabus takes the multi-faith situation seriously. We are still preparing people for 1945 – when the oldest person in our school was born nearly ten years after the war ended and the youngest will not be much more than thirty in the year 2000.

Another, more important reason, is this. We cannot teach what we do not know, or to teach Islam with a Muslim in your class, even with knowledge, demands courage. The teachers in our multi-racial schools need competent retraining if their history, geography, home economics, literature, art. music and religious studies courses are to take seriously the Asian cultures represented in the schools so that multi-racial schools may become multi-cultural. And besides retraining they need primary school classes of no more than twenty-five children if their methods are to be anything but formal.

In-service retraining in so many things is becoming so urgent we might have to send children home for half a term while we re-educate ourselves!

What to teach

With regard to the material to be taught we must first make one general point. What has been said about the general, overall aims will apply, but the approach in a multi-faith school will differ in two respects.

First, the multi-faith element will be present from the beginning. There can be no debate when to introduce material from Islam when there are Muslims in the class.

Secondly, the multi-faith element must pervade every theme or topic as far as is possible. You cannot say to a secondary class 'Christianity this year and next – but we do Islam for a term in form three!'

Approaches

How is this to be done? I suggest in three tiers:

The Direct Concrete, from five to about nine[2]

Let me give an example.

In a reception class in Batley a teacher did a theme homes and families. The children discussed their homes – their brothers and sisters and other relatives – very soon they were talking about the extended family system (though not in so many words!). They talked about foods they liked – chapatis, jellabies, ladoo, as well as fish and chips or baked beans. Clothes – the sari and shalwarkameeze – were discussed.

The time was late January – and the muslim children were away from school for a couple of days for Idd (ul-Adha). The teacher encouraged them to describe their parties, and show their new clothes. She mounted some Idd cards. The muslim children had been enjoying one of their festivals rather as other children in the class had been enjoying Christmas.

This is what I call the direct concrete experience stage, from about five to nine. During it children can gain a simple awareness of each other's culture and can begin to realize that differences exist and are acceptable – that different means neither superior nor inferior. These differences can also be discovered to be interesting and enriching.

The content would be to do with foods, language, dress, homes and families, and holidays.

The direct experiences can be supplemented by stories from each other's heritages but these must be used with care. Myths are not fairy tales. Perhaps simple biographical stories or stories of caring, forgiveness and courage (moral courage) are the safest to use.

In the example described the Wendy house curtains became saris, in the class shop children were asking for a chapati and two jam tarts, please! Clearly experience spoke more strongly than stories.

We must take seriously the prejudices which can be fostered in the reception class. 'Manjit – what a funny name!' can be upsetting; sikh boys are often called cissy and have their hair pulled; my younger daughter was still four when she came home singing 'Jew, Jew, dirty old Jew'. Teachers should be aware of these things; they can overcome them. Similarly, non-eating of pork, or beef perhaps, and an awareness that Iqbal goes to the mosque, Bucksinder goes to the Gurdwara and speaks Punjabi at home and in the playground.

The Vicarious Concrete, from nine to thirteen

The content would not differ greatly from that in tier one: customs, costume and food, places of worship, festivals – but in more detail. One can begin to help the children accumulate more information – a character portrait of Mohammed, making a model of a mosque, listening to a record or tape of the call to prayer, making a jewish scroll, visiting a synagogue but still largely descriptive, informative, related to sense-experience rather than to beliefs.

Many themes can be used, for example, journeys (including Hajj and Exodus), books, India, oil.

One could use in this connection extracts from *Religion How and Why* or *Quest* or *Man–India* by BBC schools radio – but the point must be made here that the BBC has not yet gone beyond trying to cover a whole religion (founder, ritual, beliefs and all) in a twenty-minute programme! Quest Passover is the best I have come across – but they still had to throw in Bar Mitzvah and Kiddush for good measure.

Regarding filmstrips: Concordia and EP have useful ones for these age groups.

One can also, at this stage, explore such themes as courage or caring – if so, then Bhai Ghanaya, Gandhi and Martin Luther King must have a place, as well as the West Riding lists of white Christians.

The Third Tier, Beliefs, from thirteen onwards

The third tier, from thirteen onwards, is that which has to do with beliefs and, for the first time, an attempt to systematize religious studies.

From places of worship we can move to what worship is.

From a character portrait of Jesus as a man we can move to beliefs about his person and work. So too with Mohammed or Moses.

From the bible or guru granth sahib within the context of worship one can move on to the ways in which they are to be understood and the basic teachings enshrined in them – beliefs about God, man, death, and the meaning of life.

So much for detail. We can discuss and argue about that for hours. What I want you to consider seriously is the three tier programme I have put forward.

It seems to me that religion in schools is vitiated by two wrong desires from which come almost all our sufferings. (I acknowledge the Buddha's influence.)

The desire to bring children to a religious view of life, hence the ambivalence already mentioned.

The desire to introduce beliefs at a much too young age.

We must programme our subject, not too inflexibly I hope, from direct experience, to the study of beliefs. Consequently, I hope you will feel that the three tier programming I have put forward merits careful thought.

Different beliefs

If we are honest, however we programme our courses and whatever their content, we must recognize that students will, at the point where we examine beliefs, if not sooner, be faced with the fact that not all people believe the same thing. In the BBC school programme on Gandhi, broadcast in June, 1972, one heard of him being 'imprisoned unjustly' by the British for taking salt from the sea shore and being shot by a Hindu for muslim sympathies. Aurangzeb is to the Muslim pious but to the Sikh a murderer. Jews and Christians cannot explain the meaning of Jesus' death in the same way. Jew, Muslim and Christian cannot agree upon the person of Jesus. Yet intellectual integrity, not to mention human tolerance, demands that the divisive elements in religion are examined at the appropriate place, in the upper school. Sometimes one hears teachers doubting their ability to do this, or to present Islam or Judaism in a fair way. I am aware of the problems but I wonder whether they really know what they are saying about themselves and their objectives.

Church or denominational schools may fall outside my talk but if we are apprehensive about the creation of Muslim schools how can we encourage the survival of Jewish or Quaker establishments?

Assembly

Finally, one must say a word about assembly, though this is a lecture topic in its own right.

To be objective in the classroom and to ask for worship in the hall is either to be woolly in our thinking (or perhaps evasive of thought altogether), or to suggest that our objectivity is a sham. It is in the school hall that our ambivalence of intention is most clearly seen.

If the assembly is to survive, perhaps one can make three points, relevant to the multi-faith school including the all-white Christian and the secularist. The assembly cannot be an act of worship: it may provide opportunities for sharing common awarenesses or concerns: it may provide occasions when Jews can explain Passover, or the Sikhs a Burpurb, or Christian Easter, to the rest of the school.

Ultimately, however, in viewing assembly as anachronistic, I return to one of my first points – it is not because of the presence of Jews and others that I ask for the abolition of assembly; it is because of my philosophy of religion in school.

In conclusion I would suggest that for far too long the principle of educational change has been 'ad hocery'. I therefore ask that we look at religion in this multi-faith school first in terms of philosophy, secondly in terms of the child's needs and experience, and thirdly, in terms of tolerance and understanding, but above all, I ask that we will not permit the multi-faith situation to bring religion in schools back under the domination of the confessionalists from which it is only just being rescued – whether they be Christian, Muslim or humanist.

Notes

1 This paper was presented at the Leicester DES course 39, July, 1972, and to delegates at the British Council of Churches conference on Inter Faith Dialogue.

2 The example of the Direct Concrete was written up by a student of the James Graham College, Mrs Marjorie Gee, and was included in full in the mailing, No, 4, of the CEM primary association scheme.

*The Multi-Faith Situation in the Secondary School**

Robin Minney

Kenya and Britain

Minority religions are increasingly found in British schools. For some this presents a serious problem, and one answer is to step up the teaching of Christianity, usually on the cultural argument that this is the faith of our country. The situation is not new, however, in East Africa, where school integration since independence, and in a few cases before that, has brought together Muslim, Hindu, Sikh and Christian, both children and teachers. Yet when I revisited Kenya in August 1972 in order to do some in-service work for teachers of religion I was asked for guidance, particularly by secondary school teachers, on how they might teach religion in a multi-faith situation. Of course if one broadens one's brief to mean the teaching of world religions (at the very least for part of the time) the whole thing ceases to be a problem and becomes a great opportunity.

Yet very few secondary school teachers in urban Kenya had really assessed the situation. One Nairobi teacher showed some excellent children's work along the lines that I am about to suggest. As I teach world religions in a British college of education, I was glad of this opportunity with them to put out a series of ideas which now find expression in this article.

The basic outline was a scheme with five stages. Each stage represents a year at secondary school, or that part of a year devoted to world religions. A favourable chance for course continuity might suggest starting in the primary school, and for a middle school the first two or three stages might be ideal. This would need to be tried.

Stage one: collecting

The first stage is purely inductive. Teachers were shocked when I said

*This article first appeared in *Learning for Living*, Vol. 13, No. 1, September, 1973.

they did not really need to know anything about the various religions, although under questioning I had to admit that some background does help. For this stage is one of collecting. If the children come from several religions, then they themselves provide a clear starting point. Unless they are very shy, and individual shyness does need to be handled gently, they can be asked to contribute from their home and community environment songs, pictures, perhaps objects like a shawl, garland or prayer mat, strictly on loan of course, and later encouraged to retell orally or in writing some of the ceremonies and festivals.

This kind of approach aims to achieve two things: the first is as far as possible an experience of the religion concerned. Music live and recorded, readings, even clothing and smells like joss sticks, perhaps food also, can provide something of the atmosphere. This is already being done in primary schools in Britain sometimes for assembly, but if well planned could also be a classroom activity at secondary level without asking other staff to redraw the timetable. In addition a kind of scrap-book is collected, not just writing and pictures, but also tapes and colour slides, with information about each of the religions represented: this is the second aim.

Of course anyone can object that such an approach is unsystematic. Important things may be left out, vital world faiths be quite unrepresented. But there are on the other hand some very big advantages. Christianity is pretty complex in its doctrines and its manifestations, and it is not really accurate to present other religions either as if they were straightforward and uniform, although some have more, and more important, variations than others. Consequently the teacher need not worry too much about presenting an unbalanced picture. All material collected by children is likely to be relevant because they will be attracted to those aspects which they find interesting. The theologically educated may want to separate what is strictly religious from social custom and national and regional idiosyncrasies. I am sure that it would be a mistake to do this with first year children. At a later stage the complexities of religious and cultural dialectic will become clearer. The teacher should accept everything the children contribute, unless something is actually misleading and likely to cause confusion at a later stage – and it is worth remembering that this is envisaged as only the first of several stages.

One of the Nairobi teachers had in fact encouraged secondary girls to make project-books, with pictures, cuttings and their own compositions, each about one of the various religions represented in the class (in every case their own). There was in fact a good balance, and Christian, Muslim, Hindu and Sikh were represented. They certainly made colourful and informative scrap-books, and encouraged teachers to be even more ambitious in future. Activities could include visits to places of worship, getting outside speakers, perhaps parents, to the school, and getting children to go out in pairs or small groups with a camera and tape recorder to witness festivals or interview people.

These activities, of course, need very careful preparation. Religion is often a sensitive area, particularly among minority groups, and it is not only recent immigrants who can feel they are being got at. Consequently the interviews need preparation by the teacher, not only for the children, but even more for the individuals to be interviewed. The same is true for a visit to temple, synagogue or mosque, and not only must care be taken to build a friendly relationship with religious leaders, but children must learn to respect the scruples and pieties of strangers with sensitive politeness. In Britain one of the problems in getting outside speakers to the school has been that even in large immigrant areas it is hard to find a Muslim imam or Hindu priest who speaks clearly enough in English to ensure a successful meeting with the children. In Nairobi, of course, this is no problem as there are many educated men and women of all faiths who speak English well, and some of them are also themselves teachers and so know what they are likely to be in for. This will become the situation in England too eventually, and the arrival of East African Asians (some of them teachers) is speeding the process.

The real advantage of the inductive approach to religion is that with few exceptions whatever interests the children will be suitable material for their age. What they themselves collect they will assimilate in the form which matches their development. This will be true both for the class and for individuals, and they will learn more of the feel of religions from each other than from the teacher.

The main hurdle is the psychological one which seems to nag most teachers at some stage, that somehow, somewhere, there is a complete and perfect series of lessons on any subject (dare one call it a syllabus?) which will suddenly show them up and find them wanting. Personally I feel that this is a hangover from Platonist philosophy, and that not only is it not true for world religions, but that even the idea that it might be true is positively harmful as it robs religion of life and movement and meaning, in fact the very things that make it important. It is good to try to be systematic at some stage (a later one) especially in academic study, but it is hypocrisy to pretend that any presentation can be perfectly balanced or complete. If this were possible the perfect textbook would have been written years ago, and most of us would be out of a job. In practice the best textbooks are the books you make yourself. This does not imply that they are complete, but their production represents a sustained learning process.

Stage two: how it all began

The collections children bring in the first stage are going to include stories of saints and founders, and some historical material. This is the basis for stage two. Not only are the stories interesting in themselves, but they match a desire many children feel to find out how things began and why they are as they are today. This does not of course only depend on their origins. A study of founders and others can be made together with dates and as much or little social and historical background as seems appropriate for the children concerned. But background in some measure is important because it helps to develop in children two important concepts: first that religion is (hobbies apart) closely integrated with political and economic conditions, and second, it gives them a sense of historical change and development. Saints and leaders are important in this way too, where they can be disentangled from the sort of timeless legends which are (in my opinion) better reserved for project work later. The idea of historical expression and development is powerfully expressed in art. Pictures of the Buddha, for instance, and scenes of his life can be found from Chinese silk paintings, frescoes in India, and relief carving and statuary. In using these pictures, sculptures, manuscripts or whatever, it is well worth pointing out their origin, both in time and country, because this emphasizes the need which all religions have for cultural expression which is particular to a time and society. Similarities and differences in style and emphasis can teach a lot about a religion, for recurrent emphases suggest aspects which were felt to be important in spite of changes in the life-situation of the faithful. There is plenty of scope in this stage also for inductive work, but the teacher has to provide more guidance than at the first stage, and probably a good deal of the material.

This stage too is probably the best for introducing the scriptures of the faiths under study. Many texts relate to founders and events. The scriptures will of course be found relevant and important at all stages after this. If a study of the scriptures is undertaken which is going to be more than short extracts – and this is a decision which a teacher can only take with particular children in mind – then he should emphasize the time span of the writing process. Different books belong to different periods which entail different material backgrounds and stages in theological and philosophical development.

The third stage: longing and fears

The third stage grows naturally out of the previous work, and in some cases can hardly help being anticipated. The basic idea is to use the art and mythologies of different religious traditions in order to explore human ideas on creation, life, evil and so on, the basic human enquiries which recur in myths and art. Undoubtedly there will be some discussion work at this stage, but the intention is to begin firmly with actual examples of what people have felt and wanted to express (verbally and non-verbally) as a preparation for a more speculative approach to life's problems at fifth and sixth form level.

Both art and myth – in some ways they are forms of each other – express man's longings and fears. Many of these are universal, as first Frazer, now Levi-Strauss maintain, but others, especially in their detail, belong to a particular situation. Where rituals relate to myths (using this word now in its Old Testament sense), it would be right to make a deeper study of worship and also of religious custom. This can be an extremely creative period of adolescence, particularly where children's emotions are involved, and children ought to be exposed to beauty and poetry, and helped to appreciate and nurture their own sensitivities. This kind of approach can have useful spin-offs for other subjects. From such beginnings might grow an absorbing interest in Siamese dance, Persian art, or Indian architecture. The possibilities for inter-disciplinary work are unbounded.

The fourth stage: problems and responses

The development of the next stage depends a good deal on the leanings and abilities of the group concerned. This often happens as children are grouped in different types of learning ability. The basic idea is the kind of discussion and project work often undertaken in years four and five. In addition to the Newsom-inspired activities often and rightly undertaken at this stage, academic students should be encouraged from time to time to take a philosophical look at the kind of issues which underlie all or any human projects and interrelations. The philosophies of Buddhist and Hindu sages, Christian and Muslim saints and thinkers can be drawn on to illuminate such problems as love and war, right and wrong. Alternative answers can be discussed, and the students encouraged (as always) to formulate their own. The only criterion is that the problems themselves should be relevant; and here, as in the first stage, the best guide to relevance is provided by the students themselves. The teacher does not need to be an expert in philosophy, but should know where to get information and illustrations, and he needs to understand that one religion can harbour several philosophies, and one philosophy reclothe itself in different religious societies. Confession and life-view do not go hand in hand. The Penguins on Buddhism, Islam and Hinduism provide ideas in this field, and Smart's *The Religious Experience of Mankind* gives a good introduction to the philosophers who have been most influential within the major faiths.

Most students, however, would gain more from a less verbalizing approach. For them the philosophical and theological ideas must be expressed in the vivid images and examples used by the sages themselves, and these can give an extra depth to projects like sharing, or poverty. But the examples need to be well chosen, and the less academic the students, the more diligent the teacher will have to be in searching through the commentaries and writings for suitable material which can be used or adapted for use.

The first stage in this scheme will have made clear how difficult it is to separate religious practices from social custom, and it is really not necessary to try and make fine distinctions. It seems to me perfectly natural and legitimate for the fourth stage to concentrate on social practices and cultural forms, which are easy to see in a multi-faith society, and philosophical analysis need go no further than discussing the reasons for what is observed. This can be done by a more sophisticated version of the interview technique suggested at stage one, and it is presumed that the course will now be sufficiently established as a serious venture for parents and others to be encouraged to co-operate. This indeed can be a very valuable social experience, and not just for parents who have come from abroad. Another advantage of parental participation is that the children are helped to see the older generation in a new and co-operative light.

The final stage: one religion

The fifth stage is rather specialized. It is perhaps asking more of both teacher and students than any of the others. In reality, of course, the whole course in world religions has been an exploration of the religious dimension of life, but at the fifth stage this becomes explicit, and students are intended to specialize in one religion, not their own. Psychological and sociological aspects are to be studied, phenomena of priesthood and prophetism, ritual and religious expression, with the aim of isolating the quality or activity which religion is: that which underlies all religion.

This is not by any means to suggest that all religions are the same, but rather that religion for all its many forms and manifestations is something basic and essential to what is human. The attempt to express this theologically also will, or at least ought to, emphasize that most of these forms are in fact non-verbal. They are wordless because they are too deep, arising from the depths of the human and divine encounter. Even within the allegiance to one faith there are countless forms and expressions, and yet what gleams through the differences is precisely the unity of mankind in our primal destiny and in our relation to God. In practice students have quite spontaneously declared that an understanding and respect for the religions of other men has deepened and clarified their personal faith within their own religious tradition. Conversions from faith to faith are few. I know of none which can be ascribed to a course of this kind.

The whole inductive approach should make clear that the aim of such a course is not religious knowledge. There will be plenty of knowledge in fact but the aim is a depth of feeling of and for the divine and the properly human. This is basically why only those who wish to be academic need to be systematic in their theology. Consistence is a good thing, but consistence in outlook and relationships is worth more than a well-argued library. The course should encourage a growth in religious awareness. This growth need not stop on leaving school. The beauty of a truly inductive approach is that the questions are always faced at the level on which the children actually are. In this way both interest and relevance keep pace with their development.

*Teaching the Bible in School**

Paul D. Fueter

The way Bible stories are taught very often vaccinates young people against it instead of liberating them from false religious categories. Teachers should encourage their pupils to communicate biblical texts. This develops the children's creativity and introduces them to different media (print, drawing, cartoons, drama, sound recording, slide series, films) so that they may master them instead of being seduced by them.

Pedagogical presuppositions for a responsible use of the Bible in the classroom

Whatever the churches may teach concerning the necessity of putting the Bible in the core of Christian education, we dare only introduce it into the classroom on sound pedagogical grounds. This presupposes a proper understanding of the role of religious education (RE) in schools.

When a teacher says to his pupils: 'What I am saying may be boring you today, but in a few years you will discover that it all was worthwhile', he is not realistic. When we say this about RE and (worse about Bible teaching) we may find a few who later may be vocally thankful, but the majority will wonder why we invested so much effort in giving them useless information about an irrelevant book.

To hope that RE and especially regular study of the Bible in school has something to do with 'bringing young people to Christ' is a delusion. It is problematical to encourage any religious experience in the competitive and hierarchical atmosphere of the classroom. The best news will be perceived as bad news when one is forced to listen to it.

It is beside the point to suppose that the aim of RE is to impart knowledge

*This article first appeared in *British Journal of Religious Education*, Vol. 2, No. 1, Autumn, 1979.

concerning the geography, history, languages and cultures of certain groups in the Middle East two to four thousand years ago. Today's travellers and television viewers know much more about life in the Lebanon and Egypt than their forefathers, yet much less about what it means to be a Christian.

The aim of a RE curriculum is not simple to describe. It must be based on the general pedagogical principle of helping the new generation to make informed and responsible choices in a complex world. But it is unwise, in our view, to encourage religious choices within the school system. The power position of the teacher, the competitive relation between the pupils, the necessary discipline within the four walls of the classroom tend to prevent 'free decisions' which are, in our thinking, the specificity of religious choices.

But the moment pupils leave the school precincts, they will inevitably be confronted with religious problems. They meet adherents of different faiths, they see various religious rites on television, they are invited to join various sects and movements. At home, their parents may have refused to sign a paper dispensing them from attending RE on the grounds: 'I may not be a practising Christian, but I want you to be able to choose for yourself. . . .'

The main aim of RE is therefore not as some say: 'to help pupils to understand the function of religion in European history.' What we want is to give our pupils the necessary tools for making their present or future religious choices as meaningful as possible. They should learn to assume their own religious experience and verbalize it.

In other words, teachers should enable their pupils to come to decisions based on reflection. But our religious choices will only become conscious when we try to communicate them to others. An experience, whether spiritual or sentimental, of which we cannot speak will remain in the limbo of the subconscious. The mastery of words and the understanding of symbolic actions is therefore an essential element of religious education. Teachers should create the type of environment where self-expression is the norm, and provide vocabulary and media to achieve this end.

A practical example

This approach has been practised under Bible Society auspices and has proved successful. The following example illustrates how this has been done by a teacher of religion in a German school, with 11-year-old pupils (sixth year of school) when dealing with the parables of Jesus.

The teacher began with a lesson on the role of pictures and gestures, proverbs and aphorisms in human communication. The pupils were then invited to read and act a play on 'The King and the Governor', a modern transposition of the parable of the Unforgiving Servant (*Matthew* 18.21–24) from a RE textbook.

In the following lesson the way the textbook presented the story was criticized, since it failed to set the biblical story in its context. The teacher thus retold the story of Peter, asking how many times he should forgive (seven times?) and how Jesus answered. The pupils wrote down a short question–answer summary of the conversation, highlighting the aim of the parable. Their homework consisted in finding modern situations making an equivalent point. Their results were presented and discussed in class later.

The next parable to be studied was the story of the Unfruitful Fig-Tree (*Luke* 13.6–9), which was treated on the same pattern as before. The teacher then asked the pupils to recall what they knew of the Prodigal Son (*Luke* 15.11–32) and distributed worksheets with cartoon strips on the story (one prepared in the Philippines and another in West Africa) in which the speech bubbles had been blanked out. The pupils were asked to fill in the bubbles as they thought best. A discussion on this homework elicited an exchange on the frustrations pupils experience at home and at school. The task of creating a dialogue between the father and the older son had revealed the seeming injustice of the father's action, and the pupils identified themselves with the jealous first-born. After discussing the different symbols and techniques used by the cartoon strips in dealing with the subject, the pupils were then asked to draw their own actualizing cartoon strip of the parable. This they did, some even producing a tape with a dialogue and music and others writing a contemporary story. In many cases they revealed themselves in an unexpected way through that creative work.

This was school work, so it had to be evaluated. After a period recalling the method, the pupils were formally tested on the parable of the Publican and the Pharisee (*Luke* 19.9–14). They were given the text with questions concerning the symbols used by the author. One-third of the pupils added the outline of a valid transposition of that story, which they had never studied before. This was then marked by the teacher.

We should note the following points when reflecting on this experience:

1 The Bible as a book was not introduced into this class but parables were read from a school textbook, recalled from memory, presented in cartoon strips addressed to two modern, yet alien target audiences.
2 The teacher took the pupils' actual situation seriously and tried to get them to work two by two (comparing the Prodigal Son's cartoons) or as groups. Bible background was only discussed in answer to the question: 'How can we communicate this faithfully to our neighbours and elicit reactions which would be equivalent to those of the original readers?'
3 When speaking about the Bible, the full context was respected,

past communication situations and symbols were made explicit, and the rudiments of structural analysis were taught as a tool for communicating.

4 The pupils were given the opportunity to express themselves creatively in the process of communicating a story from another culture into their own culture.

5 This communication process triggered the type of personal discussion through which pupils expressed some of their deepest concerns. In this case, the introduction of the Bible (though not as a book) into the classroom did not hamper self-expression; on the contrary. Words like forgiveness, punishment, jealousy, God's love, parental love, change of life, were used existentially.

6 Various media (a play, cartoon strips, story-telling) were introduced and pupils were encouraged to use these techniques in expressing themselves.

Why and how can the Bible be introduced in the classroom?

In the previous section we have described a special case where the Bible has been introduced responsibly in the class situation. Before describing general methods of using the Bible in religious education, some of the reasons for doing so should be presented.

The Bible consists of two collections of books. The first is the cultural heritage of the people of Israel, the second contains the witness of the first Christian leaders to the life and work of Christ. The secular interest in both collections, and their influence justifies the place which many teachers of history, art, languages and philosophy allot to it in their lessons. But we have to take seriously the opinion of religious educators that present Bible teaching practice vaccinates many against it though it may interest a chosen few. At the same time, more and more discover that pupils are becoming increasingly fed up with modern approaches to RE, which leave out the Bible in order to concentrate on social and ethical questions. We shall adduce three reasons for using the Bible in school, which, in our view, might be helpful:

1 Pupils will best be helped to understand the nature of religious choices by speaking about those of other people. In retelling a story in our own way, we prove to ourselves that we have understood it, but we also use words and symbols creatively. The exercise becomes all the more valid if it is based on a text translated from another language written two to three thousand years ago, in a totally different culture from our own. In transposing a text into his environment, the pupil is not directly involved in its message. He can choose whether it speaks to him or not. He can later recall the class experience without

necessarily feeling concerned with what was communicated.

2 European culture has been moulded by biblical thought patterns. Christians have used the media of their time to tell the stories about the Patriarchs and Jesus for centuries. By learning how to communicate those self-same stories today, pupils may understand better how Bach, Rembrandt and Dorothy Sayers did it, and acquire criteria for the proper appreciation of their own traditions. Meaningful religious choices cannot be based on the blind acceptance of past attitudes. Thus, it is not easy today to claim that Adam and Eve were the first humans walking on earth. When the authors of *Genesis* spoke of their ancestors as having met God in the garden of Eden six thousand years ago, they had a notion of time, space and genealogy very different from ours. When our fathers tried to transmit their understanding of these texts, they had to contend with nineteenth century idealism. How can we help our pupils to discover how the story of Adam and Eve challenges their own presuppositions?

3 The authors and redactors of the gospels and epistles, the Psalms and prophecies, the historical and wisdom literature of the Bible, wrote in order to communicate God's message to their fellow men in a language they could understand. Their attempt is exemplary; it shows how it is possible for human beings to be told about God's actions. It is not simply what they wrote, but the way they dealt with the problem of God's relation to humanity, which is the reason for the permanent influence of this collection of books. Any attempt at transposing the biblical message into our own culture confronts us with God's acting in the world as an existential question, not as a dogmatic or philosophical speculation. When the teacher, for himself or together with his pupils, is translating (or better, transposing) a biblical text into their own situation, he helps them to overcome the dogmatic and intellectual approaches which often prevent them from taking the Church seriously.

The method of using the Bible in order to develop the pupils' creativity in expressing themselves among their peers can be described in a few sentences:

Introduce the text by inviting the pupils to try and communicate its message to others.

Read the text together with the pupils as it is, naïvely and simply.

Invite the pupils to answer the following four questions in relation to the text:

1 What is the communication situation revealed by the text: 'Who says what to whom and why?'

2 What are the verbal symbols and the symbolic actions found in the text, and what would be their significance in that particular culture?

3 Who would today correspond to the persons mentioned and what verbal symbols and symbolic actions would elicit an equivalent reaction from them?
4 What would be the media through which we could make our experience accessible to our specific audience?

In the course of asking these four questions within the context of 'We want to communicate this story to others', pupils will be motivated to seek the information they need to understand the original communication situation and its use of symbols. Rather than impart this formally, resource material should be put at their disposal.

The best way of proceeding is to create groups of six to eight pupils. Questions can also be given as homework so that the answers can be shared by all. Group work will develop personal relations amongst students who will discover that one has to think in order to communicate meaningfully.

The Bible in the media in schools

If we want to help our pupils to communicate meaningfully, we have to examine critically how they perceive the world they live in. They are, consciously or unconsciously, oppressed and even seduced by the multitude of the information they receive every day through the various media used in our society. This is not a new problem. The children of the industrial revolution were also seduced by the development of cheap books and newspapers. But the school system of the time was geared to teaching essay-writing, introducing the main information media into the classroom. The pupils of the village school thus learned the basic skill of the writer.

Electronic communication has now displaced writing from its unique position and our school systems are beginning to face this new situation. Now is the time for teachers of religion in school (or in catechumen classes) to take advantage of their relative freedom from traditional curricula. By inviting our pupils to transpose the biblical text into our cultural situation and symbols, we give them an opportunity to communicate what they really feel in a society which often puzzles and oppresses them.

When they write creatively, use a paint brush or a pot of glue, record Bible readings with musical background or prepare a drama based on their understanding of a biblical text, they can 'be themselves'. They will also learn that the media which puzzle them so often in daily life are there to be used and not to be submitted to.

The primary function of the Bible in school is therefore to enable pupils to express themselves in a world where religious symbols are, for good or evil, taken from the Bible.

There are also two secondary functions of the Bible in our schools:

1 In order to express themselves meaningfully in their society, the pupils need '*basic information*'. When it comes to biblical communication, they should have access to the biblical text itself, faithfully translated at their language level and attractively printed. They also need adequate helps for understanding the history and the nature of the biblical books, as well as the cultural background of their first readers. This they can learn through seeing films, studying maps, hearing records. There is no end of education tools available for this purpose.

2 The world in which we live generally looks at the media productions as entertainment. Our pupils are constantly confronted with the media at home, in the cinema or in the discothèques. Usually they look at them as entertainment. But churches, schools and politics use them also for teaching, and the Bible is often presented in one way or another. Our pupils must learn to look at such presentations *critically*. The teacher's aim is to help his pupils to resist the seduction of the media. He wants them to understand what the world or the Church do to the Bible when they present it in films and pictures. The new generation should become aware of what the Sunday school, the catechism classes, the Sunday services and the evangelistic meetings do in fact communicate.

Our search for a meaningful use of the Bible in school has therefore led us to a study of the different media through which the pupils can express themselves. In order to try and put some order in what has been called 'the media jungle', we have listed seven different approaches and shared some of the experiences made by teachers in different schools in Northern Europe. We have tried to indicate methods for self expression, their use for information and criteria for critique for each of them.

1 Writing and printing

To be understood, the biblical text has to be translated from Hebrew or Greek into the pupils' own language. This is creative work with paper and pen, which presupposes some knowledge as to what was written in the original languages. Pupils can for instance be asked: 'How would you put the following sentence:

> 'Yahweh is my shepherd, I will not want;
> He leads me to green grass'

into your own language?' To do this or similar exercises, word for word rendering of chosen texts can be submitted in typed or printed form to fifteen-year-old pupils. To learn how to translate past and present biblical jargon into one's own language is to learn to communicate.

But a good Bible translation will respect the strangeness of the social structure and symbolism of the original text. Pupils can be invited to transpose a modern translation into their own cultural situation. Typed or printed 'transpositions' into other contemporary cultures can spur the pupils on to write their own, which can in turn be reproduced on the blackboard or through an overhead projector.

If a student is to learn how to translate or how to transpose a biblical text, he needs to be *informed* about biblical languages and cultures. Printed material, introductions, explanations of biblical texts are necessary. But such printed information must be easily accessible. The traditional school Bible distributed to the pupils may have made sense in a society where the 'Good Book' was regularly handled at home and in the church, and not reserved for taking an oath in court. . . . Today the printed Bible should function in school as a resource book and be conceived as such. It should be found in the library (possibly in the classroom for religious education). Pupils should not be obliged to carry it from the home to the school.

Pupils should also learn to *discern the merits* of the various Bible translations and editions on the market. Criteria for a good Bible translation and presentation should be established in class. A study of 'how the Bible was produced and published through the ages' not only illustrates the history of communication and printing, but demonstrates how the attitudes of people towards the reading of the Bible have changed. The big family Bible in the seventeenth century had a very different function from the pocket edition of the twentieth.

2 Drawing and painting

For Jews and many Christians, the biblical text is the first 'icon', the first holy image. But it was often necessary to use words to describe objects which can best be visualized through a plan or a model. The tabernacle described in Exodus, Solomon's or Ezekiel's temple can be drawn or even cut out in cardboard. Prophets like Isaiah, Daniel or the author of the Book of Revelation wrote down visions which become impressive when one draws or paints them.

Children and pupils love to illustrate Bible stories and communicate themselves freely through using colours and paint. The teacher, however, should give the pupils an opportunity to share his thought without conditioning their self-expression. Colouring pre-drawn black and white pictures or copying models may be counter-productive. A child should be allowed to be creative, more, he should be invited to explain in his own words why he represents what he read in this particular way. Our pupils should be given an opportunity to ask each other what they meant so that they can reveal how they understood the text. Most children tend to idealize, or even moralize, a message.

It is therefore necessary for the teacher to tell the story in a way that remains faithful to the author's intent. He must have understood it before he tries to retell it at his pupils' language level. He should remember that the biblical narratives are not all of the same kind. Some are the witness of the apostles or the evangelists, others are ancestor stories or folklore. Some are to be memorized ritually, others to be understood factually. The children of the people of Israel heard all of them, sometimes around a fire, or at other times, at the occasion of a sacrifice. To retell them to a captive audience in the classroom may distort them so that the aim becomes lost. The teacher's presentation should not result in pupils drawing pictures which go against the message itself.

When a class discusses the pictures drawn by pupils, each one's creation must be respected, like the pupil himself. The interpretation given by the 'artist' can, however, be analysed, and possibly critized, for example, by a question: 'Would it not have been better to draw this another way to make your point?'

Illustrated biblical texts can convey *information* in a way print on its own can never do. Many scholars have based their Bible illustrations on detailed archaeological knowledge of the ordinary objects and customs of the past. It is important to bring the Holy Land down to earth. Palestine is not a 'never-never-land'. In the classroom it should become a geographical area like any other. It is the country where certain events important to Jews, Christians and Moslems have taken place.

All through our history, *great artists* have tried to communicate the biblical message through painting on walls, glass panes, and canvas. We can help pupils to appreciate, understand and criticize their work. The painters of the middle ages did not necessarily believe that angels were blond youths with wings and long curly hair, they followed an artistic convention of their time. They mastered their art and some had deep insights into what the Bible teaches. Others, however, were rather superficial. Our pupils will learn to understand the text, their own culture and history as well as the medium in a new way when comparing, for instance, how the crucifixion was depicted through the ages.

3 Cartoon strips and caricatures

A picture of Jesus healing the daughter of Jairus cannot communicate what the Lord said to the mourning family or the words he addressed to the young girl. The cartoon strip has the advantage of combining text and drawing in such a way that it allows the flow of time to be visualized. It can become a satisfactory medium for communicating the biblical message in a society where the moving image with sound has invaded the sitting room. Cartoon strips are films printed on paper, hence their appeal to our generation.

Bible cartoon strips are very useful in developing self-expression through Bible communication for they need little equipment (a ruler, paper, pen and colours) and can be reproduced in print or sound slide series. As in the case of making a film, the script must first be written down with indications to the artist concerning the position of the imaginary camera: important sentences will be stressed through close-ups, panoramic views will introduce the biblical background of the story. To be true to this particular medium, suspense has to be created before bringing out the point of the message. To do this, special attention should be given to the communication situation. For instance, the text's indications concerning the public who listened to the parables of Jesus should be part of the cartoon strip.

The major problem is, however, how to transpose supernatural events without creating the impression that 'it is all science fiction' or that Jesus was a 'superman'. For cartoon strips have their own ways of dealing with symbols. When their authors try to communicate a story, they introduce caricature, exaggerating certain aspects of reality in order to communicate their message. There exists no real Charlie Brown, though he really lives in each one of us. This communication device has already been used by the biblical authors. To an ordinary reader, they exaggerate when they speak of what is behind our ordinary perception, what does not belong to the observable cosmic phenomenal universe. They had to go beyond the visible and tangible world in order to speak of God's mystery. The speck in your eye and the beam in mine, the voices of heaven saying to the shepherds 'The Messiah has been born', the darkness from the sixth to the ninth hour at the crucifixion, all extend our reality to communicate the reality of God's love. Pupils should understand this positive aspect of the medium, and be encouraged to caricature when expressing themselves through it.

In class the teacher can for instance tell his pupils: 'Decide how many frames you will need to make a cartoon strip of this story. Write the texts to be put in the bubbles for the various people in the story. Indicate, for each picture, what you will draw, from what angle it should be seen, and what should be the central person. Then, take a ruler, make six squares per page, and try to draw these pictures, communicating this message to your neighbours.' To introduce such an exercise, the pupils may well be given a Bible cartoon with empty bubbles, so that they can insert their own dialogue. This exercise will help them to see how to develop the use of this medium.

Bible cartoon strips can also be used as a source of *background information* for the pupils. The advantage of the better Bible cartoons on the market is that they introduce biblical stories with information known by all first readers of the Bible. The detailed study of such productions in the classroom may do more for an understanding of the real strangeness of the biblical *milieu* than hours of tedious explanation.

There are, however, real problems when using Scripture cartoon in the school. In the previous paragraph we noted that the written text itself is an 'icon' or holy image through which God's message has been communicated. Writing leaves our imagination free to create our own images, but illustrations tend to bind us. In films and cartoon strips, our freedom may be limited by the pictorial dimension dominating the text. A cartoon narrative of Moses and the people of Israel crossing the Red Sea with huge walls of water on their right and left may beg questions which the reading of Exodus does not suggest. An angel telling Zachariah he will have a son may be perceived as a visitor from Mars. Some cartoon publishers increase the number of words per bubble in order to avoid such misunderstandings. But professional designers criticize this as a violation of the medium's own principles. We should say all we can through the drawing, and only add words when absolutely necessary.

To understand the limitations of this medium, a *critique* of existing cartoons is therefore essential. Pupils who have created their own will best be able to criticize what others have done. Various criteria for judging can be formulated, and these may be helpful not only to understand the Bible but also the ideology of Asterix and Lucky Luke, which in some way conflicts with the realism which the biblical text itself applies to the so-called 'heroes' of the Bible.

4 *Drama and play-acting*

Writing, drawing, printing are purely visual media. They transform and stifle life so that it becomes two-dimensional. One of the most universal media is drama or play acting. Mime, songs, dance, musical comedy and theatre plays allow a group to communicate a message dynamically and forcefully.

This medium is extensively used in religious education. Many teachers tell their pupils to play 'the story they read in the Bible'. In that way, they can understand better the original communication situation (What type of person was Judas, or Peter, or John?), the content of the dialogues (What did Jesus really say to Nicodemus and what was the answer?) and the symbolism of the text (What does it mean to have one hundred sheep, and one gets lost?). But such a transfer of the text into life situations and dialogues is but a first step in understanding the text. It is not yet 'self-expression' and 'communication' in the full sense of the term.

The real aim of play-acting should be to create in the spectator a reaction which is similar to the one the author wanted to create in his first listeners. This is as difficult as the first step may have been easy and simple. Yet it has its own rewards, since it allows the presenting group to find a new identity and can result in a dialogue between the actors and the public. The aim of play-acting is to encourage the participation of the spectators.

But straight drama may not be suitable for all ages. Children in the higher age groups may find such self-expression too direct. It would be a contradiction in terms if teachers were to enforce the use of media for self-expression.

Many other less personal media can be introduced and used:

puppets: when children are not seen (hidden in the box) and engage in dialogues by means of self-made puppets they manipulate with their hands.
shadow plays: when young people are unrecognizable behind an illuminated white sheet and act symbolically. Slides can also be projected on to the sheet, and recorded music accompany the performance with great effect.
mimes: when the group expresses itself without words, the body uses its own language in prearranged movements.
dance and music: this is another form of miming, but can be accompanied with repetitive movements to the sound of music, in this way the actors reassure each other.
choir singing: biblical songs can be created and written, sung by individuals on the guitar with accompanying choir.

Whatever form such a presentation takes, it does not need elaborate preparation, though it will be a collective experience. Ten minutes may be enough for discussing a meaningful improvization. A more reflective play needs not only actors but also props and costumes. Puppets may have to be manufactured, music will have to be recorded and played. All this can give those who find it difficult to communicate verbally an opportunity to discover ways of expressing themselves. By agreeing to be part of a group presentation, pupils may take meaningful steps towards their involvement in their own class. The more advanced students may also discover the gifts of the 'silent third'.

Before introducing group media to his pupils, the teacher will have to structure his class for group work, linking the media-minded with the 'literary types'. This may be religious education at its best, for attitudes will only change if group dynamic processes allow room for the pupils' self-expression.

A drama, mime or dance may be moving, but spectators must have an opportunity of asking questions and explaining their reactions. This may become a confrontation between the performers as a group and the rest of the class. The teacher may act as a moderator or delegate this task to one of the pupils. He will in any case have ample opportunity of *informing* them concerning the cultural background of the text. The pupils will also feel free to *criticize* each other.

5 Recording words and music

Any text, any illustration can be reproduced millions of times through printing techniques, but with the discovery of the electronic media, it is now possible to do the same with sound. Most pupils handle tape or cassette recorders. They have a collection of records and know how to mix music and words. A purely oral repeatable communication calls on the imagination of the listener. The absence of visual experience linked with what we hear has a liberating effect. The fact that the Bible can be listened to, not only read on one's desk or laid by one's bedside, can be a revelation.

Many biblical texts were chanted, recited and memorized before they were written down and edited. They were meant to be understood without visual support. This aspect of the biblical record can be rediscovered through the use of electronic media.

A teacher can easily find out whether a pupil has understood the meaning of a text when he listens to him reading it aloud. The pupil himself will be able to understand this himself when listening to a tape-recording of his own reading voice. He will also recognize the difference between a literary text and a message accessible to illiterates. 'Translate and read this passage aloud so that any occasional listener will immediately understand its message' is a fruitful group exercise. Some voices are more suitable than others, redundancy has to be introduced, additional explanations concerning the symbolic value of certain words must be given.

A text can be communicated orally at four different levels of transposition. There is no clear division between them but this analysis has proved useful:

The reading aloud transposition: reading a Bible passage aloud with or without musical background is the simplest way of transforming a text from script into another media. It is performed every Sunday in church from a lectern. It can be recorded on cassette and addressed to specific audiences (children, old people, etc.).

The didactic transposition: can include the recording of an interview or group discussion giving all the explanations necessary for the understanding of the text. The preparation of such a programme can be a very rewarding exercise for older pupils who have chosen the Bible as a subject.

The dramatizing transposition: the biblical narrative can be retold or replayed as if the speakers were living in today's culture but without attempting to actualize the symbols used by the original writers. Dorothy Sayers' radio play *The Man Born to be King* is an example that can inspire pupils to create a radio play.

The actualizing transposition: a group of six to eight pupils can apply the questions outlined at the end of Section 3 (page 196) to a biblical text in order to create a radio programme, which will communicate how they understood the message of the text through symbols used by their own society.

Music and background noises play an essential role in the creative use of these media. Whereas illustrations and pictures focus attention and shape our imagination, music creates moods, can underline important parts of the message and enlarge our inner vision. When pupils create an audioprogramme, they become aware of the possibilities of this media which the oral society of today has not yet learned to master. The teacher may play his proper role as educator when advising his pupils on the elaboration of such transpositions.

What we. call 'didactic transposition' can be very helpful in communicating Bible *background information* to the pupils.

Music has been used throughout history to communicate the biblical message. There are many versions of Psalm 23 set to music from pre-Reformation chants to beloved nineteenth-century hymns. There are records of biblical passages such as the 'Sanctus', the 'Magnificat' or the 'Kyrie Eleison' sung to classical, romantic, pop, African or Latin American tunes. To *evaluate and compare these compositions* may help pupils to understand their own culture better, and discover the universality of religious experience.

6 *Illustrating a sound-recording with slides*

The development of photographic equipment and slide projectors has introduced new forms of audio-visual communication into our society. Our friends can now hear our enthusiastic description of our last holidays recorded with suitable background noises.

The creation of a slide series to illustrate a sound recording can be a formative group experience for a class of pupils. The biblical text read and studied in class will come alive the moment pupils are invited to choose slides that may convey the intention of the original author to their friends. They can work in groups of six or seven, some manipulating tape-recorders and microphones, others choosing slides from private or school collections. The more creative pupils will want to make their own slides. Various techniques can be developed; they can paint greaseproof paper of slide size with water colours or indian ink. They can introduce cut-out paper shapes, twisted paper clips, dried flowers and leaves, etc., between the two glass panes of the slide.

To prepare a good sound filmstrip (or slide series), the text must fit the picture. The script writers and photographers must work together from the word go. The style of the slide should be homogeneous throughout unless special effects are expected, for example, introducing a cartoon in the midst of a series of photographs in order to stress the difference between Jesus' parables and his ordinary discourses. The pictures must fit the style of the recordings and the background music. For instance, a series transposing the trial of Jesus from Jerusalem to the wild West will be underlined by folk music. Pop pictures call for pop music.

The creative use of slide series presupposes a real knowledge of visual symbolic communication. The connotation of a photograph or a design can make or mar the message the group wants to present. The collective experience of 'seeing it together' will be a discussion starter and the teacher has to understand the momentary connotation of a police helmet, a Coca-Cola bottle or a dustbin. He will find that it is easy to symbolize sin, evil and exploitation, but very difficult to depict goodness, salvation and freedom. The cross, for instance, is one of the most misused religious symbols in Western society. It is the first image pupils use to denote different concepts such as death and salvation in Christ, the Church or even love and grace. They do not realize that they are using a deep-seated universal, not a specifically Christian visual symbol. To the early Church, the cross was not an object of veneration, on the contrary, it was the image of the oppressor condemning innocents to death.

Biblical slide series can be used to illustrate transpositions of the biblical text at all four levels:

1 A simple reading aloud of a text with symbolic photographs can help meditation or enhance the shock effect of the message.
2 Explanatory Bible readings, *ex cathedra* lectures, interviews of recorded discussions on a text can be illustrated with Bible background slides.
3 The retelling of a Bible narrative in contemporary situations: biblical symbolism can be very effectively communicated through modern photographs. The Good Samaritan can become an American negro, the priest a pastor, the Levite a choir leader, but as long as the story line is respected, this is not yet a full actualization.
4 The moment modern symbols are used (the priest of the parable can symbolize the institutionalized Church, the Levite the free churches), the illustrations play an even more important role.

Slide series are very useful to convey the *information* necessary to understand a biblical text. Archaeological, geographical, historical and ethnological data are conveyed through many well prepared slide series on the market. Teachers of religion, history and art are making increasing use of them.

The *critique* of past and present efforts at transmitting the biblical message through art can best be exercised through well-prepared slide series. Christian painters and sculptors of all ages have tried to convey their understanding of the same text to their own generations. The study of the evolution of the 'halo' on the heads of the apostles, of the way a messenger tells Mary she will become the mother of Christ, and the posture of the risen Christ, can be most illuminating. African, Asian, Latin American and western artistic Bible interpretations accompanied with adequate music can be compared. European children, who still tend to consider non-Europeans as 'primitive' can discover their mistake. Here again, many existing slide series can well be introduced into the classroom for discussion.

Paul D. Fueter

7 *Films*

The aim of the television manufacturers and programme producers will soon be reached: at least one colour television set will be in each house: if possible, one for the kids and one for the parents! Our society has been transformed by this tremendous commercial drive. More impressive, however, is the fact that when different programmes are offered to the public, most spectators turn to sports events and films, especially old ones. Educational and informative productions, musical or talk-shows tend to have smaller audiences. The films the people see have a deep and unconscious influence on their attitudes to life. We are in danger of being seduced.

Our pupils sometimes see biblical films on television. The latest, 'Jesus of Nazareth', produced by Zeffirelli, is shown in the cinemas of Europe. They have become a box-office success. Many teachers of religion have presented such films to catechumens and pupils . . . but Bible films can also be seductive.

Specialists tell us that the best way of resisting the seduction of the media (especially of films) is to discover how it is done by trying to do it oneself. Schools do generally not have the equipment to use filming techniques creatively. When video-tape recorders are found on the premises, they are not likely to be handled by religious educators. But when it is possible in a class dealing with the Bible, the opportunity should be used to record acted transpositions, whether they be a drama or a puppet play (puppets are very effective on television), a musical comedy or a singing choir.

Film is an ideal medium for group communication. It should not be used for individual discourses. It gives an opportunity to a wide public to see the fellowship existing between the pupils (and possibly the teachers) in the school. Transposition of biblical texts can make excellent two to three minute television spots. A carefully rehearsed mime with proper music can do more to communicate the biblical message than the words of well-meaning priests or pastors on Saturday evening to prepare us for a Sunday on which few will go to church.

One of the difficulties in producing sketches representing actualized scenes which do not refer directly to the text that has inspired them, is how to show that 'it's all in the Bible'. Various devices have been used for this, such as reading a parable at the end of the presentation, or adding a 'sermonette' to the play. None have proved true to the medium. More experiments in this direction are necessary and we should not be afraid of recognizing our frustration in this respect.

Many film producers have tried to reconstruct the background of the Old and New Testament stories they retell. Millions of dollars have been spent to create the impression of what Egypt was like at the time of Moses, or Jerusalem at the time of Jesus. Pupils and teachers, however, should not be cheated by these expensive props. They rarely show the squalor of life of these countries at that time. They miss out the flies and mosquitoes, the diseases and the dirty water. They contribute to the fairy-tale imagery which the Bible induces in so many children and some adults. We do not really know how kings and slaves were dressed from studying mummies and sculptures in pyramids and sacred temples. Though the differences between 'life then' and 'life today' are often well indicated as far as the media allows it, the very vitality of the drama represented on the screen may lead to totally false conclusions.

Background is only a help for the actors who impersonate Jesus or the apostles. A careful analysis of the various films on the market will reveal the danger of such interpretations. It is easier to play Judas than Jesus, and easier to represent orgies and riots than temple worship. Film producers know that, but spectators, unless they are specially alert, will easily think that the Bible only speaks of interesting 'baddies' and boring 'goodies'. Moses may be too stern for many, though he was said to be the most patient man on earth. Jesus, on the other hand, may look sweet, whereas he was a 'strong Son of Man'.

Other biblical films pretend to communicate what the Bible says, but are in fact personal interpretations of a producer. They may or may not be true to what the text has to say. They often only reveal the theological or philosophical background of the author. 'The Gospel of Matthew' by Pasolini is an impressive reflection of a confessed Marxist on the life of Jesus. 'Jesus Christ Superstar' is an attempt to make the best of a musical comedy that was a great stage success because it was a good show. Cecil B. de Mille's 'The Bible' tried to tell the stories of Genesis, but succeeded only in making them totally unrealistic, so that they tend to become fairy tales.

The question of Bible films remains open. Zeffirelli's 'Jesus of Nazareth', 'The Media Bible', Marcel Carné's 'La Bible' should be presented in class. They belong to our society. They should become a basis for discussion, which may extend from the school to the family at home.

It is fitting to conclude this rather extensive study of 'The Bible in School' by commenting on films, since film is the most seductive medium of all, specially when seen on television. But films are also the best discussion starters. They can be the common experience of our pupils, linking them together the day after a programme which they have been asked to see, in order to discuss it later. Maybe, by learning how to speak through the media of our times, the next generation will know better even than their teachers how to live in tomorrow's society.

Notes on Contributors

The Reverend David G. Attfield is Team Vicar of St John's Drypool, Hull. Previously he lectured in philosophy of education at the College of St Hild and St Bede, Durham, and in religious studies at the College of All Saints, Tottenham. His articles have appeared in the *British Journal of Educational Studies, Learning for Living* and *Education for Teaching.*

Dr W. Owen Cole was Head of Religious Studies at James Graham College, Leeds, for ten years until its closure. During that time he was also Vice-Chairman of the Yorkshire Committee for Community Relations and of the Council of Christians and Jews, Leeds branch. He is a member of the Standing Conference on Inter-faith Dialogue in Education, represents the World Congress of Faiths on the Religious Education Council and is Chairman of the Shap Working Party on World Religions in Education. His publications include *The Sikhs: their Religious Beliefs and Practices* (Routledge and Kegan Paul), *World Faiths in Education* (Allen and Unwin), and *Five Religions in the Twentieth Century* (Hulton). He now teaches at West Sussex Institute of Higher Education, Bishop Otter College, Chichester.

Edwin Cox is Reader in Education, Head of Religious Education Department and Chairman of the Humanities Consortium at the University of London Institute of Education. His writings include *Changing Aims in Religious Education* (Routledge and Kegan Paul, 1966), *Sixth Form Religion* (SCM Press, 1967) and *This Elusive Jesus* (Marshalls Educational, 1975).

John Elliott, M.Phil., is Tutor in Curriculum Studies at the Cambridge Institute of Education and Director of the Schools Council Project on Teacher–Pupil Interaction and the Quality of Learning. His publications include *Me, Other People and God* – a text book for CSE (Mowbrays, 1965); with Ian Birnie (eds) *Confrontation,* RE material for sixth form and colleges (McGraw Hill, 1975); and with Eric Pain (eds) *Life Cycle* vols. I and II, RE material for CSE (Lutterworth 1975).

The Reverend Dr Leslie Francis studied theology at Oxford and Nottingham and psychology at London and Cambridge, where he also trained as a teacher. Currently he holds a research fellowship at London Central YMCA and an honorary research fellowship at the Westminster Medical School. He is also non-stipendiary priest-in-charge of two small parishes in

Suffolk. As a result of his research he has produced a programme of Christian education for Church Primary Schools and Sunday Schools, *His Spirit is With us* (Collins Liturgical Publications, 1981.)

The Reverend Paul D. Fueter, B.Sc., BD., was born in Switzerland in 1919. He was education secretary, theological teacher and publisher in East and West Africa (1947–66). He was study secretary for the Conference on Christian education in Africa (Salisbury 1962). He is now consultant on Bible communication and distribution for the European Bible Societies and lives in London. He is the author of various articles on the transposition of biblical texts.

David W. Gooderham is Senior Lecturer in Curriculum Studies, Department of Educational Studies, Teesside Polytechnic. He has taught Religious Studies at Doncaster College of Education and Humanities Curriculum at Teesside. His current research interest and work is in hermeneutic theory and its application in curriculum enquiry and theorizing.

The Reverend Daniel W. Hardy is Senior Lecturer in Modern Theological Thought in the Department of Theology of the University of Birmingham. An American long resident in Great Britain, he has contributed articles to *Learning for Living, Theology* and the *Scottish Journal of Theology,* and has written on creation, christology and personality for recent books. He has also served as a consultant in religious education to the City of Birmingham.

Dr J.M. Hull taught in schools and colleges in his native Australia and in England before taking up his present post as Senior Lecturer in Religious Education in the University of Birmingham Faculty of Education. He is Vice-Chairman of the Christian Education Movement and has been Editor of the *British Journal of Religious Education* (formerly *Learning for Living*) since 1971. With Dr John Peatling he is founder and Co-Chairman of the International Seminar for Religious Education and Values (ISREV). His publications include *Sense and Nonsense about God, Hellenistic Magic and the Synoptic Tradition* and *School Worship, An Obituary* (SCM Press) and he was drafting secretary and editor of the two British Council of Churches reports, *The Child in the Church* (1976) and *Understanding Christian Nurture, A Sequel to 'The Child in the Church'* (1981).

Trevor Kerry was co-ordinator of the DES Teacher Education Project and is co-ordinator designate of the Schools Council enquiry 'Project Work in Primary Schools' based at Nottingham University. He holds Masters degrees in Theology and Education from Nottingham University and is co-editor of *Mixed Ability Teaching* from Croom Helm, and author of *Teaching Bright Pupils* to be published by Macmillan.

Henry E. Lupton, M.Litt, M.Ed., is Senior Lecturer in Psychology of Education at St Martin's College, Lancaster. He has taught Religious

Education in Technical High, Secondary Modern and Grammar Schools, and for some years was a Chief Examiner in Religious Education for the Certificate of Secondary Education.

Mr J. Marvell, BD., M.Ed., is a Senior Lecturer in Religious Studies in charge of the County Religious Education Centre in Essex. He is author of various published articles on religious education.

Robin Minney is a lecturer in Religious Education at Durham University. After many years in inner-city schools in London, he worked in adult education in East Africa, and on returning to England took up teacher education. Since then he has undertaken in-service work at home and overseas, and his writing includes *Of Many Mouths and Eyes* (Hodder and Stoughton, 1975). He has degrees in Philosophy and Theology.

Bishop Lesslie Newbigin, CBE., DD., was formerly with the Church of South India and the Selly Oak Colleges. His more recent books include *Christian Witness in a Plural Society* (British Council of Churches, 1977) and *The Open Secret* (SPCK, 1979).

Dr John H. Peatling is Director of Basic Research in the Union College Character Research Project, Schenectady, New York State, USA. He is Editor of *Character Potential: A Record of Research.* His recent books include: *Religious Education in a Psychological Key* (Religious Education Press, Birmingham, Alabama, 1981) and *Annual Review of Research: Religious Education – Vol. 1* (Character Research Press, Schenectary, NY, 1980). With John M. Hull he is Founder and Co-Chairman of the International Seminar for Religious Education and Values (ISREV).

Edward Robinson is Director of the Religious Experience Research Unit at Manchester College, Oxford. His publications include two books on the religious experience of childhood, *The Original Vision* and *Living the Questions,* and one, *The Image of Life,* (written in collaboration with Brenda Lealman) on modern religious sculpture. He has for some years been concerned with the reinterpretation of traditional religious ideas in modern visual idiom: an exhibition of his most recent work in this field is to be held at Vaughan College, Leicester in October 1981.

Dr E.B. Turner is Principal Lecturer in the Department of Education, Stranmillis College, Belfast. His publications include articles dealing with religious attitudes and the comprehension of religious language, which have appeared in the *British Journal of Religious Education,* the *Irish Journal of Psychology,* the *Irish Journal of Education,* and *Catholic Education Today.*

John Wilson is Lecturer and Tutor in the Department of Educational Studies, and Fellow of Mansfield College, Oxford. He is the author of *Education in Religion* and *The Emotions* (Heinemann, London, 1971), *Religion* (Heinemann, London, 1972) and other works on religious, moral and educational philosophy.

Author Index

Adamson, J.W., xvi n. 8
Allport, G.W., 45, 75 n. 9
Alves, C., 36, 45, 139 n. 1, 140
Argyle, M., 75 n. 2
Association of College and University Examiners, 140
Attfield, D., 52, 77–84

Bambrough, R., 84 n. 5
Barth, K., 145
Bloom, Krathwohl, *et al.*, 134
Bourne, L.E., 45
Bowles, J.W.
 see Carter and Bowles
Brattems, C.E., 45
Bruner, J.S., 21 n. 42, 45
Busia, K.A., 75 n. 2
Buttmann, R., 45

Cambridgeshire Syllabus of Religious Teaching for Schools, xvi n. 11
Carlyle, T., 153 n. 6
Carter, J.P., 18 n. 7
Carter, J.W. and Bowles, J.W., 38, 45
Cassirer, E., 145
Chadwick, O., 101
Chardin, Teilhard de, 145
Childs, H.G.
 see Terman and Childs
Christian Education Movement (CEM), 134–5, 140, 177 n. 2
Clayton, R.D., 76 n. 22
Cohn, W., 76 n. 22
Cole, W.O., 157, 171–7
Cox, E., xiv, 33 n. 2, 52, 53–7

Denbigh School Board, xii
Dennison, A.R.
 see Kerry and Dennison
Dixon, W.J., 18–19 n. 15
Douglas, J.D., 37, 45
Douglas, M., 75 n. 9
Durham Report, 139 n. 1
Durkheim, E., 75 n. 9

Edwards, A.L., 33 n. 7
Eliade, M., 71, 73, 75 n. 12
Eliot, T.S., 101
Elliott, J., 121–2, 123–32, 153 n. 9
Elmore, C.M., 45
Elmore, C.M. and Gorham, D.R., 45
Elvin, H.L., 140 n. 9
Evans, K.M., 33 n. 10
Eysenck, H., 29, 30, 33 n. 8 and n. 13

Feifel, H., 38, 45
Feifel, H. and Lorge, J., 38, 45
Francis, L., 23–33
Frazer, J.G., 183
Fueter, P., 157, 187–203

Gates, B., 75 n. 20
Gee, M., 177 n. 2
Gerstein, R.A., 45
Giddens, A., 153 n. 3
Glock, C.Y. and Stark, R.S., 76 n. 22
Goldman, R., xiii–xiv, 3, 5–21, 45, 52, 62–3, 70, 74, 75 n. 8, 76 n. 23, 170 n. 1
Gooderham, D., 122, 143–53
Gorham, D.R., 36, 45
 see also Elmore and Gorham
Gouldner, A., 153 n. 4 and n. 10
Graham, C., 45
Green, B.F., 38, 45
Grimmitt, M., xiv, xvi n. 13
Guttman, L., 42, 45

Hamlyn, D.W., 84 n. 9
Hardy, D.W., 96, 109–18, 118 n. 1 and n. 2
Hays, W.L., 45
Heim, A., 45
HM Inspectorate, 170 and n. 5
Hirst, P., 77, 84 n. 1
Hirst, P.H. and Peters, R.S., 68
Hoge, D.R., 14, 20 n. 23
Holm, J., xiv
Horder, D.
see Smart and Horder
Husserl, 71
Hyde, K.E., xiv, 3, 37, 45–6
Hull, J.M., xi-xvi
Huxley, J., 140 and n. 9

Jeremias, J.Eg., 84 n. 8
Jones, J., 30, 32
Jones, R., 88

Kaplan, E.
see Werner and Kaplan
Kay, W., 29–30, 32
Kellaghan, T.
see Macnamara, O'Cleirigh and Kellaghan
Keller, A., 91
Kerry, T., 157
Kerry, T. and Dennison, A.R., 170 n. 2
Killeen, C., 14
Krathwohl
see Bloom, Krathwohl *et al.*
Kristensen, W.B., 71, 73, 74, 75 n. 10
Küng, H., 111

Laabs, C.W., 10–11, 12, 13–14, 18 n. 14, 19 n. 16 and n. 20, 20 n. 30 and n. 37
Lee, R.S., 46
Lemon, N., 33 n. 7
Levi-Strauss, C., 183
Likert, R.A., 33
Lord, F.M., 46
Lord, F.M. and Novick, M.R., 46
Lorge, J.
see Feifel and Lorge
Loukes, H., xiii, xvi, 36, 46, 52, 62, 70, 74, 75 n. 7, 76 n. 24, 139, 140 n. 11 and n. 12
Lupton, H.E., 122, 133–41

Macnamara, J., O'Cleirigh, A. and Kellaghan, T., 46
Martin, D., 75 n. 2
Marvell, J., 52, 69–76
Marx, 38
Mauriac, F., 90
Meadows, P., 30, 32
Merrill, M.A.
see Terman and Merrill
Mill, J.S., xi–xv, xvi n. 1, n. 2, n. 3, n. 4 and n. 5, 157
Minney, R., 157, 179–85
Munby, D., 101
Murphy, J., xvi n. 6 and n. 7

National Society and Church of England Board of Education, 140
Naylor, D., 139 n. 2, 141
Newbigin, L., 95–6, 97–107
Newton, T.B., 9, 11, 18 n. 13 and n. 14
Niblett, R.W., 153 n. 5
Nicholls, W., 69, 75 n. 1
Nielson, K., 84 n. 5
Novick, M.R.
see Lord and Novick

O'Cleirigh, A.
see Macnamara, O'Cleirigh and Kellaghan
O'Faolain, S., 85, 87–8, 90, 91 n. 1 and n. 3
Ong, W., 145, 153 n. 2
Otto, R., 70, 71–2, 75 n. 4, n. 14, n. 16 and n. 18, 76 n. 25
Owen, H.P., 84 n. 4

Papania, N., 46
Peatling, J.H., 3, 5–21, 33 n. 14
Peel, E.A., 11
Peters, R.S., 53, 84 n. 9, 153 n. 5
see also Hirst and Peters
Petrillo, C., 14, 20 n. 23
Phenix, P.H., 140 n. 10, 141
Piaget, J., 6, 7, 8, 11, 12, 15, 16, 19 n. 22, 20 n. 24, n. 25 and n. 27, 63, 82
Pikas, A., 46

Polanyi, M., 101, 105–6, 117
Portnoy, B.
see Stacey and Portnoy

Radnitzky, G., 144, 153 n. 1
Ramsey, I., 46
Read Mumford, E.E., 3, 4
Religious Experience Research Unit (Oxford), 86
Richardson, A., 37, 46
Robinson, E.A., 52, 85–91
Robson, J.M., xvi n. 1
Rosenthal, R., 33 n. 3
Russell, D.H. and Saadeh, I.Q., 46
Rowse, A.L., 102
Rust, J., 30–1

Saadeh, I.Q.
see Russell and Saadeh
Schools Council, xv, 70, 73, 74, 75 n. 5 and n. 6, 76 n. 21, 139 n. 1, 141, 148, 153 n. 7, 159
Seuss, D., 5, 17
Sharpe, E., 71, 75 n. 13
Siegel, S., 46
Smart, N., xiv, 62, 74, 76 n. 22, 183
Smart, N. and Horder, D., 75 n. 20
Smith, J.W.D., xiv, 3, 4
Sockett, H., 153 n. 8
Spinks, G.S., 91 n. 4
Stacey, C.L. and Portnoy, B., 46
Stark, R.S.
see Glock and Stark
Stephens, T., 3, 4
Stouffer, S.A., 42, 46
Stubbs, M., 29, 32

Tamminen, K., 9, 11–12, 19 n. 17 and n. 18, 20 n. 29 and n. 36, 21 n. 45
Terman, L.M., 35, 37, 38, 46
Terman, L.M. and Childs, H.G., 37, 46
Terman, L.M. and Merrill, M.A., 38, 46
Thompson, E.P., 102
Thouless, R.H., 75 n. 9
Thucydides, 89
Tillich, P., 70
Torgerson, W.S., 42, 46
Tucker, L.R., 42, 46
Turner, E.B., 3, 35–47
Turner, H., 71–2, 75 n. 15, n. 17 and n. 19, 76 n. 25

University of Sheffield, Institute of Education, 36–47

van der Leeuw, G., 71, 73, 74, 75 n. 11

Wach, J., 76 n. 22
Ward, K., 84 n. 2, n. 3 and n. 7
Wechsler, D., 38, 46
Werner, H. and Kaplan, E., 46
Wesley, B., 30–1
Wilson, B., 75 n. 2
Wilson, J., 52, 59–68
Wisdom, J., 84 n. 5
Wright, D., 75 n. 9

Yeaxlee, B.A., 3, 4
Yinger, M., 75 n. 9, 76 n. 22

Subject Index

academic approaches
to religious education, 145–53
affective objectives, 136–7, 140 n. 6
aims
of religious education, xi–xvi, 55–7, 77, 113–14, 124–32, 133–41, 187–8
anxiety, 88, 89
assembly
in multi-faith schools, 176–7
attitude
of teachers, 138–9, 151
attitude questionnaires, 5–21, 22–33
see also measurement
awe, 52, 63–4, 65

Bible, 3, 157, 187–203
Bible study, 187–203
biblical language, 36–47
Birmingham Agreed Syllabus (1975), 95–6, 97, 99–101, 103–7, 130, 133, 143, 148
Britain, 8, 23–33, 35–47, 69–76, 85–91, 95–6, 97–107, 123–32, 133–41, 143–53, 157, 161–70, 171–7, 179–85
Buddhism, 131

Cambridgeshire Syllabus (1924), xiii
checklists
and religious education syllabus, 133–41
Christianity, xii–xv, 57, 66–8, 73, 77–84, 97–107, 111, 122, 123–32, 133–41, 157, 172–7, 179–85, 186–203
Church of England schools, 28, 31
cognitive demands
on pupils, 161–70
cognitive development, 6–7
cognitive objectives
and religious education, 135–6, 140 n. 6
communication, 117–18, 190–203
Communism, 63
comparative study of religions, 98, 112
comprehension
testing of religious language, 35–47
concepts
and religious education, 78–83
conceptual framework
and religious education curriculum, 143–53
conceptual research, 77–84
confessional approaches
to religious education, 145–53
content
of religious education, 59–68, 74, 77, 80–1, 127–32, 133–41, 149–51, 172–4, 179–85
criticism, 159–60
CSE religious syllabuses, 125–32
curriculum, xiv–xv, 17, 52, 83, 95–6, 119–53, 170, 172–7

democracy
and syllabus construction, 123–32
differentiation
in religious education, 158–9
Durham Commission, 134

Education Act (1944), xii–xiii, xvi n. 9, 51–2, 97–8, 124
empirical method, 1–47, 52, 70–1

Finland, 9, 11–12, 16

hedonism, 103
Hinduism, 98, 100

Hindus, 172–7, 179–85
history
of religion, 73
humanistic approaches
to religious education, 145–53

innovation
in religious education curriculum, 152–3
integration
in religious education, 159
International Seminar for Religious Education and Values (ISREV), 3
Islam, 98
see also Muslims

Jews, 172–7

Kendall's Co-efficient of Concordance, 44
Kenya, 179–85
King John School, 163–70
Kolmogorov-Smirnov test, 43
Kuder-Richardson Reliability Co-efficients, 44

language
religious, 35–47
Lutherans, 10–11, 13–14

Marxism, 63, 78, 97, 98, 99, 100–1, 103, 203
meaning of 'religion', 97–101
measurement
and religious education, 1–47
media
and Bible study, 192–203
Methodists, 9
methods of teaching, 70–1, 155–203
multi-faith schools, 171–7, 179–85
multi-religious society, 171–7, 179–85
Muslims, 172–7, 179–85
see also Islam

National Association of Episcopal Schools (NAES), 7
North America, 5–21
Northern Europe, 193–203

numinous experience, 52, 70, 71–3

objectives
of religious education
see aims
objectivity, 99–101

phenomenological method
of studying religion, 52, 69–76
pluralism, 53–4, 69, 93–118, 123–32, 144
'progress'
in religious education, 157–60

racism, 103
rationale
for religious education, 49–91
religion
and development, 98–9
religious language
testing of comprehension, 35–47
Religious Language Comprehension Test, 35–47
religious thinking
development of, 5–21
religious traditions, 110–18
research, 77–84
role
of religious education, 187–90
see also aims; objectives
Roman Catholic schools, 28
Roman Catholicism, 13, 14

Scale of Religious Thinking, 5–21, 30
secular characteristics
of society, 53–4, 69, 97–107, 110
secularization, 51–2, 144–6
Sikhs, 172–7, 179–85
social context
of religious education, 93–118
spiritual experience, 85–91
Stanford-Binet Intelligence Scale, 38
State
and religious education, xi–xiii
syllabus, xii–xiii, 123–32, 133–41

Teacher Education Project, 162–70
teachers, 172–3
teaching

context of, 163–4
teaching methods, 97, 103–7, 123–32, 155–203
testing
and development of religious thinking, 5–21
of religious language comprehension, 35–47
see also measurement
theological method
of studying religion, 52, 70–1
translations
of the Bible, 193–4
truth
and religious education, 109–18, 129

United States, 8–11, 13–14, 16
see also North America

verification
in religious education, 159
vocabulary, 36–47

Wechsler Intelligence Scale for Children, 38, 40–5
West Germany, 188–90
worship, 52, 63–4, 65